challenging
behaviors

in early childhood settings

challenging behaviors

in early childhood settings

creating a place for all children

by

Susan Hart Bell, Ph.D.
Georgetown College | Georgetown, KY

Victoria Carr, Ed.D.
University of Cincinnati | Cincinnati, OH

Dawn Denno, M.Ed.
Ohio Department of Education | Columbus, OH

Lawrence J. Johnson, Ph.D.
University of Cincinnati | Cincinnati, OH

and

Louise R. Phillips, M.Ed.
University of Cincinnati | Cincinnati, OH

with invited contributors

·P A U L·H·
BROOKES
PUBLISHING CO®

Baltimore • London • Sydney

Paul H. Brookes Publishing Co.
Post Office Box 10624
Baltimore, Maryland 21285-0624

www.brookespublishing.com

Typeset by International Graphic Services, Inc., Newtown, Pennsylvania.
Manufactured in the United States of America by
Edwards Brothers, Inc., Ann Arbor, Michigan.

The stories in this book are based on the authors' experiences. Some of the vignettes represent actual people and circumstances. In these cases, individuals' names and identifying details have been changed to protect their identities. Other vignettes are composite or fictional accounts that do not represent the lives or experiences of specific individuals, and no implications should be inferred.

Second printing, March 2006.
Third printing, February 2012.

Library of Congress Cataloging-in-Publication Data

Challenging behaviors in early childhood settings: creating a place for all
   children / by Susan Hart Bell . . . [et al.].
      p.   cm.
   Includes bibliographical references and index.
   ISBN-13: 978-1-55766-682-6
   ISBN-10: 1-55766-682-2
   1. Behavior modification.   2. Early childhood education.   I. Bell, Susan H.
LB1060.2.C42 2004
370.15'28—dc22   2003065588

British Library Cataloguing in Publication data are available from the British Library.

Contents

About the Authors vii

Invited Contributors ix

Acknowledgments... xi

Chapter 1   Clarifying the Elements of Challenging Behavior
             Susan Hart Bell and Sheryl Quinn...1

Chapter 2   Developing Centerwide Support
             Victoria Carr, Lawrence J. Johnson, and Connie C. Corkwell.....................21

Chapter 3   Engaging Parents as Partners in Changing Behavior
             Anne M. Bauer, Monica Battle, and Lawrence J. Johnson...........................33

Chapter 4   Creating a Supportive Classroom Environment
             *Dawn Denno, Louise R. Phillips, Helene Arbouet Harte, and
             Sally Moomaw*..49

Chapter 5   Seeing the Challenge More Clearly
             *Louise R. Phillips, Joyce Hensler, Mef Diesel, and
             Andrea Cefalo*...67

Chapter 6   Determining the Teacher's Role in Further
             Assessment and Intervention
             Susan Hart Bell, Amy Clancy, and Erin N. Gaddes....................................97

Chapter 7   Implementing Individualized Behavior Plans
             Susan Hart Bell and Victoria Carr...121

Chapter 8   Evaluating and Revising Intervention Plans
             Susan Hart Bell and Christine M. Gilkey..137

Chapter 9   Planning for Crises
             Victoria Carr, Helene Arbouet Harte, and Louise R. Phillips......................149

Chapter 10   Determining When Outside Help Is Needed
             *Mary B. Boat, Victoria Carr, Lawrence J. Johnson, and
             Dawn Denno*...169

Chapter 11   Putting it All Together
             Susan Hart Bell...185

References...193

Index..209

About the Authors

Susan Hart Bell, Ph.D., Associate Professor and Chair, Department of Psychology, Georgetown College, 400 East College Street, Georgetown, KY 40324

Dr. Bell earned a master of science degree in clinical psychology from Eastern Kentucky University and a doctoral degree in school psychology from the University of Cincinnati. She has coordinated an interdisciplinary team serving preschool children with disabilities in Raleigh, North Carolina, and consulted with preschools in the Greater Cincinnati area. She directed the Ohio Early Childhood Intervention Project at the University of Cincinnati. With David Barnett and Karen Carey, she co-authored the book *Designing Preschool Interventions: A Practitioner's Guide* (The Guilford Press, 1999). Dr. Bell's son Chad has Down syndrome and continues to provide her with great joy and challenges. Her daughter Sarah plans to help families of children with disabilities through the social work field.

Victoria Carr, Ed.D., Director, Arlitt Child and Family Research and Education Center, University of Cincinnati, One Edwards Center, Post Office Box 210105, Cincinnati, OH 45221

In addition to serving as Director of the Arlitt Child and Family Research and Education Center, Dr. Carr is Faculty Chair for the Early Childhood Education Program at the University of Cincinnati. Her research and writing interests include teacher education and instructional strategies, curriculum-based measurement, and programming for children who challenge the system. She is active in the Council for Exceptional Children's Division for Early Childhood and in Head Start Programs.

Dawn Denno, M.Ed., Consultant, Assessment and Program Evaluation, Office of Early Childhood Education, Ohio Department of Education, 25 South Front Street, Columbus, OH 43215

Ms. Denno is a consultant to the Ohio Department of Education's Office of Early Childhood Education, where she coordinates assessment and evaluation in early childhood programs. She has worked in the field of early childhood education for 30 years as a teacher and an administrator. In addition, Ms. Denno has worked extensively with Head Start, public preschools, and preschool special education programs. She earned her master of science degree in early childhood education.

Lawrence J. Johnson, Ph.D., Dean, College of Education, Criminal Justice and Human Services; Professor of Education; Executive Director of the Arlitt Child and Family Research and Education Center, University of Cincinnati, 401 Teachers College, Post Office Box 210002, Cincinnati, OH 45221

Dr. Johnson earned his doctoral degree in working with at-risk populations, statistical analysis, and research methods from the University of Illinois. He has published extensively, having written 11 books, 27 book chapters, and 67 refereed journal articles. In addition to his publications, Dr. Johnson served as principal investigator or primary author of 200 grant proposals, which were funded for a combined total in excess of $100,000,000. These projects have had an impact at the local, state, and national levels, as evidenced by the recognition that Dr. Johnson has received from the states of Illinois, Alabama, and Ohio for his contributions to their citizens. In addition, he has been recognized by the Council for Exceptional Children (CEC) for his contributions as President of the Teacher Education Division and by the CEC's Division for Early Childhood for his contributions as Chair of the Research Committee. Dr. Johnson is completing 6-year terms as co-editor of the *Journal for Teacher Education and Special Education* and as chair of the State of Ohio University of Education Deans.

Louise R. Phillips, M.Ed., Coordinator of Inclusion Services, Arlitt Child and Family Research and Education Center, University of Cincinnati, One Edwards Center, Post Office Box 210105, Cincinnati, OH 45221

Ms. Phillips holds bachelor of science degrees in kindergarten–primary education and in child development, family life, and preschool education, as well as a master's degree in early childhood education from the University of Cincinnati. As Coordinator of Inclusion Services for the Arlitt Child and Family Research and Education Center, Ms. Phillips coordinates disability and mental health services for children and families and has presented on various topics, including children with challenging behaviors, inclusion, diversity, transitions, talking with children about difficult topics, the screening and assessment process, and communicating with families. Prior to teaching at the Arlitt Center, Ms. Phillips taught in a preschool program in Alabama and kindergarten and preschool programs in the Cincinnati area. As an Early Childhood Education Teacher Specialist at the Arlitt Center, she has facilitated children's learning through the Home Base and Center Base programs. In addition, she has been a cooperating teacher, resource advisor, and mentor to early childhood education students at the University of Cincinnati. Ms. Phillips and her husband Ray have two children, David and Tracy.

Invited Contributors

Monica Battle

Anne M. Bauer, Ed.D.
Professor
College of Education
University of Cincinnati

Mary B. Boat, Ph.D.
Assistant Professor
College of Education
University of Cincinnati

Andrea Cefalo
Family Advocate
Arlitt Child and Family
    Research and Education Center

Amy Clancy, B.A.
Master's Degree Candidate
Lehigh University

Connie C. Corkwell, M.Ed.
Associate Director
Arlitt Child and Family
    Research and Education Center

Mef Diesel, B.S.
Early Childhood Teacher Education
    Specialist
Arlitt Child and Family
    Research and Education Center

Erin N. Gaddes, B.A.
Special Education Teacher
Fort Mitchell, KY

Christine M. Gilkey, Ph.D.
School Psychologist
Cincinnati, OH

Helene Arbouet Harte, M.Ed.
Early Childhood Teacher Education
    Specialist
Arlitt Child and Family
    Research and Education Center

Joyce Hensler, M.Ed.
Early Childhood Teacher Education
    Specialist
Arlitt Child and Family
    Research and Education Center

Sally Moomaw, M.Ed.
Associate Director for Professional
    Development
Arlitt Child and Family
    Research and Education Center

Sheryl Quinn, Ph.D.
School Psychologist
Syracuse, NY

Acknowledgments

Susan Hart Bell acknowledges the overwhelming support and confidence of Dr. David Barnett of the University of Cincinnati. Without the opportunities provided by his mentoring, her contribution to this book would not have been possible. Many of the ideas throughout this book can be directly or indirectly traced to his influence. She also thanks the Henlein family for a grant that supported research for this book in Spring 2002 and Dr. William Pollard, Provost of Georgetown College in Georgetown, Kentucky, who made this grant available. Finally, Dr. Bell thanks her students Amy Clancy, Jessica Groves, and Heidi Sorrell—two future school psychologists and a future pediatrician. This book would have been much shorter without their contributions.

Victoria Carr acknowledges the professional influence of her co-editors and the staff of the Arlitt Child and Family Research and Education Center, as well as the support of her husband, Jerry Huebener, in the writing of this book.

Louise R. Phillips acknowledges the contributions of Helene Arbouet Harte, Lowellette Lauderdale, Kim Rioux, and Amy Webre, teachers from the Arlitt Child and Family Research and Education Center who helped develop the Classroom Application checklists in Chapter 5.

For my husband Jeff with love and gratitude
and in celebration of our 25 years of marriage—
always remember
SHB

To my two wonderful children, Dylan and Shannon,
who continue to teach me how to be a parent and
connect me to the world according to teenagers
VC

To Amanda, Jason, Lia, and Skeeter—
the children in my family
DD

challenging behaviors

in early childhood settings

Chapter 1

Clarifying the Elements of Challenging Behavior

Susan Hart Bell and Sheryl Quinn

Attempting to define the challenging behaviors displayed in early childhood classroom settings runs the risk of overwhelming or insulting the reader. A professional who is new to the field may despair at the thought of implementing an early childhood curriculum and creating a classroom environment that addresses severe challenging behavior. A seasoned professional may quickly reply, "I've tried it all. Let me tell you my story." Regardless of experience, early childhood teachers often feel inadequate, frustrated, and desperate when confronted with these serious and frequent classroom disruptions.

When faced with a child who poses significant behavior challenges in the classroom, the teacher's first task is to step back and clarify the elements of the problem situation. This chapter seeks to structure that process by placing child behaviors within the context of child, home, and classroom factors, as well as behavior characteristics. Throughout this book, vignettes about children serve as examples of problem situations. Classroom application sections provide questions that allow the early childhood professional to revisit important concepts and apply them to disruptions in his or her classroom environment.

WHICH CHILD FACTORS NEED TO BE EXAMINED?

Educators must investigate a broad range of child factors. These characteristics are detailed in the following subsections.

Identified Health Conditions or Disabilities

When seeking to understand a problem situation, an early childhood teacher must first consider whether the child has obvious health concerns or sensory impairments. Usually, this issue is addressed by a medical screening that is conducted before a child is enrolled in an early childhood program. It is critical to identify any physical limitations, psychological characteristics, or side effects from treatment or medication that commonly accompany such diagnoses (Brown & Anderson, 1999) and can have behavioral significance (Boekaerts & Roder, 1999; Feldman, Hancock, Rielly, Minnes, & Cairns, 2000; Miceli, Rowland, & Whitman, 1999).[1] However, it is important to understand that children with similar medical conditions may have different behavioral reactions to symptoms, treatment, and medications (Brown & DuPaul, 1999; Brown & Macias, 2001; Lee & Guck, 2000; Miceli et al., 1999).

A child who enters an early childhood program with a previously diagnosed health condition may 1) experience frequent absences; 2) tire easily or experience pain that limits classroom performance; 3) require exceptions to classroom routines, including mealtimes and gross motor play; and 4) express frustration with classroom limits (Brown, Tanaka, & Donegan, 1998; Schuman & La Greca, 1999; Thies, 1999). Overprotectiveness from parents may contribute to noncompliance and resistance within the classroom routines (Thomasgard & Metz, 1997; Thomasgard, Shonkoff, Metz, & Edelbrock, 1995). Medications may limit participation in more demanding classroom activities (Phelps, Brown, & Power, 2002).

It is important for early childhood teachers to understand that individual children vary widely within a given diagnostic category (Boekarts & Roder, 1999; Lee & Guck, 2000; Miceli et al., 1999). Knowing the characteristics and continuum of abilities and skills that generally accompany a specific illness or disability may provide teachers with a range of expected behavior around which they can plan (Mukherjee & Lightfoot, 2000; Roberts, Brown, & Rickards, 1996). However, although it is helpful to know whether a child has a diagnosed medical condition or an identified disability, teachers are strongly cautioned to remember that each student is a child first, with all the uniqueness that temperament and life experiences provide. The following vignettes of two children with Down syndrome illustrate this diversity. As suggested in the vignettes, teacher strategies for addressing each child's learning and behavioral issues will be vastly different.

> Lacey, age 4, is happily engaged in dramatic play with two typically developing children. Lacey gestures for one girl to place a hat on her head and giggles as she picks up an oversized purse and hands it to another friend. Although her verbal communication is limited to a few words, which are largely unintelligible except to her teachers and immediate family members, Lacey's facial expressions and animated body movements make her intentions clear. She has an extensive sign vocabulary,

[1]*Health-Related Disorders in Children and Adolescents* (Phelps, 1998) gives concise descriptions of frequently encountered medical conditions, along with the psychoeducational implications of these disorders. The book explains physical conditions that occur in childhood (e.g., asthma, childhood cancer, organ transplantations) as well as genetic (e.g., Down syndrome, Williams syndrome) and other complex disorders (e.g., autism, traumatic brain injury). *Children with Disabilities, Fifth Edition* (Batshaw, 2002), also provides complete, readable descriptions of the medical aspects of children's disabilities.

and her friends have learned a few of the signs that Lacey uses most often. Her social skills are her biggest asset. Lacey's teachers also make accommodations for her serious heart defect by protecting her from extreme temperatures and excessive activity demands.

Joey, also age 4, seems disinterested in his classmates. He rarely communicates with them or his teachers, although he vigorously protests when a teacher physically assists him through the classroom routines. He prefers to rock by himself in a red chair in the book area or to lie on the floor, arms outstretched, rolling a car back and forth and humming softly. Many of Joey's play actions seem infantile or toddler-like. His health is excellent, however, and he does not have any accompanying organ system defects or sensory impairments.

Unidentified Disabilities or Sensory Impairments

A child with an unidentified disability or impairment often demands extraordinary adult attention because he or she does not display skills expected for his or her chronological age (Bell & Barnett, 1999; Brown, Odom, Li, & Zercher, 1999). The child may act much younger, displaying global developmental delays in language, social, cognitive, motor, and self-help skills. This behavior necessitates calling in local resources to determine the level of assistance required to maximize the child's progress in the program (Barnett, Bell, Gilkey, et al., 1999). This topic is discussed further in Chapter 10.

Less marked health differences also may occur. A child who presents a behavioral challenge may have a previously unidentified sensory impairment that limits his or her participation in classroom activities. Diminished hearing sensitivity due to chronic otitis media (i.e., repeated ear infections), for example, can result in language and learning problems and should be considered by early childhood professionals as a possible contributing factor to inattention or inappropriate behavior (Shriberg et al., 2000; Trivette, 1998). Visual impairments also may contribute to atypical classroom behavior and limitations in social skills (Holbrook, 1996; McGaha & Farran, 2001). Collaboration with skilled medical, speech-language, or other professionals is essential for a program to meet the needs of children with identified health concerns or developmental disabilities.

Staggered or Uneven Development

Typically developing children often mature in fits and starts—for example, moving ahead in language and cognitive ability while lagging behind in motor and social skills. Behavioral challenges may emerge from staggered developmental skills, as highlighted in the following vignettes.

Mario, age 4, is able to visualize the way that he wants his drawing of a chipmunk to appear on paper. However, he cannot adequately transfer the image from his memory to the paper. He wads the paper into a tight ball, throws it to the ground, and screams, "I hate art!" The other children in the classroom stare fearfully at his unpredictable behavior.

Lauren, age 3, is able to construct intricate block towers and complete simple jigsaw puzzles. She also listens to her teacher reading for long periods of time. Yet, the simplest verbal communication is beyond Lauren's capability. Instead, she moves aggressively to shove away a child perceived as interrupting her storytime with the teacher. She pinches a child who moves in to watch her build a tower and hovers protectively around her creation. The other children protest and call for help when Lauren nears a play area. Thus, Lauren usually plays alone or with a teacher.

Jonathon moves from classroom activity to activity with awkward clumsiness. He is tall for a 4-year-old and towers over his classmates. He is enthusiastic and lunges unpredictably toward activities that interest him, leaving tumbled block structures, scattered puzzle pieces, and stepped-on toes and fingers in his wake. He is most successfully engaged with other children on the playground when he joins in chase games.

Children with uneven or atypical developmental courses require careful observation and planning from early childhood teachers. The road to typical behavior may seem unending and the process to intervene with these children confusing. The classroom climate is often unpredictable, as the other children are affected by the day-to-day challenges of the child's behavioral puzzle.

CLASSROOM APPLICATION

Is the child healthy?

Is the child's medical evaluation up to date? What illnesses or developmental problems are mentioned?

Do the child's parents have helpful medical information?

What additional information is needed about any medical condition or treatment regimen?

Do the parents suggest modifications to the child's daily routine?

Does the child demonstrate staggered development? In what area(s) is the child lagging behind?

Should screenings for cognitive, language, social, or motor delays be initiated?

Should the child's parents be contacted regarding professional evaluations in any of these areas?

Does the child have an identified disability? What information is needed from parents and related professionals to assist the child in this educational setting?

Adequacy of Social Skills

Diverse social competence levels and temperamental predispositions may be found among children in a given classroom (Carey, 1998). Young children differ in their exposure to social interactions, often depending on whether they have siblings or neighborhood friends. For many children, the early childhood classroom is the first opportunity for peer interactions; play partners previously may have been limited to parents, grandparents, or other adult caregivers. For the first time, these children must share limited play materials, negotiate entry into play, sustain cooperative play with peers, and compromise by turn taking during desired activities.

Play entry is a complex activity for young children, and there is evidence that repeated experiences of peer rejection may affect a child's subsequent classroom activity engagement as well as his or her social and emotional adjustment (Buhs & Ladd, 2001). The teacher may notice that a particular child has difficulty maintaining appropriate physical boundaries when approaching another child or a group of children. This child may burst into a classroom center activity, touching carefully arrayed play materials and interrupting ongoing play themes. At times, this behavior results in overt peer rejection as frustrated children protest the disruption of their play activities. Children with identified disabilities also experience social interaction difficulties and attempt fewer play entries and spend less time in child interaction without adult support (Brown et al., 1999; McGaha & Farran, 2001; Roberts et al., 1996).

Some young children experience particular difficulty with self-regulation (Bronson, 2000; Kochanska, Coy, & Murray, 2001). Difficulties in self-regulation can be expressed as limited impulse control and frequent noncompliance (Sethi, Mischel, Aber, Shoda, & Rodriguez, 2000). These children may have trouble remembering the daily classroom routines, requiring repeated reminders for entry activities (e.g., hanging up one's coat, turning over one's name tag on the board at the classroom door), transition activities (e.g., cleanup or lining up procedures), daily group or circle-time participation (e.g., sitting on a carpet square, sitting with one's arms and legs folded), or snack-time participation (e.g., waiting until all are served before eating). They may impulsively rush to classroom play centers, seemingly oblivious of cleanup responsibilities or posted limits about the numbers of children allowed in a classroom area at any one time.

Other children may find sustained engagement in age-appropriate activities a continuing challenge (McWilliam & Bailey, 1995). They may move quickly from area to area, spending mere seconds on one task before moving to the next. These children may have a shortened attention span, continually be distracted by the activities of other children, and impulsively move from one play activity to the next. This combination of behaviors often has been described as attention-deficit/hyperactivity disorder (ADHD)—a psychiatric diagnosis of much interest (American Psychiatric Association, 2000; Anastopoulos, Klinger, & Temple, 2001; Barkley, 1996). Teachers may be challenged to provide intensive scaffolding, guiding these children through the completion of simple activities and encouraging them to spend more than a few seconds at each activity center (Malmskog & McDonnell, 1999).

Some children may have little experience with certain play themes (e.g., playing post office or pet shop) and need considerable guidance from teachers and peers regarding appropriate play actions for the pretend play setting (Peters, 1995). Lack of knowledge of related play actions may be reflected in a child's disorganized approach to the play area and aggressive or destructive play with thematic materials. The teacher can highlight other children's play activities, encouraging the inexperienced child to model or imitate another child's use of the materials. An experienced play partner can scaffold the use of unfamiliar toys and activities, prompting and encouraging age- and activity-appropriate play. Additional preparation can take place during opening group time through the use of stories, songs, or games that give information about the novel play activities.

For some children, it may be important to encourage engagement in various activities and types of play throughout the day. Some children may avoid challenging or less preferred activities (e.g., writing activities) or spend most of their time in functional, repetitive play activities (e.g., at the sensory table) (Kontos, Moore, & Giorgetti, 1998), as exemplified in the following vignettes.

> Maribeth rushes to the sensory table each day upon entry into the classroom. She is the last to leave the table when her teacher signals a transition to group time, snack time, or outside play. Maribeth inevitably returns to the table whenever free activity choices are offered. She scoops beans, rice, or sand, playing beside the other children and ignoring their play activities at the table. When there are too many children at the table, she becomes agitated, attempting to pull another child away or take a participating child's smock. When the sensory table activity is "closed" for the day, Maribeth returns continually to the table, asking her teacher if she can play there.

> Juan spends each free play period wandering from one activity center to another. He occasionally dumps out puzzle pieces or a basket of manipulative toys, fingering the pieces for a few seconds before moving on to the next area. He resists teacher efforts to support him in completing simple puzzles or fitting blocks together. From classroom observations, it seems that Juan spends an average of 4 seconds per activity. His teacher is breathless from following him around the classroom, assisting him in cleaning up spilled materials and encouraging him to follow a simple activity to completion (e.g., covering the surface of a paper with sponge-stamped forms). Juan seems happiest on the playground, chasing other children and running from play structure to play structure.

Inappropriate Play Themes

Children play out what they have seen and experienced in an attempt to take on adult roles and to make sense of personal experiences. For some children, these experiences include exposure to sexually explicit or violent media (e.g., movies, television programs, or video games with mature themes). In more tragic cases, children have directly experienced violence or sexual exploitation. These children may bring this into the classroom, as they pretend play with story lines of violent gun play, drug use, or sexual activity. Even when gently redirected, these children may seem compelled to return to these highly salient play themes (Horton, 1996). A preference for engaging in violent pretend play has been linked with social interaction conflicts and teacher-identified behavior problems in early childhood settings (Dunn & Hughes, 2001). Highly detailed and precocious knowledge may be displayed during these play activities and may prompt questions of the possibility of parental neglect or abuse (Davies, Glaser, & Kossoff, 2000). Teachers must be prepared to discuss concerns with parents and, if appropriate, to seek assistance from social services agencies to investigate the child's safety at home. This dilemma is illustrated through the following vignette.

> Mickey is never left to play alone out of the sight of one of his teachers. Nearly 5 years old, he particularly likes to play with Sierra, a 3-year-old who is small for her age. He often leads Sierra to a pillow in the book area or the bathroom or encourages her to crawl under the math table with him. Once there, he places his hands inside her clothing. Sierra generally seems to enjoy playing with Mickey but actively resists these inappropriate touches. She is mostly nonverbal, however, so the teachers must watch continually to prevent Mickey from leading her to these more remote areas. In addition, Mickey often laughs as he makes sexually sophisticated comments while playing with dolls in the house area. His teachers are concerned about the compulsive quality of these sexual play themes and have contacted social services. Mickey's mother denied that he has been exposed to sexually explicit media or placed in situations with potential for sexual abuse.

Separation Anxiety

For some children, the first weeks of the school year are filled with excitement and novelty. Each day brings the joy of exploration and challenge, and these children eagerly leave their mothers and fathers at the classroom door—with the parents being more hesitant than their children to separate for the day. Separation from caregivers causes daily sadness and fearfulness for other children. The tearful leave-taking extends beyond the first few days of school, continuing well into the ensuing weeks. A child may persuade his or her parent to stay longer each day and engage in play. When the parent eventually leaves, however, the child may become so preoccupied with the separation that he or she clings to a teacher and repeatedly asks, "When will Mommy (or Daddy) be back?" This dependence on adult reassurance and physical proximity may seriously affect the teacher's accessibility to other children in the classroom. Daily crying also may become frustrating as the teacher seeks an effective way to separate the child (e.g., at the center's door, on the bus before coming to the center, after 5 minutes of classroom visiting) from his or her parent with minimal distress.

Violations of Safety Limits

Unsafe behaviors are challenging to early childhood professionals because of the risks involved for the individual child and his or her peers. Regardless of the child's individual abilities, skills, or temperament, he or she may display numerous behaviors that demand immediate teacher attention to ensure classroom safety (Barnett, Bell, & Carey, 1999; Barnett, Bell, Gilkey, et al., 1999). These behaviors may be exacerbated by specific child ability or skill impairments (e.g., cognitive, language, social, attention) and may be learned responses to situations that are frustrating or confusing for the child. A child may respond to a teacher direction (e.g., "It's time to clean up") or a peer's action (e.g., taking turns using the computer) with unsafe actions or inappropriate verbal behaviors. He or she may engage in tantrums, cry loudly, and resist teacher efforts of reassurance and redirection. Excessive crying and angry demands disrupt the activities of the entire classroom, diverting teacher attention from peers. The tantrums may include actions that could injure the child, nearby peers, or adults who attempt to calm the child. Functional behavioral assessment has emerged as a method to disentangle the factors contributing to and maintaining these behaviors (Gresham, Watson, & Skinner, 2001). Functional behavioral assessments are discussed more thoroughly in Chapter 6.

Aggressive and antisocial acts are relatively common in early childhood classrooms (Harden et al., 2000; Kupersmidt, Bryant, & Willoughby, 2000; Reguero de Atiles, Stegelin, & Long, 1997; Willoughby, Kupersmidt, & Bryant, 2001). A child may use physical aggression to meet his or her needs or to express frustration. Instrumental aggression—hitting, pushing, shoving, scratching, grabbing, or pinching others or throwing classroom materials to obtain an end (e.g., to get a desired toy)—is more commonly observed in classrooms serving young children than in later educational environments. Biting, in particular, occurs frequently in early childhood settings and often is associated with limited language facility (Reguero de Atiles et al., 1997). Hostile aggression involves attempts to establish dominance or power in the classroom and requires intensive teacher monitoring and proactive strategies to prevent injury to the child, his or her classmates, or adults (Crick, Casas, & Ku, 1999). Relational aggression in the form of cursing, taunting, ridiculing, or name-calling often accompanies physical aggression. Left unchecked, these behaviors can escalate, becoming increasingly disruptive to classroom activities, exhausting the teachers, and, eventually, pervading the classroom climate (Goldstein, 2001). As a result, other children may express to parents and teachers a fear of going to school.

Running is a serious safety-related behavioral challenge. It is a powerful technique that a child can use to immediately dominate the teacher's time and attention. The child may run in the classroom or leave the classroom and/or escape from the child care center building itself, requiring an adult to follow for safety reasons. This behavior is especially difficult to manage because the adult has no choice—he or she has to respond with immediate attention (Piazza et al., 1997).

CLASSROOM APPLICATION

What skills does this child have?

What is the child's complete daily routine?

Does the child successfully enter or initiate play activities?

Which play areas interest the child?

Which play areas does the child avoid or visit infrequently?

How long does the child remain engaged in preferred and nonpreferred activities?

How many activity changes does the child make within a 30-minute period?

Is it necessary to contact the child's parents or appropriate child protection agencies regarding disturbing play themes?

Are there unsafe behaviors that warrant priority for intervention?

WHICH HOME FACTORS ARE IMPORTANT TO EXAMINE?

As a teacher continues to assess a challenging classroom situation, it is critical to consider influential factors in the home environment that may be important areas for communication and consultation between the early childhood education staff and the family. A warm, nurturing, communicative home environment with age-appropriate limits that are consistent but flexible provides a child with the basic support needed for relationships with other children (Baumrind, 1967, 1996; Collins, Maccoby, Steinberg, Hetherington, & Bornstein, 2000; Maccoby & Martin, 1983). Although much of the available research focuses on the mothers' role in child rearing, the unique contributions of fathers as role models and playmates are being investigated (Sirridge, 2000). The families of young children in contemporary early childhood settings are diverse, ranging from intact biological families to grandparents serving as guardians to young children (Edwards, 2000; Karpowitz, 2000).

Parental Lack of Experience or Understanding of Child-Rearing Practices

Adolescent parents may have little knowledge of typical child development, may have unrealistic expectations of their child's behaviors, and may be more likely to have children with aggressive or oppositional behavior problems (Orlebeke, Knol, Boomsma, & Verhulst, 1998; Stormont, 1998). Inaccurate perceptions of a child's maturity level may lead parents to punish harshly typical child behaviors such as spilling food, having toileting accidents, or soiling clothing (Spieker, Larson, Lewis, Keller, & Gilchrist, 1999). Conversely, some young parents may inaccurately judge the maturity and independence capabilities of a 3- or 4-year-old, thereby exposing their child to adult themes in television or movies, giving in to unreasonable demands regarding bedtime or food choices, or inappropriately using the child as a confidante or source of support (Fine & Wardle, 2000).[2]

Some parents, regardless of age, may be overwhelmed by child demands, relying on ineffective and inconsistent disciplinary practices. Children of these parents quickly learn to calculate the odds of punishment or escape. They may capitalize on parental vulnerabilities or indifference by "trapping" their parents into meeting unreasonable demands (Patterson, DeBaryshe, & Ramsey, 1989). Some parents may fear that placing limits on behavior may cause them to lose their children's love. Others may rely on abusive or harsh disciplinary practices, methods with which they are familiar from their own childhoods (Fine & Wardel, 2000; Herrenkohl & Russo, 2001; Patterson et al., 1989). Parenting

---

[2]For more in-depth information on research regarding adolescent parents and their children, see Whitman, Borkowski, Keogh, and Weed (2001).

strategies that rely on angry and aggressive responses to the disciplinary infractions of young children have been linked with behavior problems during early childhood, especially when implemented by fathers (Carson & Parke, 1996; DeKlyen, Biernbaum, Speltz, & Greenberg, 1998). Inconsistent and ineffective disciplinary methods with young children have also been associated with increased reports of behavior problems as the children enter school (Brenner & Fox, 1998; Herrenkohl & Russo, 2001; Kaiser & Hester, 1997). Different caregivers may have different child-rearing philosophies, requiring a child to adapt to varying behavioral standards and disciplinary methods from each caregiver (Edwards, 2000; Mahoney, Jouriles, & Scavone, 1997). Marital conflict often is related to harsh and intrusive parenting strategies that, in turn, are linked to behavior problems in young children (Frosch & Mangelsdorf, 2001; O'Leary, Slep, & Reid, 1999). The influence of conflicting parental approaches is illustrated in the following vignette.

> Leah is a precocious and creative child. In the housekeeping activity center, she describes wildly imaginative play themes to her peers. She entices the other children to participate by laying out the play scenario, explaining the roles and the dialogue that she envisions. The other children are eager to play along. Within moments, however, Leah becomes frustrated because the other children embellish the plot, adding their own dialogue and actions. Leah reacts to the variations by screaming at the other children and hitting them with play materials. The teacher rushes to the activity center, comforting the other children and asking Leah what is wrong. During a later parent–teacher meeting, Leah's mother explains that she takes a behavioral approach to child rearing—that is, detailing the guidelines for acceptable behavior and the consequences of aggressive or defiant acts. Conversely, Leah's father believes that his creative and intelligent child needs freer range to express her talents. He advocates talking to Leah at length, exploring the underlying reasons for aggression and noncompliance. He explains to the teacher that he can empathize with Leah because as a child, he was similar to Leah.

Financial Concerns

Some parents face limited economic resources, having to work two or more jobs and/or late-night shifts to pay for home and child care expenses. These financial strains can negatively affect the quality of parenting, especially for single parents (Jackson, Brooks-Gunn, Huang, & Glassman, 2000). Long work hours limit the time that parents have to spend with young children. Valuable play and cuddle time can be sacrificed as the exhausted parents cope with household responsibilities (Karpowitz, 2000). Parental frustration with mounting bills or work time lost in caring for sick children can erupt into harsh discipline, inappropriate permissiveness, or neglect (Herrenkohl & Russo, 2001; Jackson et al., 2000). Children may spend time with less dependable or attentive caregivers, and anxiety about unpredictable daily routines may spill over into the classroom. Maternal employment issues are contributing factors to the challenging behavior described in the next vignette.

> Elisha arrives at the child care center at 7:15 A.M., tugging tearfully at her mother's coat. Her mother must be at work at 7:30 A.M. and dreads

her daughter's daily protests. Elisha anxiously asks her mother, "Are you going to pick me up today?" Her mother explains, "No, remember, today is Tuesday. You go to Gramma's house on Tuesday." Elisha persists, "Which Gramma? Nana Joyce or Gramma Jane?" A little impatiently, her mother responds, "Nana Joyce. I have to leave, Elisha. I'll be late for work. I'll see you tonight." Elisha begins to cry in earnest, refusing to be separated from her mother. "What time tonight, before supper or after supper?" Her mother gives her a fierce hug and leaves. Elisha anxiously questions the teachers throughout the day, "Who's coming to pick me up?" She has great difficulty falling asleep at naptime, pleading with a teacher to rub her back for 30 minutes before she finally falls asleep.

Parental Substance Abuse or Chronic Illness

Other parents are unavailable to their children, physically and emotionally, because of drug and alcohol dependency. One or both parents may prioritize drug-seeking and drug-using behaviors above their children's daily care (Fine & Wardle, 2000). This can lead to escalating behavioral challenges, as a child may respond to distracted and ineffective parenting with aggressive tactics (Brook, Zheng, Whiteman, & Brook, 2001). Living in an often unsupervised and sometimes dangerous home environment, the child pushes for boundaries and limits. In the worst case, a child may be punished harshly as he or she exhibits increasingly inappropriate behaviors to gain parental attention (Fine & Wardle, 2000). The child may be distrustful and defiant, be unaccustomed to adult limits, and expect an unusually broad range of choices and acceptable behaviors. He or she may continually test teachers, determining whether classroom routines and limits remain consistent and predictable. The child also may use aggressive and noncompliant behaviors in an inappropriate bid to secure the attention of adults in the school environment. During parent consultation, the parent may be tearful and remorseful or defiant and defensive when asked about this breach of parenting responsibilities (Fine & Wardle, 2000).

A similar scenario may occur when one or both parents have been diagnosed with a mental illness, such as depression or an anxiety disorder (Spieker et al., 1999; Stormont, 1998; Wright, George, Burke, Gelfand, & Teti, 2000). The influence of parental chronic illness (e.g., cancer, heart disease) on subsequent behavior problems in young children has been disputed in research. The illness demands (e.g., lifestyle changes, the drain on financial resources), the availability of extended family support, and the impact on the marital relationship seem to be moderating variables for adjustment problems in young children (Kahle & Jones, 1999). The next classroom vignette highlights challenges related to overly mature developmental expectations in the home environment, stemming from neglectful or distracted caregiving.

> Marcus, age 4, climbs precariously on a small chair, reaching for the juice that had been delivered from the kitchen and placed on a high shelf. When his teacher reminds him that his feet must stay on the floor, Marcus persists in reaching for the juice container, knocking it on the floor. The next 10 minutes are spent cleaning Marcus and the floor, delaying snack time. When the children are finally seated around the table, Marcus waits

impatiently for everyone to be served. He surreptitiously eats both of his crackers, then takes a cracker from the plate of the child next to him while the teacher's back is turned. The other child cries to the teacher in protest. The teacher moves Marcus between her seat and the wall, pushing the plate away from him as she does so and admonishing him to "use his words" to ask for more food.

Multiple Family Concerns

Some families have multiple concerns, including financial stressors, parental substance abuse, and daily experience with violence (Hanson & Carta, 1996; Stormont, 1998). Ackerman, Kogos, Youngstrom, Schoff, and Izard (1999) noted that factors adding to family instability (e.g., frequent residential moves, caregivers having numerous intimate partners, an accumulation of recent negative life experiences) uniquely contribute to the development of aggressive and noncompliant behaviors in young children. Ecological or contextual approaches to the assessment of young children emphasize the cumulative impact of many risk factors on the development of behavior problems (Barnett, Bell, & Carey, 1999; Shaw, Winslow, Owens, & Hood, 1998).

Siblings

Family composition varies, and children come to school with diverse experience regarding interactions with other children. Some children must compete for attention, such as a younger child in a family with several children. Other children begin school with supreme confidence in their own worth, squarely in the center of their parent's world as the only child. Harsh reality confronts these children when they must learn that the classroom teacher devotes comparable time to each child. Some children may bring competitive, aggressive behaviors to the classroom, hoping that these actions will be as effective in the classroom as they are at home (Stormont, 1998). Children with siblings may develop sophisticated negotiation strategies and social skills and successfully apply them in the school setting (Stormshak, Bellanti, & Bierman, 1996). Some children also have learned to protect or depend on a brother or sister. Such bonds may prevent a child from benefiting from social relationships and educational opportunities at school because the child anxiously looks for his or her sister on the playground or asks daily to eat lunch with his or her brother.

Safety of the Child's Neighborhood

It is critical to examine the neighborhood and broader community contexts within which children live. They are affected by the relative risk inherent in playing within their neighborhoods (Vig, 1996). A child will respond with fear or acceptance when exposed to domestic or community violence (Shahinfar, Fox, & Leavitt, 2000). The child may become highly anxious and fearful of leaving his or her parents, anticipating that they will be harmed while he or she is at school. Another possibility is that the child becomes hardened to violence and comes to view it as a predictable and acceptable part of daily life. Adults who engage in aggressive and criminal activities may be role models, encouraging such behavior during play and in interactions with peers and adults (Vig, 1996). Although teachers cannot significantly change a child's home life, there is hope that connections can be made for family support, education, and intervention. This topic is discussed more fully in Chapters 3 and 10.

CLASSROOM APPLICATION

Does the child have a safe and attentive home environment?

Is there a method for daily communication with the child's parent(s)?

Have areas of parental concern or parental inexperience been identified?

Would participation in parenting classes or support groups be helpful/feasible for the child's parent(s)?

Does the early childhood center have a plan to address sibling interaction when brothers and sisters are enrolled in the same program?

What are the family's support needs? Should a referral to an outside agency (or agencies) be initiated?

Are there any links between parenting behaviors and child characteristics? That is, is the child hungry or tired?

WHICH CLASSROOM FACTORS ARE IMPORTANT TO EXAMINE?

Guidelines abound for the construction of center curricula and the provision of age-appropriate and enriching activities for groups of young children. The National Association for the Education of Young Children provided best practices guidelines for programs from infancy through early childhood (Bredekamp & Copple, 1997). Critical factors in providing a supportive and nurturing early childhood environment permeate the other chapters in this book. Therefore, only a brief treatment of this topic is included in this chapter.

Teacher–Child Ratio and Overall Class Size

It is imperative that young children feel safe and important with the adults who are consistently in their lives. A small teacher–child ratio helps ensure adequate attention to children who need guidance and boundaries. A longitudinal study by the National Institute of Child Health and Human Development (1998) established child care quality as one of the most important predictors of positive child outcomes. Having an appropriate number of sensitive and responsive staff members permits scaffolding for shy and hesitant children, who are often reluctant to enter play situations or attempt an unfamiliar activity.

Additional staff members within the classroom allow children to explore individual interests with appropriate supervision and assistance. Adequate staffing also allows appropriate responses for crisis situations—conflicts among children, tantrums, and health or building emergencies. The importance of planning for adequate staffing is illustrated in the following vignette.

> Lewis plays contentedly in the housekeeping area with Shondra, carefully placing the play food on the small table as he pretends to serve breakfast. She obligingly pretends to eat the banana and apple that he placed on the plate. The early morning classroom is quiet as the teacher talks with the only other staff member in the room, an assistant who is new to the program. Three other children play in the book area, "reading" aloud as they lie on the rug. At 8:15 A.M., the bus arrives and 10 children noisily troop into the room, all trying to greet the teacher at once. Lewis begins to rake the plates off the table and throws them into the basket under the pretend stove. He runs to the door to greet his friend Ben, hurriedly inviting him to go to the block area with him. Other children crowd in the area around the cubbies, shoving their coats onto hooks and their backpacks onto shelves. The teacher helps some of the children unfasten and stow their winter clothing. Ben is distracted by the activity around the cubbies. Lewis pulls Ben's hand and repeatedly yells, "You're not listening to me." The teacher attempts to help Lewis redirect his anger, but Lewis and Ben begin a shoving match. Another child, Maria, is fearful of Lewis's yelling; she begins crying for her mother. The new staff member comforts Maria, while the remaining children chase each other around the classroom.

Staff Training and Awareness of the Center's Philosophy

Classroom staff members have varying degrees of professional preparation. Although there is increased awareness of the need for personnel preparation, many individuals come to the classroom with little knowledge of early child development and early childhood educational theory (McDonnell & Brownell, 1997). It is the early childhood program's responsibility to provide adequate supervision and training for new staff members, pairing them with experienced mentors to guide their first days in the classroom and to answer situation-based questions. The center's philosophy should pervade every teacher–child interaction because children crave consistency and test staff member boundaries and experience. Firm but flexible limits reduce each child's need to establish the bounds of acceptable behavior. Child care settings in which teachers fail to set and enforce clear limits face high levels of challenging behavior (Arnold, McWilliams, & Arnold, 1998). Consistent, child-centered policies and procedures prepare staff members to act confidently in unusual or emergency situations. The importance of consistency in staff responses is evident in the following vignette:

> Matthew and Timothy are playing in the manipulatives area. Timothy is building a tall structure. Matthew repeatedly attempts to connect two blocks of different sizes to make a tower like Timothy's. The blocks will not connect, and he gets increasingly agitated. A teacher watches from

the puzzle area where she is helping another child. Matthew gives up in frustration, turns his creation sideways, and points it at Timothy, saying, "I'm going to shoot your tower down!" The teacher moves to the manipulative area and says, "Matthew, that's not safe. We don't make guns in this classroom. Did I see that you were trying to make these pieces fit? What would happen if you try the green ones?"

Staff Sensitivity and Responsiveness to Child Needs

Sensitive caregiving is the hallmark of high-quality child care, a characteristic that is closely associated with children's learning and overall development (Dunst et al., 2001; Sandall, 1997). Unstable child care arrangements (i.e., frequent changes in child care settings) are associated with increased numbers of behavior problems in young children (McCartney et al., 1997). It is important for each child to feel that staff members care about his or her interests and safety. Individual staff members must build relationships with each child, taking time to learn about the child's family, common activities, and daily life (Bredekamp & Copple, 1997). Daily conversation with each child also keeps staff abreast of important events at home and in the child's extended family. These frequent positive interactions allow the adults to build trusting relationships with the children. An intimate knowledge of an individual child allows a staff member to intervene early, preventing many conflicts from escalating into crises (Umbreit, 1996). Knowing a child's "hot spots" often allows an astute observer scanning child activities across the room to ascertain a problem, redirect the child at this critical time, and prevent an emergency situation (Barnett, Bell, & Carey, 1999; Wolery & Winterling, 1997). In turn, a child who receives frequent and positive attention may be less likely to engage in negative attention-seeking behaviors.

Cleanliness, Appearance, and Safety of the Classroom

Classroom arrangements vary given the constraints of each facility. For some programs, all activities must take place within a single room. For others, children have the luxury of outside playgrounds or indoor gross motor activity rooms, and these activities can be rotated, providing variety in the daily schedule. Regardless of the physical layout, it is important for the space to be logically divided, separating noisy and quiet areas, permitting monitoring by classroom staff, and facilitating appropriate child engagement (Lawry, Danko, & Strain, 2000; Wolery & Winterling, 1997). The materials also must be well organized, with open or clear plastic containers placed at a child's eye level to facilitate a personal sense of responsibility for cleanup. The space should be organized with safety in mind, separating the adult storage and planning areas from the child's play areas (Sandall, 1997). The number and arrangement of classroom activities should fit the interests and ability levels of the children (Dunst et al., 2001; Umbreit, 1996). Inattention during group time, inappropriate use of construction or sensory materials, unsafe climbing (on shelves or tables), or running may be addressed by rearranging classroom materials and activities (Lawry et al., 2000), as illustrated by the next vignette.

The classroom is carefully arranged for the first day of class. Activity areas are situated around the walls with plenty of space in the middle of the room for group time. The activity center and materials are arranged with special consideration for Alicia, a 4-year-old in a motorized wheelchair. The rugs are thin, giving Alicia easy access to the book area and group time space. A bench is placed next to the music area, with plenty of room for Alicia's wheelchair. Shelves are placed at a level that gives Alicia easy access to materials, whether she is in or out of her wheelchair.

When the children arrive, Ron, an active 4-year-old who is highly excited about this first day of school, rushes around the room. When the children begin to choose activity areas, Ron yells, "Watch this!" He then runs around the room, using the bench as a step to hurdle the bookshelf behind it, turning, diving to the ground, and sliding on his stomach on the highly polished floor in the open center of the room. The other children, intrigued, begin to imitate his progress through the obstacle course. The teachers quickly redirect the children to appropriate activities and start planning a new arrangement for the room.

Predictability of the Daily Routine

Another essential element of the early childhood classroom is a consistent daily schedule (Barnett, Bell, & Carey, 1999; Lawry et al., 2000; Sandall, 1997). Children flourish in the safety of predictable daily activities and learn most effectively through the comfort of repetition. Classroom limits and rules should be easily accessible to young children. This may be accomplished by posting visual cues regarding the expected child behavior in each play area. Young children establish expectations for different experiences. Frequent departures from these expectations can provoke anxiety. For this reason, it is important to plan for and warn the children about changes in routine, to introduce the children to new staff, and to assure the children that these changes are safe.

CLASSROOM APPLICATION

Is the classroom environment safe and attentive?

Is the curriculum appropriate for the chronological ages, interests, and abilities of the children within the class?

Are classroom materials arranged to promote safety, engagement, and self-sufficiency?

Are visual cues posted for expected classroom behavior?

Which classroom areas cause problems for this particular group of children?

What are the staff support needs? In which areas do staff need further training and professional development? Are additional staff members needed?

Have plans been made for adequate mentoring and supervision of inexperienced staff?

Which parts of the daily schedule need improvement?

WHICH CHILD BEHAVIOR CHARACTERISTICS ARE IMPORTANT TO EXAMINE?

This chapter conveys the need to view challenging behavior within an ecological context. The previous discussion highlighted the importance of considering the influences of child, parent, and classroom-related variables on aggressive, noncompliant, or other challenging behaviors. The remainder of the chapter discusses the defining elements of the behavior of concern. Chapter 6 details techniques for gathering information on an individual child's problem situation. For the purposes of introduction, this chapter identifies the variables that compose any summary or complete description of a child's challenging behavior.

Frequency

When discussing a child's disruptive behavior, the first question usually is, "How often does this behavior occur?" Any decision to further examine the problem situation or call for administrative consultation would be predicated on the number of times that the classroom teacher and staff has had to address the issue. Counting problem behaviors during a discrete time period or activity (e.g., three "talk-outs" during group time, four incidents of noncompliance across the school day, 17 activity changes during morning free play) can help flesh out the body of the problem (Kazdin, 2001; Miltenberger, 2001).

Duration

The time spent on inappropriate or unsafe behavior must be tracked as well (Kazdin, 2001; Miltenberger, 2001). Some behaviors (e.g., hitting, biting) happen quickly but need to be immediately and systematically addressed. The disruptiveness of other behaviors depends on the time that staff spend attending to the behavioral challenge (e.g., running, tantrums, refusal to follow a classroom routine) (Barnett et al., 1999). The behavior may occur only two or three times per week but is totally disruptive and time-consuming.

Severity

Although some behaviors may be annoying and interrupt the classroom day, they can occur frequently and at length without posing danger to the child, the other students, or the staff. The occurrence of these behaviors can vary from one early childhood program to another. Expected levels of such behaviors can be defined by a closer examination of the specific peer grouping (Bell & Barnett, 1999). Other behaviors are of sufficient severity to endanger the health or emotional well-being of the child and his or her peers (or the staff) (Kazdin, 2001; Miltenberger, 2001). Behaviors that are common in early childhood settings (e.g., hitting, shoving) may escalate as the offending child takes a no-holds-barred approach. Hitting may be intense enough to cause bruising, and single-minded shoving may cause the other child to be hurt in the fall. Using a classroom material as a weapon (e.g., throwing a chair, stabbing a peer with scissors, breaking glass containers) often constitutes a crisis situation that requires immediate, unplanned action. Destroying children's belongings or classroom materials (e.g., intentionally breaking manipulative toys, marking on other children's clothing, harming the classroom pet) jeopardizes the emotional security of other children in the program and requires immediate and consistent responses from classroom personnel. Engaging in unsafe behaviors (e.g., climbing on classroom furniture, jumping from high playground equipment, running from the building or playground) can be life threatening and precipitates immediate teacher action.

Warning Signs

Another consideration is whether it is possible to predict that a child may act aggressively or disruptively in a given activity, with a given group of children, or on a given day. These conditions are often called *setting events* because they seem to define the conditions under which challenging behaviors are more likely (Feldman & Griffiths, 1997; Kazdin, 2001). Some children give no warning at all, causing perplexed teachers to comment, "But they were playing so well together only a moment before." Others follow predictable patterns or sequences of behavior. A child may play happily with one combination of children but erupt with another group of playmates. Another child may escalate gradually from minor rule infractions to serious, unsafe behaviors. Still another child might come to the classroom in a bad mood, warning staff that giving the child extra attention will be time and effort well spent. Finally, some classroom situations might "light a child's fuse." Examples include times when 1) staff patterns are unpredictable (e.g., a substitute appears in the regular teacher's absence), 2) schedules are not predictable (e.g., on days when parties or field trips are scheduled or there is a classroom visitor), or 3) the classroom is particularly crowded (e.g., part of the center is closed, two classes are combined for a special activity).

CLASSROOM APPLICATION

Can the behavior of concern be summarized or described?

Have the behavioral outbursts or problem episodes within a 30-minute period been counted?

Has the amount of time spent addressing the problem been measured?

Has the severity of the behavior been determined? Have crisis plans and outside resources been identified?

Do warning signals predict the behavior?

Which staffing, environmental, or curricular changes might prevent future episodes?

CONCLUSION

This chapter has defined some of the challenging behaviors that are addressed throughout this book. Although it is tempting to view a disruptive situation as a discrete child problem, teachers are encouraged to examine the interplay among such factors as 1) child health, skills, and abilities; 2) parenting skills and priorities; and 3) classroom-related variables. The ensuing chapters detail these issues and suggest assessment and intervention strategies.

Chapter 2

Developing
Centerwide Support

Victoria Carr, Lawrence J. Johnson,
and Connie C. Corkwell

Marian Wright Edelman said, "We must not, in trying to think about how we can make a big difference, ignore the small daily differences we can make." Often, these small differences make teachers believe that a child care center's administration supports their hard work. Working with children with challenging behaviors is difficult. Therefore, it is important that teachers, parents, and administrators collaborate to support each other. Finding the time to do so, however, is not an easy task. This chapter focuses on the administrative leadership that is necessary for creating a place where all children can succeed. This leadership supports staff, including all teachers and related personnel, and families that are struggling to resolve issues that challenge the classroom structures. When teachers consider employment with an early childhood program, questions related to leadership should be asked during interviews. This chapter addresses leadership and the administrator's role, financial and professional centerwide support, collaborative problem solving, and the sociocultural context of the early childhood program.

WHAT IS PRINCIPLE-CENTERED LEADERSHIP?

Covey (1990) stated that synergy is the essence of principle-centered leadership. The central tenets of leadership synergy are valuing and respecting differences, building on strengths, and compensating for weaknesses. In addition, Hord (1997) stated that school leaders must create learning communities in which the entire school works together to solve problems. Furthermore, center leaders must create and support a consensus on purpose and practice that becomes the standard for staff and families. Leaders must raise questions about practice, institutionalize shared values, and motivate others by example (Sergiovanni, 1996). These elements form the challenge of creative collaboration in developing centerwide support for children, families, and staff.

When choosing an early childhood education and care center, many parents assume that they have selected a place where everyone truly cares about children. This assumption is valid in many centers, but families must explore a center's level of commitment to collaborating with children and families to foster learning and the social community of children, families, and staff. Staff seeking employment must investigate this aspect of a prospective employer as well. The processes of participation, democratic interactions, collective responsibility, problem solving, and decision making are integral to the organizational and educational structures of a center that embodies principle-centered leadership (Spaggiari, 1998). In fact, the most frequently cited reason that educational leaders lose their jobs is the failure to communicate in ways that build on positive relationships with parents, teachers, students, and colleagues (Bulach, Pickett, & Boothe, 1998). The second most common reason is the failure to make decisions that reflect a thorough understanding of the center's issues and problems (Davis, 1997). This is why administrative or instructional leaders, directors, or principals must commit to finding resources to support teachers, children, and families.

Early childhood teachers quickly learn about an administrator's levels of commitment and support when a challenge exceeds the skills and techniques of classroom staff. Key elements of principle-centered leadership include an administrator's willingness to commit time and funds to support collaboration and cooperation among all stakeholders. When challenging behavior is the issue, stakeholders include not only classroom staff and families but also administrative staff, mental health staff, and other professionals. A principle-centered leader must be able to visualize the big picture. He or she has to determine whether the stress of staffing is cost-effective in both the short and long run and must find creative ways to allocate funds for additional staff, if needed. The administrator must design programming for flexibility to allow scheduling time for collaborative problem solving. He or she must observe the group dynamic and sociocultural context within classrooms and engage families when intervention is necessary. Finally, based on assessed needs, the administrator must seek and arrange for professional development and educational support for the classroom.

Build on Habits

Covey compared effective leaders to compasses: "They are always pointing the way. And if we know how to read them, we won't get lost, confused, or fooled by conflicting voices and values" (1991, p. 19). An effective program is almost impossible without an effective leader. The administrator sets the tone and establishes standards by which staff members measure themselves. He or she must differentiate between effective leadership and management: A leader does the right thing; a manager does things right. Clearly, effective management is a part of the administrator's role, but effective leadership is the key to exemplary services. Relative to principle-centered leadership, Covey (1991) described seven characteristics of highly effective leaders, as well as seven characteristics of ineffective leaders. These effective characteristics and their counterparts are described next as they apply to effective administration of early childhood programs.

Be Proactive Instead of Reactive

A proactive administrator uses his or her resourcefulness to anticipate problems and find solutions before a problem escalates. It is not always possible to anticipate problems, but leaders should address problems as soon as they become evident. Problems rarely just go away; instead, they typically get more complicated and severe over time. One of the most unproductive administrative approaches is "admiring problems." That is, administrators describe the problem, talk about contributing factors, identify those involved, and, perhaps, muse upon its awfulness and detrimental effect on the program. Yet, a solution is not found.

Proactive administrators have the ability to assess the situation and develop a positive response. They also focus on the things over which they have influence and, in the process, often expand the area of influence. Conversely, reactive administrators often focus their efforts on areas over which they have no control. Their complaining and negative energy may shrink their circle of influence. Leaders must believe that they have the ability to take charge, plan ahead, and focus their energies on things that they can control instead of reacting to or worrying about things over which they have little or no control.

Begin Working with the End in Mind
Instead of Working without a Clear End in Mind

When people begin working with a destination in mind, they have a road map to guide daily activities. Specific opportunities and challenges should be approached with a clear understanding of their capacity to facilitate or inhibit goal attainment. Without considering the big picture, it is easy to get lost in daily activities that may or may not contribute to the primary vision. Overall, goals should be revised and refined on the basis of new challenges and opportunities, but this process should be systematic and navigational in character. The administrator should change course based on a systematic assessment of progress toward identified goals. He or she must always reference identified goals to maintain perspective on the program's progress. In the process, overall goals can be revised based on the context within which the program exists and the needs of those whom the program is designed to serve.

Put First Things First Instead of Doing the Urgent Things First

An effective administrator focuses on the issues that are most critical to the program's mission. Each issue must be assessed regarding its importance to the program and its need for action from the administrator. These two dimensions form four characteristics of an issue.

1. *Urgent and important:* These issues represent true crises that must be dealt with immediately. They are important to the program. They can be unexpected events,

such as accidents, or deadline-driven events that are encased in urgency because of the approaching deadlines. When an event of this kind occurs, the administrator must focus on it and cannot afford to be distracted or to delegate the work.

2. *Not urgent but important:* These issues are truly important to the program but do not require immediate attention. They can include long-term planning, teacher assessments, program assessments, celebrations of accomplishments, and other issues that are critical to the program's success. Although these kinds of activities are not urgent, a program will suffer if the administrator never addresses them. In fact, if the administrator ignores such activities, they can become crisis situations that must be addressed.

3. *Urgent but not important:* These activities appear to be urgent but are really not that important. Often, they relate to other people's minor interpersonal issues. Unfortunately, an administrator who gets involved in issues that other people believe are urgent can fall into the habit of mistaking unimportant matters for important ones. Thus, precious time and energy is wasted. Over time, the administrator's ability to address urgent and important issues will erode.

4. *Not urgent and not important:* Many activities require an administrator's time, so the administrator who is not careful can spend too much time on issues that are neither urgent nor important. An administrator who tends to micromanage can fall into this trap, focusing on tiny details that disfranchise employees and waste time. In turn, the administrator will be unable to give sufficient attention to more important issues.

Administrators must keep the program in mind when reviewing their priorities and deciding what needs to be attended to and in what order. For some people, this is easy, but for those whose personality traits inhibit delegation and/or releasing control of situations, this is difficult.

Think Win-Win Instead of Win-Lose

Administrators seeking a win-win orientation have to listen to others and attempt to understand their position. Administrators must shun a win-lose approach to interpersonal relations and avoid the seduction of succeeding because someone else has failed. This orientation has been promulgated by the competitiveness of our culture and is destructive because, in the long run, people have to cooperate more than they have to compete. A win-win attitude seeks mutual benefits for all involved and encourages people to participate in future activities.

Seek to Understand, Then to Be Understood Instead of Seeking First to Be Understood

When people engage in conversation, they often do not listen to understand. Rather, while the other person is talking, they are in the process of forming their reply. This internal dialogue precludes people from truly hearing what others have to say. An effective administrator works hard to comprehend another person's frame of reference. Listening does not necessarily mean that the administrator must agree with the other person's view; it only means that he or she should strive to understand that person's viewpoint. This, in turn, is critical to the administrator's being understood. The administrator can present his or her position more clearly and respectfully when he or she understands where the other person is coming from.

Synergize Instead of Going It Alone

Two or more people in creative cooperation can produce results far better than each person could produce alone. An effective administrator must display humility, recognizing that his or her own views are limited and that creative solutions can emerge from interactions with others who have different values and mindsets. Moreover, these solutions are typically superior to those that the administrator might have achieved alone. However, collaborating and problem solving with others is difficult; these activities require effort and genuine commitment. Far too often, administrators choose the easier path—generating actions in isolation. (Although Covey [1991] described this ineffective trait as "compromise," the chapter authors believe that compromising is important for synergizing. For early childhood administrators, *trying to go it alone* is a more appropriate phrase for contrasting with the term *synergize*.)

Sharpen the Saw Instead of Fearing Change and Putting Off Improvement

An effective administrator recognizes excellence as a journey and engages in a process of continuous improvement. This journey is an upward spiral of growth and change. Although change merely for the sake of change is avoided, making strategic changes based on continuous improvement data is embraced. This orientation allows the administrator to take the program to increasingly higher planes of excellence. It allows for greater awareness of which resources are needed, what is urgent, and how to support teaching staff.

CLASSROOM APPLICATION

What questions may foster principle-centered leadership?

How is the child care center or classroom staffed?

Are there resources to assist classroom staff when problems arise?

Is the director willing to do whatever is necessary to be supportive?

What can be done to promote principle-centered leadership?

How should activities be prioritized in the face of a difficult task (e.g., a large project, an external program review)?

WHEN IS FINANCIAL AND PROFESSIONAL CENTERWIDE SUPPORT NEEDED?

Administrative support typically comes in response to a problem that began in the classroom. A problem can be an immediate crisis or a chronic issue. A crisis generally results in an immediate cry for help, and the issue is addressed in a manner relative to the center's protocol and procedures. At times, however, the crisis is addressed "on the fly," without consideration of procedure. Regardless of how a problem arises, the administrator must be prepared to support staff and families during all phases of problem solving. The following vignette exemplifies a situation that occurs in many early childhood programs.

> Elijah arrives at the center at 8:30 A.M. and is picked up at 5:30 P.M. Each morning, the two classroom staff brace themselves for his screaming tantrums; abusive language, which is aimed at the teachers and other children; and physical attacks on other children without apparent provocation. In the afternoon, the staff dread naptime because Elijah resists the classroom routine. In the evening, staff worry about addressing complaints from the parents of Elijah's peers. The lead teacher has already informed the assistant director of Elijah's behaviors and how they negatively affect the staff and the other children and their families.

In this scenario, the assistant director can respond by doubting that the incidents significantly affect the classroom or, at the other extreme, by removing Elijah from the program. Each solution is drastic. The first step for the administrator is to observe the situation for adequate staffing, appropriate classroom management techniques, and a dynamic curriculum. Second, a shared observation with the family may facilitate an understanding of the family's cultural beliefs and expectations about Elijah's behaviors. The classroom staff should have well-documented information about Elijah's behavior over the course of the day. With this supporting documentation and, perhaps, a decision to provide additional support staff, the administrator may need to assign another staff member to the room for the most problematic times of the day: drop-off and naptime. This short-term solution will enable classroom modifications for all of the children, and especially for Elijah.

Long-term solutions may require an intervention plan to benefit Elijah, staff members, and the other children. More specifically, staff members may need a script of responses to Elijah's inappropriate behaviors. Creating a script is best accomplished through collaborative decision making based on collected data and family suggestions. (Script creation is further discussed in Chapter 7.) Second, staff in the classroom may need professional development or coaching from the assistant director to build classroom management skills for anticipating and responding to tantrums and aggressive behaviors. Third, when other crisis situations arise throughout the day, the other children need help developing a collective response to his aggressive behavior to ward off attacks. These responses must be supported or guided by teachers and support staff.

Create or Expand Flexibility within the Program

For short-term and long-term solutions, a flexible program must be maintained. Although this approach often presents logistical problems, flexibility is imperative for scheduling and staffing patterns. For example, providing overlapping schedules for staff during the day may give a teacher time to meet with parents and support personnel. Administrative staff may take over the classroom for a designated period of time, or parents may be asked to assist in the classroom. Such flexibility allows for implementation of what Dunst, Trivette, and Deal (1988) called the *enablement model* of helping parents and teachers problem-solve and identify contextual problems. Although the enablement model is typically applied to families, teachers who provide care and education for young children also need to feel empowered to make decisions and implement interventions that promote teacher competency and goal satisfaction. In essence, through collaboration and coopera- tion, parents and teachers can decide what is important, develop a plan of action, and effectively deal with the issues at hand. This model empowers in a way that promotes active problem solving and supports teacher and parent capabilities to jointly effect change. Creating time and space for collaborative problem solving is essential to providing centerwide support.

Outside Observations of the Classroom's Sociocultural Context

A first step to problem solving is obtaining data on behaviors as they occur within the classroom culture. If a young child's behavior is frequently stressful for teachers and caregivers, an assessment from a professional who is outside of the context can often provide insight regarding positive strategies for managing inappropriate behavior and developing individualized interventions. One key for such observation is the concept of "trained eyes." Directors, counselors, psychologists, master teachers, or others employed by the school or center should have extensive child development knowledge and well- developed observational skills. As Seefeldt stated, "Observing is probably the oldest, most frequently used and most rewarding method of assessing children, their growth, development, and learning" (1990, p. 313). However, one must explicitly know what to look for and how to record and interpret observations. Through this process, the observer can identify possible contributors to inappropriate behavior and ways that the behavior is encouraged, even if inadvertently. The observer can provide the classroom teacher with information about the overall classroom culture, teacher–child and peer interactions, and information about the particular child's social play and development. This is the first step toward developing an action plan and an ongoing process for implementing interventions. Providing resources for observing the child within the sociocultural context is another critical component of centerwide support.

Importance of Funding for Additional Staff

Providing support is a complex job, particularly when a center's budget is tight. Grant funding is sometimes available to early childhood programs and often available for pro- gramming related to mental health, disabilities, and early care and education. However, grant-writing expertise is required, and applications take time to process. If grant funds are not an option, then the budget may need to be scrutinized for accountability, identifying areas that may be adjusted to allow the hiring of additional staff. Many center administra- tors find it cost-effective to hire an additional staff member, such as an assistant teacher, who is available to cover during lead teacher absences and to help carry out interventions. Given high turnover rates among early childhood education personnel, this solution can meet several center needs, such as creating flexibility in staffing patterns.

Support may also come from parent volunteers who work with the other children while the teacher implements intervention techniques with a particular child. Another possibility is seeking assistants among college students who are majoring in education, psychology, speech-language therapy, or related fields and need volunteer experience and/ or are willing to work for minimum wage. In addition, scheduling an administrator to provide classroom support during the most difficult times of the day may be an option.

A budget that allows for such emergencies and interventions is of utmost importance. Yet, an additional staff person also is needed as a substitute when the lead assistant teachers need to meet with intervention stakeholders (parents and all applicable staff) to problem-solve and design intervention plans. Thus, it is not a question of whether additional staff members need to be hired but a question of how to make additional personnel available in a cost-effective manner. Administrators must find ways to generate funds within existing budgets, perhaps even by raising tuition rates, or through grants. Administrators also must collect data and document the center's needs to request funds from a center's board of directors. For example, documented cases of children's behavior influencing the center's staff—including high stress levels, many sick days used, and high turnover rates—may generate support for increasing staff salaries and/or tuition. Documentation of successful interventions that were implemented with the help of additional staff members may generate the continuation or extension of support staff funding.

Administrative Role in Engaging Families

Securing funding is an ongoing administrative task, but engaging families in the educational process also is inherent to any high-quality program. Administrators must recognize that they set the tone for family involvement and must make that involvement a key priority. (See Chapter 3 for further discussion of issues related to involving families in early childhood programs.) Children whose parents are involved in their educational programming tend to have the best educational outcomes. Studies have documented the relationship between parent involvement and higher test scores and attendance rates, positive self-concepts and attitudes toward school, and fewer behavioral issues (Christenson, Rounds, & Franklin, 1992). Yet, there are barriers to engaging parents, and a good administrator anticipates and minimizes the impact of these factors. Parent-identified barriers are related to logistical concerns (e.g., work schedules, time conflicts, transportation and child care difficulties), communication problems with teachers, and a misunderstanding of the educational system. Teacher-identified barriers are related to issues such as parent apathy, parent hostility, lack of time to meet with parents, and lack of expertise in techniques for supporting and involving parents. An effective early childhood program administrator provides the resources necessary to address logistical problems. At times, this requires paying baby sitters and arranging transportation so that parents can attend meetings and providing overtime pay for teachers to meet outside the regular school day. The main requirement is being sensitive to the logistical problems parents face and finding creative ways to address these problems. Asking parents to help identify solutions is the first and best step that an administrator can take toward being sensitive to these logistical problems.

Administrators are also key to addressing the barriers identified by teachers. One of the most serious challenges to family involvement occurs when parental beliefs and actions conflict with school and teacher attitudes, actions, and practices (Grossman, Osterman, & Schmelkin, 1999). Moreover, the distinctive roles of parents and teachers within their respective environments can create barriers and boundaries that further compound the problem of engaging parents. Specifically, teachers, administrators, and parents strive to protect those boundaries, separating roles and activities that are limited to parenting from those that are specific to school (Powell, 1990). An effective administrator can help early childhood professionals acknowledge their role in creating and maintaining these boundaries. For example, many studies indicate that early childhood personnel perceive that parents do not engage in child-rearing practices at the level valued by early childhood professionals (Kontos, 1984; Kontos & Dunn, 1989; Kontos, Raikes, & Woods, 1983; Kontos & Wells, 1986). In particular, Lightfoot's (1978) study suggested that teachers' stereotypes of socioeconomic and racial subgroups greatly influence staff perceptions of parental competence. If this is true for teachers in a specific program, the administrator can discuss these perceptions and help teachers understand how their attitudes inhibit efforts to enhance home–school relationships. Moreover, as Bierman (1996) emphasized, a key factor in a child's education is the communication and relationship between his or her parents and the educational program. Thus, a major function of an effective administrator is facilitating an effective communication cycle between parents and all members of the program.

Parents Who Challenge the System

Some parents challenge early childhood programs. It is the administrator's role to help teachers understand that most parents—even those who lack parenting skills, are absorbed in self-centered or destructive behaviors, and/or are abusive—want their children to be successful and well behaved. It is up to teachers and administrators to reflect on their own biases and seek to engage all families, particularly those of children who need interventions. For example, if a child abuse and/or neglect court case has been adjudicated but the parent still has custody of the child, it is important for teachers and other center staff to understand the situation. They must work to address any strong feelings that they have about this family. Parents in this situation often have a social services worker assigned to their case, and this individual may be available to help staff deal with their feelings.

Create a Family-Centered Program

Teachers and administrators need specific skills to effectively engage families. The early childhood education field emphasizes the importance of a family-centered approach, but individual programs may interpret this concept differently. Administrators must ensure that ongoing professional development discusses this family-centered philosophy and plans for carrying out these ideals in the program.

Bronfenbrenner eloquently stated the importance of a family-centered approach:

> Intervention programs that place major emphasis on involving the parent directly in activities fostering the child's development are likely to have constructive impact at any age, but the earlier such activities are begun, and the longer they are continued, the greater the benefit to the child. (1975, p. 465)

As Bronfenbrenner noted, parents are a child's greatest influence, and early childhood professionals need training and support to maintain a family-centered approach. Administrators must recognize that parents are busy and that children are often stressed as they are asked to adapt to their parents' schedules. In addition, parents and early childhood professionals have high expectations of young children. Children are expected to adapt to new surroundings, participate and problem-solve in groups, share, feed and dress themselves, follow adults' directions, and maintain composure during the day. To get to work on time, hurried parents often rush to drop their children off at child care centers or school. It takes extra effort for administrators to understand and engage these busy parents. Administrators also must help teachers learn how to calm angry parents. The administrator must support the teachers and find a way to clarify the situation so that key issues can be addressed. The following vignette illustrates some of the challenges of busy parents.

> Jintai is 4½ years old. Both of his parents are students at the local university. His father is completing an internship at the university hospital; his mother is writing her master's thesis and working 32 hours per week in the English as a Second Language Department. Jintai recently joined his parents, having spent the past 2 years in Japan with his grandparents, and the transition to the United States has been difficult. Jintai's mother hurriedly drops him off at the center between 7:30 A.M. and 8:00 A.M. each morning so she can work on her thesis before going to work at 9:00 A.M. Jintai's father usually has left for work when Jintai wakes in the morning and often is still at the hospital when Jintai goes to bed. Both parents highly value academic prowess and are taking Jintai to Saturday school. Jintai's teachers have noticed that he is crying at odd times, screaming during activities, and throwing books in the garbage can.

Elkind (1981) asserted that children ages 2–8 years perceive hurrying as a rejection—that is, as evidence that their parents do not really care about them. Children find such rejection threatening and may develop stress symptoms as a result. Jintai's behavior may reflect this hurried child concept. Although Jintai's parents are considerably involved in their son's development and education, the resulting impact of their busy schedules may be unexpected. An intervention without the family's participation would be futile. Thus, the teacher and administrator need to find a time when both parents can meet with staff to address these issues and plan for an intervention. Building on the premise that they want the best for their child, a solution is probable.

Jintai and Elijah, the two children in this chapter's vignettes, are in early childhood settings where expectations for cooperation, problem solving, and communication are valued. The extent to which each child succeeds depends on the overall group dynamic as well as the individuals' level of skill. However, parental involvement in any intervention is respectful of the social system in which the child functions. More specifically, as Bronfenbrenner (1979) asserted, human development is a dynamic process of interactions between an individual and the environment. Therefore, to develop interventions that positively involve parents in fostering their child's development, parents must be an integral part of intervention development. The administrator can assist the process of engaging families by building relationships, inviting family members to join staff observations of their child, and providing specific information related to their child's success.

Arrangements for Professional Development and Educational Support

Katz (1975) stated that professional development opportunities should be made available to early childhood educators on a continuing basis. Subsequently, Spodek and Saracho (1990) predicted that practitioners would continue to enter the field of early childhood education with a wide range of skills, that professional organizations would continue to press for higher standards of practice, and that the knowledge base of early childhood education would continue to expand through research. These predictions came true. Some early childhood teachers enter the field with a high school diploma, but many more have associate degrees, particularly in response to a national Head Start mandate for teachers with degrees. The push for baccalaureate degrees also is expanding. The National Association for the Education of Young Children approved revised standards in November 2001. These standards were most explicit about the content of educational programs (e.g., early childhood degree programs at universities) in that the programs' curricula must include instruction on the many facets of learning. In addition, in its *Position Statement on Interventions for Challenging Behavior,* the Division for Early Childhood of the Council for Exceptional Children specifically stated that many services should be available in early childhood environments, including "external consultation and technical assistance or additional staff support" (1999, p. 4).

Finally, early childhood educators and administrators are pushing for programs that put theory and research into practice. As Bruner (1966) asserted, a theory of instruction must guide pedagogy to achieve positive educational outcomes. Professional development for teachers and administrators is critical to a program's success and quality. It is particularly critical to seek professional development when unique situations present themselves. For example, when a child with diabetes, autism, or bipolar disorder enters a program for the first time, it is imperative that teachers learn best practices and routines that will ensure safety and sound programming for all children and staff. It is the administrator's responsibility to find professional development opportunities and provide support for staff to participate in those opportunities.

Professional development can occur in many ways. In-house professional development is inexpensive, utilizes internal resources, and generates dialogue. For example, one staff member may attend a seminar, then share what was presented and discuss its applications with the center's staff. College courses in early childhood education move staff up the career ladder. Some programs, such as Head Start, help offset the costs of college tuition for staff. Many university early childhood education professors assist with professional development at low or no cost to the program in conjunction with ongoing research. Early childhood conferences and seminars also provide professional development opportunities. However, "one shot" workshops do not provide the level of professional development necessary for influencing practice. The best strategy is having an early childhood professional development educator provide periodic workshop sessions with ongoing, in-house coaching. This also provides a center with the most cost-effective solution.

CLASSROOM APPLICATION

What questions help determine when financial and professional centerwide support is needed?

What are the support needs for a particular classroom?

How do classroom staff obtain the support that they need?

With whom can classroom staff discuss their needs for support?

Do some parents seem to have an ineffective approach to discipline?

Do some parents appear to lack skills or not care about their children?

Do staff members think that there is only one right way to raise children — that is, their way?

Are staff aware of cultural differences regarding parenting?

Are staff aware of their biases regarding parenting?

Does the program's administrator embrace family involvement?

CONCLUSION

Covey (1990, 1991) stated that effective administrators are leaders, not managers. Clearly, administrative principle-centered leadership is the key to providing centerwide support. This leadership must be built on honesty, respect, and a willingness to solve issues as they arise. Administrators must empower teachers and parents to work toward goals that help every child succeed. This means creating flexibility in the program; observing the cultural contexts of classrooms; providing feedback; finding funds for extra staff when warranted; developing relationships with all families; engaging parents when intervention is necessary; and implementing learning opportunities that are creative, reflective, and collegial in approach.

Chapter 3

Engaging Parents as Partners in Changing Behavior

Anne M. Bauer, Monica Battle,
and Lawrence J. Johnson

Working with and supporting families are critical components to helping children reach their full potential in early childhood programs. There are many ways to engage parents on behalf of children. Swap (1993) proposed four basic models of parent–school interaction: protective, school-to-home transmission, curriculum enrichment, and partnership.

In the protective model, the goal is to reduce conflict between parents and educators through separating their functions. The aim of this model is to protect the school from parent interference. The protective model assumes that parents delegate the education of their children to the school and that parents then hold the school accountable for learning outcomes. There is little parental intrusion but also no structure for preventive problem solving. In addition, there are no efforts to use community and family resources for enrichment.

A second method is what Swap (1993) referred to as school-to-home transmission. In this model, parents are enlisted to support the objectives of the school. The model assumes that children's achievement is improved by a continuity of expectations and values and that parents should endorse the importance of school, reinforcing school expectations and providing nurturing home conditions. The advantages are increased school success and a clear transmission of information to parents. However, there is an unwillingness to consider parents as equal partners.

Curriculum enrichment is the third model that Swap (1993) described. The goal of this model is to expand and extend the school's curriculum by incorporating the contributions of families. This assumes that continuity is important and that parents and educators should work together to enrich curriculum objectives and content. Relationships are based on mutual respect, and both parents and teachers are viewed as experts. This model incorporates the specialized knowledge of parents as a resource.

The goal of the fourth approach, the partnership model, is for parents and teachers to work together to accomplish the common mission of success for all children. This model assumes that success for all children involves collaboration among parents, community representatives, and teachers. It necessitates transforming the school culture to one based on collegiality, experimentation, mutual support, and collaborative problem solving. This model is difficult to implement because it requires changes in the way schools typically work. This chapter discusses the implementation of a partnership model by addressing the following main topics: what defines a family, barriers to parent participation in interventions, barriers to family participation, structuring an effective parent conference, and engaging parents in interventions.

WHAT DOES IT MEAN TO BE A FAMILY?

As Johnson and Hawkins (2001) asserted, the family is the basic unit that defines and binds society. Families appear in many configurations; nonetheless, it is important to understand that families worldwide are far more alike than different and that the goals that parents have for their children are nearly universal (Moles, 1993).

Family compositions have changed dramatically since the 1970s. The idea of the family being a father, a mother, and one or more children living together is not common, and data suggest that fewer than one in five families fit this description (Zinn & Eitzen, 1993). Another dramatic change that has occurred since the 1970s is that in the United States, the number of families headed by single men has increased from 1.3 million to 3.2 million, and the number of families headed by single women has increased from 5.8 million to 13.6 million (U.S. Census Bureau, 1995). Parental death, single-parent adoption, and a divorce rate that has doubled during this time period offer explanations for the rise in single-parent families. Other family configurations have emerged, involving combinations of stepparents, stepsiblings, extended family members, and common-law families (Beirne-Smith, Ittenbach, & Patton, 1998). People that make up the family may not be related by blood or marriage, and they may not live together most of the time (Turnbull, Turnbull, Shank, & Leal, 1995). To be effective in partnering with these individuals, early childhood professionals must have an expanded notion of *family* and embrace the unique configurations of the families of children enrolled in their programs. Moreover, the various types of family units with which the educational professional will come into contact often bring unique problems and challenges that must be addressed (Edwards, 1995).

A key component of all families is a commitment among family members to meet their collective and individual needs. The children attending early childhood programs are all members of families first and students second. Their families will have the most lasting and powerful influence on their development, and it is important for early childhood professionals to understand these families from a systems perspective. For the sake of simplicity, however, the remainder of this chapter uses the terms *parents* and *family* to refer to a diverse range of caregivers.

The Family System

All families function as interrelated systems. That is, if anything affects one member of the family, it affects all members of the family. Changes that occur in the broader community affect the family system as well. For example, a downturn in the economy can create additional family stress; if one parent loses a job or is less able to provide for the family, the impact on the child can be significant. Tension in the community because of inequalities or racial differences also can strain the family system and affect how a child functions in the classroom. Conversely, a child's experiences at school often have an impact on the broader family unit. Spending extra time with one child for intervention purposes detracts from other family activities. The early childhood professional must assess the family's capacity to take on additional tasks as he or she works with the family to build its capacity for parenting. Although requesting support of classroom activities can have positive outcomes, asking a parent who is already stressed by working long hours to support the family economically may actually do more harm than good.

Families Come from Diverse Backgrounds with Unique Needs

Parenting is a challenge, and each family has unique strengths and challenges that must be understood to support the family in nurturing a child's development. Poverty, substance abuse, and exposure to violence are daily concerns for a significant number of families (Hanson & Carta, 1996). In turn, families living in poverty, for example, have more than financial issues to address. Stressors associated with poverty include poor parental care, poor nutrition, a sense of lack of control over the living situation, and little hope for success in the future.

Teachers also may be from a different cultural, ethnic, or linguistic group than the families with whom they work. When this mismatch exists, working as partners becomes even more complex. The following subsections explore this topic through some broad examples.

African American Families   Harry (1992) suggested that two factors combine to challenge the participation of African American parents in their children's education. First, caregivers in these families are sometimes viewed as lacking the ability and the stability to form partnerships on behalf of their children. Combined with the deficit view of children's learning on which interventions are sometimes based, such attitudes diminish the roles of African American parents as full participants in decision making. Harry's suggestions can be applied to all parents of young children. She suggested that early childhood professionals must develop new roles for parents—roles that go beyond that of "consent-giver." Instead of simply giving information about their child's social history, parents can be included as active and official members of the assessment team. Parents can present reports, providing information that becomes part of the official record, well beyond the tacit "okay" traditionally given in response to a teacher's report. Parents also may become policy makers through membership on parent advisory committees, and they may act as advocates and peer support for other families.

Asian Families Although there is incredible diversity among Asian cultures, many Asian parents may view teachers as individuals with complete authority over their child's schooling. The parents' role, then, is not to interfere. Teachers who ask for help may be viewed as incompetent. In addition, Asian families may have difficulty accepting that their child is exhibiting behavior problems because Asian cultures sometimes view psychological distress as an indication of organic disorder, which is shameful to the family and the child. Communication in Asian cultures generally is highly contextual and does not always require verbal expression, relying instead on shared assumptions, nonverbal signals, and situational cues. Asian parents may appear polite to the point of submissiveness (Schwartz, 1995).

Many Asian families have the additional challenge of being refugees. For example, in his study of Cambodian refugee parents, Scheinfeld (1993) found reports of widespread fatigue and depression stemming from relentless economic pressures and cultural alienation. Under such stressful conditions, the Cambodian practice of physical punishment sometimes became extended and exaggerated in severity. In addition, intergenerational tensions emerged because of a parental culture that emphasized absolute parental knowledge, child deference, and traditional standards for child behavior. Furthermore, information may have been lacking among many Cambodian parents concerning American culture and society, and they experienced a decreased sense of support when structures on which they traditionally relied (e.g., the community, the extended family, the Buddhist temple) were not available.

Latino/Hispanic Families Latino/Hispanic families may be reluctant to send their children to early childhood programs (Lewis, 1993). Parents may not agree that their children will benefit from early childhood education. At home, children are usually nurtured with great care by numerous relatives, and parents are hesitant to extend the caregiving role to the child's school (Nicolau & Ramos, 1990). Nicolau and Ramos noted that many Latino/Hispanic parents with low incomes may view the U.S. school system as "a bureaucracy governed by educated non-Hispanics whom they have no right to question" (p. 13). Teachers and administrators may misread the reserved, nonconfrontational manner and noninvolvement of Latino/Hispanic parents as disinterest in their child's education—a perception that may increase each side's distrust for the other.

Language and communication also can be a significant barrier with Latino/Hispanic families. Bailey, Skinner, Rodriguez, Gut, and Correa (1999) interviewed Latino/Hispanic parents of young children and found that mothers were more aware of child-related services and took greater advantage of them than fathers did. However, family and child variables bore little relationship to awareness and usage of, or satisfaction with, early childhood programs. Although teachers are often recommended to seek information unique to each family's culture, Bailey and colleagues cautioned teachers about making generalizations about a group that may not pertain to every individual or family in that group. Similar to the findings of studies with majority culture families, program variables were more likely to determine service use and satisfaction than family factors alone. Bailey and colleagues found that Latino/Hispanic families may be somewhat less satisfied with early childhood services than their majority culture peers. However, practitioners should not assume that the traditional characteristics described in the literature are applicable to all families.

CLASSROOM APPLICATION

Have issues of family structure and partnership been addressed?

How diverse are the structures of the families of children enrolled in this early childhood program?

Does the family structure affect the relationships among family members?

Does the family structure affect staff interactions with the family?

Does this early childhood program value partnership with parents?

Is there a cultural ethnic or linguistic mismatch between the early childhood teachers and staff and the parents of children in this program?

WHAT ARE THE BARRIERS TO FAMILY PARTICIPATION?

It is important to minimize the barriers to active family involvement in early childhood programs. Some barriers are perceived and others are grounded in fact. When a family perceives a barrier and the teacher does not address it, however, the barrier—perceived or real—precludes full participation of the family. Barriers can be viewed from the perspective of the parent or the teacher (Johnson & Hawkins, 2001; Lynch & Stein, 1987). As introduced in Chapter 2, parent- and teacher-identified barriers can impede the formation of effective partnerships.

Parent-Identified Barriers

Logistical Problems

The unique logistical problems of each family must be considered as staff try to involve families in early childhood programs. Often, families must arrange for transportation to the center, babysitting, or time away from work to attend conferences, take part in observations, or visit with their child in the classroom. Although these are serious problems, early childhood programs can often minimize their effects. For example, a teacher might consider going to the family's home instead of having the parent come to the classroom, or the meeting could be held at a community center near the family's home. Transportation could be arranged by the early childhood program, such as asking a parent to ride the bus with his or her child and having a staff member drive the parent home after the meeting. A teaching assistant, another classroom teacher, or someone from the community could be paid to babysit the other children while the parent attends a meeting or visits the program. Meetings could be held at times that are accessible for working parents, such as during lunch or in the late afternoon or evening.

Communication Problems

As mentioned previously, families come in very different configurations, making effective communication difficult. For example, a child's parents may be divorced but maintain joint custody. In such family configurations that prove challenging for school–home communication, the teacher should have frank discussions with the parents to set up agreed-on structures for sharing information about their child. This discussion must happen before a problem arises. Otherwise, the challenges associated with the problem further complicate communication difficulties, thus inhibiting the development of a solution.

Increasingly, families and early childhood staff come from different cultural and/or socioeconomic backgrounds. As previously suggested, these differences must be understood or communication will prove more difficult. Early childhood professionals also must minimize the use of educational jargon and abbreviations that are confusing to some parents. Otherwise, teachers and family members will have completely different understandings of the same conversation. In addition to cultural differences, teachers must recognize different norms of communication among a particular family's members. Some families tend to be loud and emotional, whereas other families may be reserved and restrained. Professionals also have norms for communication and differing tolerances for variations in conversational style. One teacher may interpret a loud and emotional parental response as aggressive when it is merely the manner in which communication is shared in that particular family. The teacher's reaction may be intensified if he or she is sensitive and uncomfortable with assertive behavior. Another teacher with a more expansive style of communication may be unaffected by this parent's communication style.

It is imperative for early childhood professionals to understand strategies for effective communication, becoming aware of their communication tolerances as well as the varying communication styles of the families of children in the program. It is critical that staff communicate effectively with all families. Early childhood teachers should remember that nonverbal communication—such as facial expressions, body language, and eye contact—can convey meaning as well.

Although many factors help create an environment that nurtures effective communication, the most important is a commitment to active listening. A teacher who actively listens conveys the value of a parent's input. As Covey (1990) asserted, those who seek to understand before seeking to be understood are more likely to truly understand and effectively address the issue at hand.

Thus, communication is more than sending notes—it involves all of the ways in which information is transmitted to parents. Davies (1997) contended that in communicating with parents, teachers should use a variety of techniques, including the telephone, newsletters, and home visits and other personal contacts. The following guidelines can improve parent communication:

1. Create a friendly environment by encouraging all staff (e.g., secretaries, teacher assistants, custodians) to greet parents in a welcoming manner.

2. Reach out to parents by providing information in ways that are easily accessible for most individuals.

3. Plan specific ways to involve parents in program activities. Ask parents about the information that they might need to participate and their preferences for involvement.

4. Work with parents to identify resources that can help them address unique family needs.

5. Initiate interactions with parents before school begins. Introduce yourself and describe some of the projects or themes that are planned for the class.

6. Make frequent positive telephone calls and send home positive notes. Begin and end conversations on a positive note, reiterating the desired plan resulting from the interaction.

7. Focus on the family's assets and the strengths that the family brings to the program.

When communicating with parents in writing, remember that many consider all written communication "official." In addition, written communication may not be appropriate in some situations, such as when there are language or literacy issues. Furthermore, there is the possibility that the parent may fail to receive the note. When an issue is important, a telephone call or face-to-face conference is needed.

Lack of Understanding of the Educational System

American educational programs are complex organizations. Their rules can be formal and overt (e.g., the rights of children with disabilities and their families) or covert (e.g., the ways that parents can influence a program or school to place their child in a certain class) (Johnson & Hawkins, 2001). If parents do not understand these rules, then they will get lost in the bureaucracy and be unable to use the system to meet their needs or their child's needs. If the early childhood program is truly family focused, then staff members will make these rules public and work to ensure parent understanding. Early childhood program staff have to ask, "What facets of this program inhibit parents from becoming full partners in the educational process?" An increased emphasis must be placed on encouraging and empowering parents to be an important part of program decision making. This may mean teaching parents how to gain access to program and community resources.

CLASSROOM APPLICATION

Have efforts been made to engage parents?

Are meetings scheduled for parents' convenience?

Have creative ways to increase parent attendance and involvement been considered?

What are some innovative methods that can be used to effectively communicate with parents?

‖ Has the program made organizational policies and informal guidelines available and understandable to all parents, regardless of their educational or cultural background?

Teacher-Identified Barriers

Perceived Parent Apathy

It is possible that the parents' previous experiences with school have not been positive. These parents may seek to avoid future contact because they believe that these interactions will inevitably be negative as well. Parents also may believe that they have very little influence or power over what is going to happen to their children. They may think, "Whatever I do won't make a difference, so why bother?"

Although parent apathy is sometimes real, it is often overstated and can be the result of misinterpreted cultural differences or other factors. For example, it is possible that the parental behaviors interpreted as expressions of apathy may actually be exhaustion stemming from meeting numerous family challenges. To effectively address real or perceived apathy, teachers must first try to understand their own biases. They must be careful not to use perceived apathy as an excuse to avoid the difficult work necessary to keep a program family focused. As Johnson and Hawkins (2001) asserted, it is very easy for a teacher to use the excuse "The family doesn't care" when, in fact, the teacher's interactions with the family are unresponsive to the previously discussed logistical concerns (e.g., child care). Instead, teachers are advised to infuse school-related activities with a positive feeling and to encourage expectations of optimistic outcomes. If schools are viewed as positive places where positive things occur, parents are less likely to remain apathetic. A related strategy for overcoming apathy is to have parents participate as active decision makers about their children's education. Teachers must do everything possible to empower parents and let them know that their opinions matter. As parents experience the positive effects of this participation, they will be more willing to enter into an active partnership with the program.

Difficult Parents

Some parents challenge the system and prove very difficult for teachers to engage. These parents may be hostile and uncooperative and be perceived as "problems" by their children's teachers. Seligman (2000) suggested caution when making such a judgment. Although the early childhood teacher's interpretations may be correct, they also may be distorted by factors that the teacher fails to understand or recognize. Regardless, it is in the child's best interest for the teacher to find a way to work with the parent. As mentioned in Chapter 2, parents whose cases for abuse or neglect have been adjudicated and who have retained or regained custody of their children may prove particularly challenging. The teacher may not find these parents very likeable. However, he or she must find a way to get past these feelings and help such parents to support their child. White-Clark and Decker (1996) encouraged teachers to remember that parents are the primary educators of their children and that educational programs are incomplete without parent involvement. They described several rules for involving hard-to-reach parents:

1. Embody an ethic of caring.

2. Disregard stereotypes by recognizing that assumptions affect behavior.

3. Demonstrate to parents that their participation is valued. Demonstrate confidence in their potential impact on their child.

4. View parents as partners, collaborators, and problem solvers.

5. Communicate clear expectations, roles, and responsibilities to parents.

6. Address personal concerns and work actively to involve parents.

7. Understand the purpose and function of involving parents and the early childhood professional's place in facilitating that involvement.

8. Work to improve parent involvement by experimenting and being open to new ideas.

Angry or hostile parents pose certain problems. A parent may come to the teacher upset about something that his or her child said about an event in the classroom. The parent may appear defensive and not want to hear about the child's behavior. It is important to avoid escalating such a situation. Johnson and Hawkins (2001) suggested that the following steps may help to deflate the situation:

1. Listen! Do not try to interrupt the parent. Let him or her express whatever he or she came to say.

2. Do not argue, become defensive, or promise something that cannot be delivered.

3. Speak softly and calmly no matter how heated the parent becomes. Talking in this manner often calms the parent and lowers his or her intensity to a level consistent with your responses.

4. Write down key phrases expressed by the parent, and when he or she calms down, repeat these phrases to ensure that he or she knows the concerns were heard. Tell the parent you will try to get the needed information and will schedule a meeting with the appropriate individuals to address his or her concerns. If the parent seems to have calmed down sufficiently, it is possible to have the meeting immediately. Otherwise, it is better to schedule a future meeting for addressing these issues.

Lack of Time

Like parents, teachers have limited time to meet during the day; alternative meeting times in the evenings or on the weekends may be considered. Unfortunately, such meetings place additional burdens on teachers' time and take them away from their families. Although scheduling meetings to accommodate the parental needs is a primary concern, administrators have to be sensitive to the pressures and demands placed on teachers. For this reason, early childhood programs must develop creative ways to meet the needs of the teachers and families they serve. It is also important to run meetings in an efficient manner to use parent and teacher time most effectively.

Lack of Expertise in Supporting Parents

Working with parents in a collaborative manner requires a special set of skills—techniques designed to nurture a partnership with parents. Communication skills lay the foundation for active partnership. A genuine self-examination of attitudes about family participation is critical. Although many early childhood programs claim that families are important team members, the actions of individual teachers and staff sometimes communicate a different message. It is not uncommon for teachers to characterize families as "problem makers" when they make suggestions that are contrary to the program's views. This sentiment is even more likely if the families come from a different cultural background than most staff or are particularly assertive with their input.

Unfortunately, teacher actions and words may suggest that parents do not have the skills, attitudes, or resources to support their young child with challenging behavior. For instance, a parent's lack of literacy skills makes working with the child and his or her teachers more difficult and increases the amount of time spent on problem solving. In discussing families with complex needs, Taylor (1993) argued that these families are able to solve complex problems related to their own survival in difficult situations. Taylor suggested that programs appreciate and use parental input. The innate and experience-based knowledge that families bring to the problem-solving process can be a building block for working together on behalf of the child.

The way that early childhood programs schedule and conduct meetings can communicate to parents that they are not important. This is especially true when the meeting is scheduled at a time that is inconvenient for the parents or when their input is not taken seriously during the meeting. When early childhood professionals ask families to be involved but do not give them any real decisions to make, they are no more likely to become involved than professionals would be when placed in similar circumstances (Thompson, 1992). However, when parents are given a chance to make a real difference in their child's education and care, they are more likely to consistently participate in the educational setting.

Finally, early childhood professionals must work hard to ensure that their actions and words are consistent and congruent. Research suggests that the most important factors facilitating parent involvement are the teacher's attitudes and practices (Dauber & Epstein, 1993). It is important for early childhood professionals to recognize the important role that parents play in the lives of their children and to actively include parents as active decision makers. The following vignette illustrates a case in which the teachers and early childhood program staff should engage parents of a child with challenging classroom behaviors. It exemplifies the kinds of issues presented to early childhood educators.

> Jarad, age 4, joined the early childhood classroom mid-year after leaving another center because of difficulties interacting with other children there. Jarad had become increasingly aggressive. He used inappropriate language, kicked the trash can, snatched toys from other students, and kicked and hit children who tried to play too close to him. Jarad's parents removed him from that center when they discovered that the staff had unsuitably addressed his challenging behavior (e.g., restrained him improperly).
>
> When Jarad loses control at home, his parents put him in his room. He breaks and throws objects, then gradually calms down and shows remorse. Jarad's parents are especially concerned because his mother is pregnant and he is challenging them physically at home. They are afraid of what he will do with the baby because he has been saying, "I don't

want any baby." The classroom teachers want to engage Jarad's family in working on his challenging behaviors, both at home and in his present classroom.

CLASSROOM APPLICATION

Have efforts been made to fully include parents in decision making?

Do teachers encourage parents to become full partners in decision making?

Is it assumed that parents neither care about nor want to be involved in their child's educational program?

Is parental input solicited concerning perspectives on the challenges that the child presents in the classroom?

HOW IS AN EFFECTIVE PARENT CONFERENCE STRUCTURED?

Undoubtedly, early childhood teachers have many conferences with parents to discuss children's challenging behaviors in the classroom. How the teacher plans and structures such conferences contributes to his or her ability to work in partnership with parents to help children reach their potential. Parent conferences have three phases: 1) preconference planning, 2) conference implementation, and 3) postconference follow-up (Turnbull & Turnbull, 2001).

Preconference Planning

Preconference planning is perhaps the most important phase because it clarifies the issues to be addressed. Turnbull and Turnbull (2001) recommended several steps to help a teacher plan for the conference:

1. Review the child's folder and any other indicators of progress.
2. Form a clear description as to the child's current progress or the issue to be addressed. Select specific examples to share.
3. Prepare an outline of topics to be addressed.
4. When appropriate, meet with other teachers to gain additional information that contributes to a solution.

As part of the planning process, the teacher should prepare the environment where the conference will be held. Turnbull and Turnbull (2001) offered the following considerations that may help the teacher create an environment that is conducive to a successful meeting:

1. Pick a quiet, private room. Meeting in the classroom is a good idea if no one else will be using it. However, if the classroom is equipped with only small chairs, consider

bringing in an adult-size table and chairs or meeting in another room. Sitting on small chairs is uncomfortable for adults and can be distracting.

2. Try to schedule the conference at a time or place that makes interruptions unlikely.

3. If the topic for discussion is sensitive, have tissues available. It is uncomfortable for everyone involved if a parent cries and cannot wipe his or her eyes and nose.

4. Provide an interpreter if the family is not fluent in English.

The final preplanning step is notifying the parents that a conference is desired. Notification needs to be nonthreatening to encourage the parents to attend and to avoid angry and defensive reactions. In some situations, such as when the parents share custody of the child, individualized strategies must be developed to ensure that each parent is aware of the conference. The discussion may be better served by separate conferences.

Conference Implementation

Parent conferences should be conducted efficiently to avoid wasting the time of parents and staff. However, it is important to start with broad opening statements and to refrain from presenting the essential information too quickly. Good communication skills are essential; again, the use of active listening helps to clarify issues and concerns. The teacher should try to follow the agenda and avoid having the conversation stray into unrelated issues. Yet, at times, the agenda must be changed to address this new information that is garnered through active listening. This is a difficult balancing act, and every effort should be made to adjust without becoming so distracted that the task at hand gets lost. Once the conference is over, it is important to present a full summary. This allows everyone present to hear again what was decided in the conference.

Postconference Follow-Up

It is important that early childhood professionals follow up with conference participants to reinforce actions and to ensure that everyone understands the decisions that were reached. Summarizing the conference notes and providing a written copy to participants facilitates understanding and provides a common interpretation of the meeting. It also is helpful to make a follow-up telephone call to the parents, thanking them for their support and asking about the progress of the plan decided on at the conference. Following up with other key people involved with the conference, such as specialists who were consulted, provides a way to monitor progress and determine if any new information or new actions need to be taken.

Unplanned Conferences

Without question, some parent conferences will be unplanned. Recognizing this fact and engaging in some general planning can help the teacher maximize the value of these informal interactions. Although it is unlikely that a teacher will never be caught off guard, there are things that he or she can do to be ready. Being familiar with data on the children enrolled in the classroom is a great help. Keeping files well organized is also useful, allowing the teacher to quickly retrieve information that answers a parent's questions. If the teacher is asked a specific question and does not have ready information, he or she should say so and then assure the parents that the requested information will be given to them as soon as possible. In anticipation of being caught off guard, the teacher might want to have a standard phrase prepared, such as "I'm really glad that you took the time to talk to me. Let me make sure I get the right information for you and get back to you as soon as possible." Another response might be "I appreciate your interest; let's see if there's a time when we can talk in detail." If the teacher has the time and knowledge to answer a parent's question, then he or she should do so immediately. If the teacher does not have the time or the information, however, he or she should take the opportunity to clarify the question and set a time for a future meeting.

HOW CAN PARENTS BE ENGAGED IN HOME AND SCHOOL INTERVENTIONS?

According to a systems perspective, every child develops within a series of nested contexts. The home environment, with its intimate parent–child and sibling relationships, involves daily routines that have a direct impact on the child's development (Bronfenbrenner, 1979). Through the use of daily routines, parents can provide purpose and structure at home. These daily routines can give children many opportunities to practice and develop skills that they will use at home, at school, and in the community.

Studies have demonstrated that parents and teachers working together to address challenging behaviors is both time and cost efficient (Schreibman, Koegel, Mills, & Burke, 1984). In addition, programs that support families in working with their children can strengthen the family's functioning (Dunst, Trivette, Starnes, Hamby, & Gordon, 1993). Home and school interventions, then, can benefit the child and the family.

Benefits of Engaging Families in Intervention

Koegel, Koegel, Kellegrew, and Mullen (1996) described the importance of engaging parents in behavior change efforts for their children. They contended that teachers should assess children's opportunities to practice skills before interventions are designed. Behaviors and skills required only in the school setting can be practiced at school. Stremel and colleagues (1992), however, incorporated individualized education program (IEP) objectives into the daily routines of children with disabilities. The families identified the daily routines that should be used as IEP goals (e.g., increasing child vocalizations). Routines involving self-care commonly emerged as times for intervention because of their consistent, daily occurrence.

Families and homes are as unique as the children in an early childhood classroom. For interventions to be successful, they must account for various parent and home characteristics. Kellegrew (1998) conducted a series of studies with families that recognized the uniqueness of each family. Kellegrew identified parents who had previously limited their children's chances for performing certain daily tasks. These parents were invited to participate in a program to increase the number of opportunities that they presented to their children. The parents were taught to turn daily care activities into teaching situations and to monitor the amount of assistance required by their children. Through participation in the program, parents learned to increase the opportunities they presented to their children to practice skills.

In addition to home and school interventions, it is necessary for teachers to coordinate activities between home and school. One way in which these activities may be coordinated is through priming. For example, Wilde, Koegel, and Koegel (1992) found that preschoolers behaved better during circle time when they were familiar with the stories being read. Preschool teachers then began sending home each storybook the night before it was to be read in class. The data indicated that when the teachers used stories to which the children had been exposed at home, the children's behavior during circle time improved. Even with other tasks, prior home exposure reduced disruptive child behavior and increased appropriate responses.

Families from Different Cultures, Ethnicities, or Linguistic Backgrounds

When working with families from various cultural, ethnic, or linguistic groups, teachers should identify parents' perceptions of the intervention process. Linan-Thompson and Jean (1997) suggested that teachers and family members may differ in their interpretations of a disability's meaning, preferred method for dealing with problems, and manner of appropriate communication. Teachers are urged to listen to family members and to explain the assessment and intervention process in comprehensible language. Families who are unsure how a disability affects their child's ability to learn may seek other explanations and solutions for the child's behavior difficulties in the classroom. To address variations in means of communication, the teacher should identify the family's preferred method. He or she may need to use telephone calls, informal meetings, and personal notes in addition to the forms required by the early childhood program or local school district.

To exemplify how culture can affect teacher activities, Hourcade, Parette, and Huer (1997) discussed issues related to culture and the use of assistive technology for children with severe cognitive, communication, or motor impairments. The researchers found that if the family was not involved in the selection and implementation of such assistive devices, the family often abandoned the technology. Specifically, Hourcade and colleagues recommended that teachers faced with suggesting the use of assistive technology 1) understand the family's need for information about such devices, 2) recognize the impact that such technology might have on family routines, and 3) consider the extent to which family members value acceptance in community settings for themselves and for their children. It is important to acknowledge that families and teachers may have very different perceptions and values related to the incorporation of assistive technology, which are based, in part, on their cultural backgrounds.

In their sample of African American and Latino/Hispanic families, Chavkin and Williams (1993) argued that contextual fit must be considered. *Contextual fit* refers to the compatibility of the behavioral support plan and 1) the characteristics of the individual for whom the plan is designed, 2) the people who will implement the plan, and 3) the

Table 3.1.   Interview format for families to assess contextual fit

How well do you think the program addresses your child's needs at home?

How well does the plan account for your understanding of your child and his or her behavior?

How well does the plan address your priorities?

Do you understand your role in the plan? Are you comfortable in this role?

Do you understand the role of others in this plan? Are you comfortable with their roles?

Does the plan recognize and support you as a parent? Does it recognize and support other family members?

How well does the plan fit with your regular family routines? Does it cause serious disruptions?

How well does the plan fit with your parenting style and beliefs? Does it cause any stress or hardship at home or in the community?

Is the plan based on your strengths? Is it based on your child's strengths?

Does the plan make use of resources you have available to you? Are these resources available in the long run?

How difficult is it for you to implement the plan?

Do you believe that this plan will work?

From Albin, R.W., Lucyshyn, J.M., Horner, R.H., & Flannery, K.B. (1996). Contextual fit for behavioral support plans: A model for "goodness of fit." In L.K. Koegel, R.L. Koegel, & G. Dunlap (Eds.), *Positive behavioral support: Including people with difficult behavior in the community* (pp. 95–96). Baltimore: Paul H. Brookes Publishing Co.; adapted by permission.

environment and systems within which the plan will be implemented. Behavioral support plans work well when family members or other stakeholders are comfortable with the plan's goals and strategies, have the skills and resources to use the strategies, and view the plan as likely to succeed.

Parents and other family members are active collaborators in designing programs with good contextual fit. In initial discussions, family interviews are used to identify family characteristics, values, goals, and daily routines. The family takes the lead in identifying the most challenging routines and activities and in setting priorities for interventions that would enhance family life. Albin, Lucyshn, Horner, and Flannery (1996) suggested using a survey to assess goodness of fit. Table 3.1 provides a simplified interview format to assess contextual fit.

HOW ARE THESE ELEMENTS PUT TOGETHER?

The preceding sections have described methods for planning parent conferences and engaging parents in behavioral interventions. The vignette about Jarad is continued to illustrate efforts that are made to involve the parents in observations, planning, and intervention regarding their child's challenging behavior.

> Jarad's new teacher and teacher assistant and the new center's director decide that a home visit would be beneficial before Jarad's first day in the program. Jarad's parents agree, and during the visit, they reiterate their concerns that Jarad had been physically restrained at his previous center. They also express interest in play groups outside of school to extend friendships for Jarad.
>
> After the home visit, Jarad says to his parents, "I don't want to go to that new school. I hate that new teacher. I hate that school." However, at the end of his first day, Jarad does not want to leave the classroom.

His father picks up Jarad, who is screaming and kicking, and quickly leaves the center.

Jarad's parents then are invited to observe his behavior prior to departure time. They watch as Jarad is given a series of warnings (e.g., "It will be 2 minutes before Mom and Dad come to pick you up"). His parents, waiting in the nearby observation room, quickly come and pick him up as soon as the 2 minutes elapse.

Jarad's parents are asked to attend other classroom observations and to attend problem-solving meetings. During these meetings, Jarad's parents and teachers work on specific intervention plans, thus ensuring consistent responses by everyone working with him. For example, if Jarad begins to engage in a behavior that has been identified as disruptive (e.g., sitting too close to another child, using inappropriate words or touching, hitting another child or adult), the adult says, "Jarad, you're _____ [pinching, hitting, leaning on] _____ [name of adult or child]. Please stop." If another child is involved, the adult says, "You can tell Jarad, 'That's bothering me; please stop.'" If Jarad stops, then the adult points out that he has controlled his own behavior and affirms Jarad's ability to manage himself. If Jarad continues the disruptive behavior, the adult says, "I see you chose not to stop _____. Now I will choose for you." The adult then follows with a natural consequence (e.g., losing a chance to go to a special area or to sit with a favorite peer). For example, if Jarad continues to nudge a child near him, the child is assisted to move. The same language is used consistently at home and at school. In subsequent conferences, Jarad's parents report on situations in which the intervention plan is successfully used at home.

CONCLUSION

Engaging parents in efforts to change their children's behavior is challenging but profitable. A key factor in addressing behavior is a supportive environment in the home and classroom. Chapter 4 discusses practices to provide a supportive classroom environment and the design of daily routines and activities.

Chapter 4

Creating a Supportive Classroom Environment

Dawn Denno, Louise R. Phillips,
Helene Arbouet Harte, and Sally Moomaw

Teachers in early childhood classrooms work to design classroom environments that meet the developmental needs of young children. Yet, it is sometimes difficult to design classroom environments that support and respond to the individual needs of children with challenging behaviors. Although classroom environments may be appropriate for specific age ranges, many require more in-depth thought and discussion to provide *all* of the elements needed to support *all* children. Nowhere is it more important to customize supports for children than in environments that serve children with challenging behaviors. This chapter describes resources available to teachers for planning and evaluating supportive classroom environments.

Classroom environments are made of many interdependent elements. Therefore, when designing environments for individual children, the interaction of support for each child becomes critical. This natural interaction is frequently called the *ecology* of the classroom (Barnett, Bell, & Carey, 1999). Classrooms function as ecosystems; the interaction of all classroom elements determines the types of learning that children experience.

In creating classroom environments for children with challenging behaviors, teachers make many decisions. These settings require careful planning, implementation, evaluation, and reflection. Daily schedules must be predictable and responsive to children. Classroom curriculum and activities must be based on information about the interests of children as well as on a careful observation of their developmental capabilities. Groupings of children are planned based on knowledge of the social interactions of those children.

Classroom limits are reasonable, accessible, and obvious. The classroom must have cool-down areas, safe places, numerous dramatic play and sensory activity areas, as well as space for extended areas when necessary. Teacher interactions need to create a bond with children and families. Teachers can achieve this by 1) using child-directed language, 2) scaffolding new skills based on observations of a child's development, and 3) monitoring the relationships among peers to create a supportive environment. Above all, teachers of children with challenging behaviors must have time to plan creative, flexible solutions for environments that do not work (Lara, McCabe, & Brooks-Gunn, 2000).

HOW CAN EDUCATORS CREATE A CLASSROOM ENVIRONMENT FOR ALL CHILDREN?

A supportive environment for children is constructed much like a quilt. Children and families come to school with individual patterns of strengths and needs. Just as quilters select pieces of fabric to create designs, teachers carefully select classroom elements as pieces of the supports needed to address these strengths and needs. Pieces of the classroom environment are tailored to support the individual needs of the children, teachers, and classroom. These pieces are then sewn together to produce the complete array of supports required for the children's and families' unique patterns of strengths and needs (Kutash & Duchnowski, 1997). The finished product is wrapped around each child to support appropriate behavior and protect against threats to success.

To construct the complete pattern of supports, teachers need to find and use as many different environmental elements as possible:

1. Daily schedule
2. Curriculum and activities
3. Space and room arrangement
4. Grouping
5. Limits and boundary setting
6. Teacher and family interaction

Teachers can develop many variations on each element and can create new ones as well. The important thing to remember is that the final support system will be a creative, individual product that enhances the strengths of children, families, and teachers and supports identified needs.

HOW CAN EDUCATORS CREATE A DAILY SCHEDULE THAT FITS THE NEEDS AND STRENGTHS OF ALL CHILDREN?

Educators need to follow best practice guidelines for creating a classroom schedule. The right daily schedule can provide a basic structure that helps children move through the day with minimal confusion and frustration. The daily schedule reflects the individual needs of children, families, and teachers, as well as the needs that are accepted as being appropriate for specific age ranges. Generally, a quality classroom schedule for young children contains large blocks of time for child-selected activity. The schedule also includes smaller blocks of time for activities selected by teachers, outside play, and routine classroom maintenance activities (e.g., putting toys away, cleaning lunch tables). Activities are balanced between quiet and active play (Koralek, Colker, & Dodge, 1995).

General quality indicators for classroom schedules provide important guidance for scheduling the day. Yet, planning based on general rules may not alone be enough to support all children. The amount of time allocated and the sequence of activities used are determined by the individual needs of children and teachers. Schedules that are predictable decrease stress by allowing teachers and children to plan for the next activity and to move through the day without confusion. Schedules allow teachers to match the types and tempos of activities to the needs of individual children as well as those of the group.

Match the Classroom Schedule to the Needs of Each Child

When schedules closely match those naturally occurring in children's families, children find it easier to move through routines. Talking to parents and other caregivers about family routines provides important guidance for planning classroom schedules. For example, when children attend afternoon preschool classes, appropriate behavior can be supported by planning quiet activities at times that children would ordinarily take a nap.

Teachers must pay close attention to the children's behavior throughout the day. Completing anecdotal records and observation checklists provides information for making decisions about the schedule. Teachers must weigh the needs of the group against the needs of the individual. When problems with an existing schedule emerge, teachers must decide whether to alter the sequence of activities and/or to alter the amount of time allotted for specific activities. To do this, teachers have to reflect on the known strengths and needs of children at home and at school. Answering the following questions can help teachers navigate a change of this type:

1. Is this activity a problem for one child or for more than one child?
2. Do problems seem to occur at one time of day only or at various times?
3. Could changes be made to other elements of the classroom that would be less intrusive?
4. Does the existing schedule have benefits that must be preserved?
5. Are the difficulties greater for children or for teachers?
6. What is known about the affected child(ren) that might help clarify this situation?

Change the Length and Sequence of Classroom Activities

It may be more practical to lengthen or shorten specific activities rather than to change the entire daily schedule. Altering the amount of time allotted for specific activities modifies only the times of day that produce problematic situations. Elements of the day that work well are not changed, so the schedule essentially remains predictable.

Sometimes it is necessary to change the sequence of activities. Again, observation and discussion are the keys to making a smooth transition from one sequence of activities to another. Matching the schedule with the natural patterns and rhythms of children in the group is essential.

Help Children Predict the Daily Routine

Some children need more help than others in understanding and predicting the classroom schedule. Picture schedules can be helpful. With this strategy, teachers use drawings or photos of daily activities to prompt children when it is necessary to wait or to make transitions. Picture schedules of the daily routine can be posters, books, or wristbands (i.e., a wristband containing photos of the child engaged in daily activities or catalog pictures that represent routine activities). The following vignette illustrates the use of picture schedules.

> Sarah, age 4, loves to play in the gross motor room at her preschool. Because this area is a shared classroom, Sarah's class does not get to use it until 2 hours into the program day. Sarah frequently becomes impatient when she has to wait for the scheduled time. Each day after arrival, she stands near the classroom door, hoping to go to the gross motor room. Because Sarah is so worried about missing time in the gross motor room, she does not engage in the curriculum or play with other children. Sarah's teacher believes helping Sarah understand the routine will make it easier for her to wait. Using an instant camera, Sarah and her teacher take pictures of the other children participating in the daily schedule of activities. Sarah's teacher uses the pictures to make a book entitled "Sarah's Day." After Sarah becomes familiar with this book, her teacher can refer to the classroom routine depicted in the book. Soon, Sarah can tell her teacher and peers about the sequence of events leading to gross motor room time, and she begins engaging in classroom activities. The book is kept in Sarah's cubby so she can refer to it when needed.

Limit Children's Choices, When Appropriate

Sometimes, teachers find it useful to reduce the number of choices that children can make during specific routines. A child may have problems making choices on certain days or at certain times of day. Providing more structure may help the child calm down. For example, the teacher might say, "It's story time now. You choose a book, and I'll choose one."

Although skilled observation and flexibility are required, changing the classroom routine can tremendously improve the working life of the classroom. Designing the day's schedule around the needs of children and families provides a setting for appropriate behavior. Children, teachers, and parents benefit from this extra consideration of contextual fit between the daily classroom schedule and the needs and interests of individual children.

Address Limited Access to an Activity Center

Daily schedules should be designed to minimize the amount of time that children wait to participate in an activity. When waiting is unavoidable, such as for high-interest areas, teachers can use "waiting lists" to help children. The teacher adds names to the list in the order that children come to the activity area, and names are crossed off as children finish the activity. With this strategy, waiting children are able to track their name advancing to the top of the list.

CLASSROOM APPLICATION

Does the daily schedule match the developmental characteristics and preferences of the children?

Is there sufficient time for child-selected activities?

Is there a balance between active and quiet play centers?

Is the schedule predictable?

Will a change in the sequence or length of activities address specific problem situations?

Do some children need prompts?

Do any of the children need help with choices?

Are strategies needed to help children wait?

HOW CAN CLASSROOM TRANSITIONS BE FACILITATED?

Teachers frequently report that transitions between activities (Barnett, Bell, & Carey, 1999) and play partners (Stormant, Zentall, Beyda, Javorsky, & Belfiore, 2000) create difficulties in the classroom. Some researchers estimate that 20%–35% of classroom time is spent in transition from one activity to another (Sainato & Lyon, 1989). Therefore, approaches to classroom transitions for young children require a great deal of thought and planning.

Expect Developmentally Appropriate Transitions

Expectations for behavior during transitions must be realistic. Transition routines must be both developmentally and individually appropriate (Bredekamp & Copple, 1997). To design effective routines that are developmentally and individually appropriate, teachers need information about their students, which can be obtained by 1) talking to parents and other caregivers, 2) observing throughout the day, 3) learning the principles of child development, and 4) keeping informed about developmentally appropriate practice.

Just as classroom schedules are designed to be predictable, transitions must be planned to predictably communicate expected behavior. Once reasonable expectations are clarified, teachers can use a variety of methods to communicate them consistently to students.

Give Effective Signals for Transitions

Teachers communicate transition routines to children by verbally describing the routines, prompting and modeling the routines, and providing feedback to children. A warning given just before a mandatory transition allows children 1) to complete their activities and then clean up or 2) to make plans for activity continuation at a later time and then clean up. For children who are still reluctant to stop playing, discussing upcoming activities and requesting a choice commitment might provide motivation (e.g., "Lee, I remember that you haven't had a turn at the easel yet. When we get back to the room, would you like to paint at the easel or build with blocks?"). A picture board depicting the routine's steps also can be an effective communication device. Singing often helps children move from one activity to another or helps them wait when necessary. Using name cards to denote assigned seats decreases confusion and gives the children chances to recognize their names. Placing an adult in crucial areas during transitions can help facilitate movement between activities. As noted previously, it is important to customize transitions by using such strategies as applicable.

Teachers may find it useful to embed learning activities in transition routines. For transitions to work, however, they must fit the needs of children. One research study found that embedding learning activities into transitions may exacerbate inappropriate behavior for children who frequently display noncompliant behavior (Wolery, Anthony, & Heckathorn, 1998).

Help Children Who Are Engaged in Play Make Transitions

"Save notes" are used when a child's activity is interrupted for another activity or event. These notes, which state "Save for [child's name]" and are placed on the activity material, are helpful when children need more time to complete an activity than the schedule allows. This technique provides teachers with a mechanism for individualizing the schedule without making large changes to the group's schedule. For example, Tony is building a block structure, and it is time for lunch. Writing a "Save for Tony" note reassures him that he can continue building after lunch, thereby making him more willing to interrupt his play.

Modify Ineffective Transition Routines

Sometimes transition routines do not work. When changing transition routines, teachers should use the informed decision-making steps that are used for changing classroom schedules. Teachers monitor transitions, gather information, discuss alternatives, decide how to change the transition, communicate the routine to children, and monitor the success of the change. This process, as well as appropriate expectation, is illustrated in the following vignette.

Three-year-old Julie is working in the art area. She is gluing glitter onto a milk carton when her teacher signals that it is time to clean up. Julie begins cleaning up but accidentally spills the glitter onto the table. A few minutes later, Julie's teacher sees that Julie has not yet put the materials away. She prompts Julie that the class needs to go outside in 2 minutes. Julie cries and throws some art materials. When the teacher moves to the art area, she sees that Julie is trying to clean up but cannot: Every time Julie attempts to sweep the glitter in a pile, it swooshes around the table and sticks to her arms. The teacher offers a wet cloth for wiping the table, and Julie finishes cleaning up without further assistance or frustration.

CLASSROOM APPLICATION

Are transition times contributing to challenging behavior?

Is the transition routine developmentally appropriate and consistent?

Are the transition signals effective for all children?

Would transition-based teaching help structure transition periods for some children?

Should we institute a "save note" strategy?

HOW ARE EFFECTIVE CHILD GROUPINGS CONSTRUCTED?

The way that children are grouped affects their behavior. Teachers often report that some children engage in a cycle of aggressive, noncompliant, or oppositional behavior when paired with other children exhibiting those behaviors. Also, researchers have documented that when children behave aggressively, they are rejected by their peers. This, in turn, generates more aggression or withdrawal (Newcomb, Bukowski, & Pattee, 1993). Research on children who exhibit a "difficult" temperament found that they frequently receive negative reactions and rejection from their peers; the outcome of this rejection can be aggression (Chess & Thomas, 1991). Additional research documented that although children may be rejected by one social group due to aggressive behavior, they frequently form new social groups of other aggressive peers (Cairns & Cairns, 1991). These new social groups tend to increase the level of aggression in the classroom.

Preschoolers often stratify into different social groups based on their relative dominance (Farver, 1996). Children develop social preferences for particular peers. Some variables that determine preference include gender, age, and social dominance. Children who are highly preferred are considered to have high social status. Children of lower social status frequently conform to the rules established by the higher status, more dominant children. In addition, children exhibiting aggressive and competitive behavior are imitated by their peers more often (Strayer, 1980). The social structures and hierarchies in the group reinforce and promote an increase in challenging behavior.

Administrators and teachers make decisions about how to group children. Typically, administrators place children in particular classrooms. Administrators plan the social structures, and factors such as age, gender, and play style are important determiners. Interventions for a child who exhibits challenging behaviors are more effective when they focus on the group. Administrators have many options for changing the grouping of children to support appropriate behavior. Interventions can be as minor as changing the seating of children in groups or as complex as moving children from one room to another. Decisions about interventions are based on observation and discussion with staff and parents. Once children are placed in particular classrooms, teachers determine how to group the children for optimal learning.

CLASSROOM APPLICATION

Does child grouping contribute to the problem situation?

Do specific children consistently become aggressive when playing together?

Does one child tend to imitate the aggressive actions of another?

Does peer rejection trigger aggression in a particular child?

Should the seating arrangement during group or snack time be changed?

Does a specific child need to change classrooms?

HOW IS CLASSROOM SPACE EFFECTIVELY DEFINED?

The design of the classroom space affects the behavior of teachers and children. In general, well-organized, clearly defined spaces serve as prompts for appropriate behavior. Furniture that is organized into easily supervised learning areas, shelves that are labeled so that children can replace materials, and spaces that separate quiet and active play are all part of the classroom system to support the success of children.

Consider General Factors

When arranging the classroom space, teachers must consider the amount of space needed for children to complete an activity, the flow of traffic in and out of areas, and the visibility of areas for adult supervision. Because of classroom size constraints, it may be necessary to limit the number of children allowed in an area at one time. Such limits should be logical and easily understood (e.g., the number of children working at a table is limited by the number of chairs, the number of children playing at the sensory table is limited by the number of smocks). Bracelets or necklaces can control numbers in more open areas such as dramatic play. With this strategy, different color bracelets or necklaces are associated with certain activity areas, and children must be wearing the correct bracelet or necklace to play in those particular areas.

Furniture arrangement can allow space for children to move as appropriate or can isolate an area for quiet work. Furniture placement also can break up large areas of open space that might encourage unwanted running or other active behaviors. For safety purposes, it is vital that all areas are visible to adults from any vantage point. High shelves or other equipment should not be put in places that block vision or create safety hazards for active children.

Meet the Needs of Children and Teachers

Balancing teacher needs for classroom spaces that are easily supervised with the child needs for private, smaller learning areas is tricky. As mentioned previously, teachers of children with challenging behaviors often design the room so that all areas can be seen at all times. Teachers usually do this to ensure the safety of all children in the classroom. However, it is important to remember that if teachers can see the whole room at one time, children usually can, too. Some children are overstimulated by the noise and activity levels created by this type of room arrangement.

Create Private Space

Some children may need a "cool down" area in the classroom. Cool down areas should be private and free from negative associations. Teachers can prevent such negative attributions by planning the classroom space to accommodate privacy in many areas at once. Private spaces can be designed by using low shelves and rugs to define the space.

Although safety is a priority for all areas of the classroom, teachers must be particularly cautious to ensure that cool down spaces are safe. Shelves must be secure enough not to be tipped. Knowing the behavior of children in the group will help teachers to plan both the layout of the physical space and the materials needed to support appropriate behavior in these situations.

Assess the Effectiveness of the Classroom's Arrangement

Teachers must pay close attention to the use of classroom space. Anecdotal records and checklists that log the number of children in various areas during the day may be helpful. The following signs indicate that the room arrangement is not working: running, excess noise, involvement in only a few activities, excessive requests for adult help, and inappropriate use of materials. When these behaviors are observed, teachers must use problem-solving strategies to encourage appropriate behavior. When changes are made, teachers must give them time to work. Just as changing the routine can cause confusion and frustration, changing the classroom space frequently causes problems for some children. Observation and communication is the key to deciding the type and rate of change needed in the classroom.

CLASSROOM APPLICATION

Does the physical arrangement of the classroom promote aggressive or disruptive behavior?

Does the traffic flow need to be assessed?

Do clearly defined limits need to be instituted for activity areas?

Does the arrangement of materials promote self-regulation?

Will rearranging the furniture or activity areas address the problem situation?

Do children need more intensive scaffolding in certain activity areas?

Is a "cool down" space needed?

HOW CAN AN EFFECTIVE CLASSROOM CURRICULUM BE DEVELOPED?

The types of classroom activities that teachers provide support the success of children with challenging behaviors. Since the early 1980s, curriculum and classroom activities have been studied extensively as variables influencing the behavior of children in the classroom (Roberts, Marshall, Nelson, & Albers, 2001). The difficulty of the activity, the type of instructions given, the preferences of a particular child, and the opportunity that the child is given to make choices affect behavior change (Dunlap & Kern, 1996; Ferro, Foster-Johnson, & Dunlap, 1996). Teachers can influence each of these variables.

Tailor Curricular Activities to Meet an Individual Child's Needs

Through careful observation, teachers can determine the elements of the curriculum and activities that encourage inappropriate behavior. If teachers watch closely as a child moves among learning activities, they can determine whether the child needs a different type of instruction or whether the activity is too difficult. Teachers can then design the curriculum to match the child's needs. If the task is too difficult, then teachers can scaffold success by planning activities that support the child's learning at different levels. If the child seems to do better when preferred activities are presented, then teachers can embed learning in preferred activities. Such careful attention to the causes of the inappropriate behavior supports learning.

Facilitate Active Learning

Sensory exploration is a primary source of cognitive and social learning for young children (Boyer, 1997). Most young children enjoy this activity as well. Advances in brain research support the notion that active sensory stimulation reinforces learning and can be physically calming (Rushton & Larkin, 2001). Therefore, teachers can provide additional supports for children with challenging behavior by planning extended activities in the sensory area. Integrating sensory activities throughout the room promotes self-regulation, as children can select the activities when they need to calm down. Playdough and water play are examples of sensory activities that can be a regular part of a classroom. In addition, a sensory table can provide a variety of materials, including sand, rice, and beans.

In addition to sensory activities, dramatic play provides support to children's cognitive and social development (Petrakos & Howe, 1996; Shim, Herwig, & Shelley, 2001). During dramatic play, children enact various roles and personal experiences (Howe, Moller, Chambers, & Petrakos, 1993). Dramatic play activities can include familiar (housekeeping) or unfamiliar themes (going to a pet shop). It is important to plan the types of experiences and intended learning from each activity (Bagley & Klass, 1997).

Match Curricular Activities to Developmental Stages

Children move through stages of dramatic play themes. The earliest form develops around domestic play. Then, children develop rescue themes. The final common theme that develops includes play activities that portray sudden threat (Howe et al., 1993). Each theme can be used to teach important skills and support social development.

As discussed previously, research indicates that children tend to stratify into groups based on their relative dominance (Strayer, 1980). Dramatic play provides opportunities for children to try new roles if sufficient attention is given to child groupings. Grouping children to increase their role-playing repertoire supports their development without directly controlling the play. Teachers can support new ways of interacting by grouping children in various combinations, providing play props that encourage a variety of roles, and structuring themes so that all children can be successful.

Select Classroom Materials with Child Behavior in Mind

Teachers also support appropriate behavior by planning the types and quantities of materials found in the classroom. Research has documented that 61%–73% of aggression episodes in the classroom are preceded by a dispute over property (Stormont et al., 2000). Providing adequate amounts of preferred, developmentally appropriate materials is clearly important. Planning interaction with these materials is important as well (Hartle, 1996).

Inappropriate behavior can result in situations that require turn taking. Sometimes children need help understanding how to take turns using materials. Waiting lists and timers give children concrete information that helps them learn appropriate ways to wait for their turn. Providing duplicates of favored toys also decreases the need for negative intervention. Rather than creating negative situations that do not allow for teaching, providing two identical toys allows children to play with the desired toy until the teacher has time to purposefully teach or facilitate needed strategies for negotiating the use of one toy. The following vignette highlights the use of materials that address a child's needs.

> Max has been a kindergarten teacher for 5 years and has never before worked with a child like Sean. District administration expects children to identify, read, and write upper- and lowercase letters by the end of kindergarten, but Sean refuses to complete exercises that Max has designed for this purpose. When presented with alphabet activities, Sean throws materials, strikes other children, and refuses to participate. Sean is falling behind the other children, and Max has become discouraged about meeting the district expectations. However, after observing Sean and documenting the activities that lead to and follow Sean's behavior, Max sees some patterns. Sean seems to avoid tasks specifically related to letter identification.

Max decides to assess Sean's skills in more detail and finds that Sean is even further behind the other children than expected. Max designs activities that will allow Sean to be more successful and, in turn, decrease his inappropriate behavior. Max examines the difficulty of the activities, the length of the activities, and the specific teaching materials used. To make activities meaningful, Max decides to start them by using the letters in Sean's name. Max uses manipulatives rather than paper and pencil to work with Sean, and he sets aside a short period of time each day to give Sean extra help. After several weeks, Sean no longer resists the activities he once disliked and is catching up with the other children in his class.

CLASSROOM APPLICATION

Are classroom activities and materials developmentally appropriate for all children?

Should certain toys be incorporated to provide decreased or increased challenges for an individual child?

Should pictorial or verbal prompts be provided for certain activity centers?

Would individual children benefit from increased time with sensory activities?

Is there sufficient access to highly preferred materials and activities?

HOW CAN CLASSROOM LIMITS BE COMMUNICATED?

Teachers can guide behavior by setting and communicating classroom limits. Once established, classroom limits help keep children and materials safe. They facilitate the smooth classroom operation, and, when applied evenly, ensure fair classroom management (Bredekamp & Copple, 1997).

Classroom rules and limits provide the basic structure for classroom behavior by setting the minimum standards for everyone. Therefore, rules and limits must be carefully considered, explicitly taught, and evenly applied (Paine, Radicchi, Rosellini, Deutchman, & Darch, 1983). Many confrontations between children and adults can be prevented by carefully planning classroom ground rules. Only rules that are necessary for safety, preservation of materials and equipment, and basic classroom functioning should be considered (Marion, 1995). Examples of typical ground rules include

1. We all walk in the classroom.
2. We all tell people when we are upset.
3. We all call people by the names that they like.
4. We all put materials back on the shelf when we are finished using them.

Help Children Learn the Classroom Limits

Once the essential rules are selected, they can be communicated in various ways. It is extremely important that everyone in the classroom fully understands the rules. Teachers communicate rules by modeling desired behavior, designing the classroom to communicate behavioral expectations, prompting, and providing consequences.

Whenever possible, teachers should initially use the least intrusive method to communicate rules. This allows teachers to focus on positive learning opportunities. For example, arranging the classroom furniture to discourage running means that teachers are not forced to monitor running. Furthermore, when teachers model appropriate behavior, they give children concrete information about how to behave within the boundaries of the classroom.

If teachers break the rules, children notice and then see the rules as arbitrary and unfair. In turn, it becomes more difficult for teachers to credibly enforce the limits with children. Rules that teachers commonly break are "Sit in chairs rather than on tables," "Walk over to speak to someone rather than yelling across the room," and "Put materials away." Teachers need to help each other remember and abide by such rules. Having children and adults help each other remember the rules is another way to prevent mistakes from happening.

Sometimes, children need direct communication about classroom rules and limits. Verbal or pictorial prompts can provide this communication. If a teacher is prompting children consistently, however, he or she should consider why this is occurring. Children break rules and violate limits for many reasons, which frequently fall into the broader categories of obtaining or avoiding something. Without understanding the reasons for noncompliant behavior, teachers can inadvertently increase the behavior that they seek to decrease. Behavioral supports should set the situation so that the behavior becomes "irrelevant, inefficient, and ineffective" (O'Neil et al., 1997, p. 66.)

In some cases, children become dependent on prompts. It is important for teachers to consider in advance how they may lessen a child's dependence on teacher involvement in rule maintenance. Paying attention to the times of day and setting events that lead to the behavior and the reasons a child may exhibit the behavior gives teachers information for planning decreased involvement.

As noted previously, pictures can prompt appropriate behavior. For example, pictures of materials placed on shelves can prompt children to follow cleanup procedures. Teachers can provide verbal prompts, in person or via taped recordings, to remind children of expected behavior. Each method should be considered an element of a classroom plan to move children from concrete, direct prompting to increased self-regulation.

Respond to Children Who Consistently Break Rules

Even in well-planned environments, rules are broken. These situations must be used as opportunities to teach appropriate behavior. As a result, the consequences for misbehavior must be naturally and quickly linked to a learning objective. Understanding the function of the offending behavior will lead to the design of positive behavior support plans. For example, conflicts over the use of toys erupt regularly in preschool classrooms. Rather than removing a toy to end a conflict, the teacher can use the situation as an opportunity to scaffold appropriate behaviors. By holding the toy and guiding children through negotiations, the teacher can support the learning of communication and turn taking.

CLASSROOM APPLICATION

Does the classroom have developmentally appropriate limits?

Are only essential rules presented?

Are the limits positively stated?

Are the limits applied consistently to children and adults?

Do some children need pictorial or verbal prompts regarding classroom limits?

HOW ARE EFFECTIVE TEACHER–CHILD RELATIONSHIPS ESTABLISHED?

Teachers must never underestimate their influence on children and parents. To support children with challenging behavior, teachers must have strong, positive relationships with these children and their parents. They must develop safe environments in which children and families feel comfortable and willing to trust (Malaguzzi, 1993).

Research on young children's developing brains highlights how a classroom's emotional tone affects children's behavior (Rushton & Larkin, 2001). High levels of stress and perceived threat inhibit children's learning. A relaxed environment that still presents activities that challenge children has been linked to more positive developmental outcomes. Furthermore, research has documented that teachers with warm, responsive affective interaction styles are likely to engage children for longer periods of time and at higher levels (Raspa, McWilliam, & Ridley, 2001).

View the Classroom From a Child's Perspective

Children can perceive threats from the physical classroom space, from other children, and from the teachers and staff. To prevent stressful situations, it is sometimes helpful for teachers to sit in the classroom and look at it from the children's point of view. Sitting in child-size chairs or working with the children's materials may give teachers insight into the emotional tone of the classroom from the children's perspective. For example, teachers can visually scan the room to determine whether the materials are haphazardly placed or are well organized and easy to use. Teachers can listen to determine whether the noise level in the room might be threatening to some children. Finally, teachers can carefully watch the social interactions of children to ensure that children feel safe with and trust other children in the classroom.

Determine Expected Child Behavior

In addition to setting an appropriate emotional climate in the classroom, teachers must be aware of their beliefs and expectations for children. An individual's culture, ethnicity, race, gender, age, religion, geographic location, life experiences, and socioeconomic status play roles in shaping his or her views of the world (Coll & Magnuson, 2000). Teachers bring their views to the classroom, and children, parents, and other classroom staff members bring their views as well.

Studies in the United States and other countries demonstrate that the beliefs of teachers are linked to the behavior of children (Arnold, Griffith, Ortiz, & Stowe, 1998; Czaja, 1999; La Paro & Pianta, 2000). Teachers enact their beliefs by 1) designing curriculum for children, 2) deciding when and how to communicate with children and parents, 3) choosing how to design the limits within the classroom, and 4) determining consequences and rewards for behaviors. Each element has been determined to affect behavior (Roberts et al., 2001).

Communicate with Parents

As discussed previously, sometimes the beliefs and perceptions of children, parents, and teachers are mismatched. For this reason, it is important that teachers work to understand the points of similarity and difference between themselves and the people with whom they work. As mentioned in Chapter 3, parents from some cultures revere teachers and believe that it is disrespectful to disagree with them. When teachers make recommendations, these parents may listen and nod, even when they do not agree with the recommended course of action (Coll & Magnuson, 2000). Then, teachers cannot understand why parents do not follow behavior support plans at home. To be considered complete, all support plans and interventions must be created with careful attention to the values, beliefs, perceptions, and expectations of all of the individuals involved.

Research has demonstrated that the beliefs of teachers affect not only the behavior of children and parents but also the beliefs and expectations of parents (Donohue, Weinstein, Cowan, & Cowan, 2000). Parents listen to teachers' opinions about their children, especially when children are young. Teacher opinions about academic performance and behavior can predict the perceptions of both fathers and mothers. In addition, the parents' perceptions of their children's performance has been linked to the beliefs and behavior of children (Fagan, Newash, & Schloesser, 2000).

Monitor the Impact of Personal Biases

Some negative trends in teacher perception have been documented for children of certain ethnicities and for boys. Research has documented that Latino/Hispanic and African American boys are perceived as being less positive and as having more behavior problems (Arnold et al., 1998). Many studies have documented the overrepresentation of these children in special education placements (Coutinho, Oswald, Best, & Forness, 2002).

Several studies have found that teachers' beliefs about how children learn affect the way that the teachers interact with children. In one study, teachers who believed that social development is inherent in children tended to present activities to all children the same way and to refrain from designing interventions because these teachers believed that social development would occur naturally in the classroom (Lieber et al., 1998). Teachers who believed that social behavior is learned were more likely to consider social supports to children, such as pairing children with a staff member or another child, placing other children or adults in proximity of the child, scaffolding social skills, and explicitly teaching social skills.

Teachers and children sometimes have different goals and objectives for the classroom. Brown, Bauer, and Kretschmer (1995) found that teachers tend to focus on the educational or learning tasks in the classroom, whereas children tend to focus on social activities. The teachers observed in this study impeded social interaction while redirecting children to learning tasks. The difference between the goals and objectives of children and teachers created conflict that sometimes resulted in confrontations.

The distinction between a task focus and a social focus is important. When teachers do not consider classroom social activities part of the curriculum, they may not use all of the supports that are available. Challenging behaviors in the classroom can come from multiple sources: Some are initiated by learning activities and some are initiated by social activities (Taylor, Ekdahl, Romanczyk, & Miller, 1994). Children can act out to escape either social or learning activities. Conversely, children can act out to obtain social or learning activities. Teachers must observe children to understand how their own expectations about how children react in situations affect the structure of the classroom for each child.

The relationship between teachers and children is dynamic; teachers affect children, and children affect teachers. Interaction is subjectively experienced. For instance, teachers also seek comfortable situations and try to escape situations that make them feel uncomfortable. When the behavior of certain children makes teachers feel uncomfortable, they may avoid contact with these children or the situation that creates the behavior (Carr, Taylor, & Robinson, 1991). For children to receive the needed interaction and responsiveness, teachers must be aware of their tolerance for various behaviors and situations. It may be necessary to work with team members to provide supports for teachers so that they can provide consistent care to all of the children in the classroom (La Paro & Pianta, 2000).

By maintaining a positive, responsive relationship, teachers set the stage for appropriate behavior and for positive support of children. To develop this relationship, teachers must reflect on their values, beliefs, and expectations. They must work hard to understand the beliefs and expectations of children, families, and coworkers. Sometimes, they may need to override their initial impression about the behavior of a child or parent. Other times, they may need to reach out to team members (e.g., administrators, other teachers, resource staff members) when they recognize a mismatch between themselves and certain children and their parents. Teachers can be supported by talking through situations with other staff members, asking staff members to observe and give feedback, or asking for direct assistance.

CONCLUSION

The classroom ecosystem sets the stage for the types of learning that children experience. To plan effectively, teachers sew together many pieces of the classroom ecosystem to protect against threats to children's success. Daily schedules predictably cue children regarding upcoming activities and provide the flexibility needed to support the appropriate behavior. Elements of the curriculum and class activities are used to fit learning expectations to the individual learning styles and needs of children. Purposefully constructed groupings of children enhance the capabilities of children and prevent unnecessary problems. Classroom rules and limits are important elements of predictable, individually appropriate supports. Thoughtfully arranged materials and equipment allow children to self-monitor and follow through on tasks with little adult supervision. Finally, carefully nurtured relationships between children and adults encourage appropriate behavior. By providing these items, teachers create classrooms that support individual children, benefit the classroom as a whole, and accommodate diversity. Only by considering all of these elements can teachers design classrooms that truly respond to all children.

Chapter 5

Seeing the
Challenge More Clearly

Louise R. Phillips, Joyce Hensler,
Mef Diesel, and Andrea Cefalo

A growing number of children exhibit behaviors that require intervention. Aggression in children is appearing at younger ages and at escalating levels (Campbell, 1990; Hawkins, Catalano, & Miller, 1992). Webster-Stratton (1998) reported that 7%–25% of preschool and early school-age children meet the diagnostic criteria for oppositional defiant disorder and/or conduct disorder. High rates of aggression, noncompliance, and defiance in young children are reported as predictors of future conduct problems (Campbell, Shaw, & Gilliom, 2000; Webster-Stratton, 1990a, 2000).

As introduced in Chapter 1, research suggests that certain family characteristics put children at particular risk for developing conduct disorders: low socioeconomic status; limited parental education; maternal teenage pregnancy; isolation from family, community, and/or other social support systems; high levels of stress; single parenthood; parental psychiatric illness; parental criminal history or substance abuse; and high levels of marital discord (Webster-Stratton, 1990b, 1998). Interventionists, however, view families as part of the solution rather than as part of the problem. Family intervention programs that support collaboration, learning, and information sharing reflect a positive problem-solving approach to helping families and children (Boulware, Schwartz, & McBride, 1999; Webster-Stratton, Reid, & Hammond, 2001).

Many factors need to be considered when deciding how to clarify the challenging behaviors of children. The Division for Early Childhood's concept paper on identifying and creating interventions for children with challenging behavior states, "Many young children engage in challenging behavior in the course of early development, [but] the majority of these children respond to developmentally appropriate management techniques" (Brault et al., 1999, p. 63). Brault and colleagues cautioned that "care be given to consider cultural and community beliefs, developmentally appropriate expectations, and one's own beliefs about behavior, in the identification of children's behavior as 'challenging'" (p. 63). These factors are of primary significance when observing and documenting the behaviors of children (Lieber et al., 1998; Lynch & Hanson, 1998).

Examining the daily schedule of a child with challenging behaviors often reveals patterns of difficult times and/or activities (Barnett, Carey, & Hall; 1993; Barnett, Ehrhardt, Stollar, & Bauer, 1994; Barnett et al., 1997; Crosser, 1992; Welch, 1994). It is important to identify which factors in the child's environment contribute to the behavior (Slaby, Roedell, Arezzo, & Hendrix, 1995). As suggested in Chapter 4, the child's response to the daily schedule often provides needed information. A close look at the schedule can reveal that the child has difficulty when making transitions, during a specific activity, or at a particular time of day. These "hot spots" in the daily schedule give early childhood educators the opportunity to develop individual proactive and reactive strategies that provide support to a child with challenging behaviors (Lawry et al., 2000). These strategies provide a predictable backdrop for seeing the challenge more clearly—that is, seeing the possibilities that structuring the environment, individualizing instruction, and meeting individual needs can yield in terms of supporting a child's success.

Teachers follow a specific process when presented with a behavior challenge in the classroom. The process begins with informal information gathering. Proactively, early childhood educators implement preventive strategies to provide support where hot spots surface (Crosser, 1992). Early observation and documentation of the child's behavior can often increase the effectiveness of the preventive strategies in place for an individual child (Brault et al., 1999; Umbreit & Blair, 1997; Wolery, 1994).

The teacher's documentation of the behavior is then shared with the child's parents (Brault et al., 1999; Katz & McClellan, 1997). Input from the parents is encouraged, as a collaborative relationship is formed (Bailey, 1994; Barnett, Bell, & Carey, 1999; Bredekamp & Copple, 1997; Hewitt, 1995). This initial stage of observation, documentation, and collaboration lays the groundwork for clear definition of the challenge and encourages communication (Brault et al., 1999). If the child's challenging behaviors persist over time, escalate significantly, or present safety concerns, further collaboration and consultation is indicated.

Building on Chapter 4, this chapter encourages teachers to assess the specific factors contributing to the behavior challenges presented by an individual child. When clarifying the challenge, teachers must collect data to determine the appropriate next steps for developing an intervention strategy (Hewitt, 1995). This chapter encourages further examination of 1) times in the daily schedule when the challenging behaviors occur and preventive strategies that teachers can implement to understand those behaviors and support the child, as well as 2) methods that teachers can use to collect specific, objective information as the behavior occurs and to share that information in a way that fosters communication and mutual respect among all stakeholders.

WHICH PARTS OF THE DAILY SCHEDULE MAY BE HOT SPOTS?

Identifying "hot spots"—the times or activities during which challenging behavior surfaces—may help teachers understand the causes and/or purposes of the behavior. It is essential that the daily schedule reflects best practice in early childhood education (Bredekamp & Copple, 1997). This means that a daily schedule must provide each child with consistency, predictability, and a balance between active and quiet activities (Bredekamp & Copple, 1997; Hewitt, 1995). Examining when challenging behaviors occur often can give early childhood educators and parents the information needed to develop a plan that effectively addresses the needs of the child, the family, and the classroom community (Barnett et al., 1997). For some children, the behaviors of concern are limited to transition times or are related to specific activities (e.g., group time, naptime). For other children, the challenging behaviors are more generalized, seeming to occur throughout the day with little provocation or connection to the daily schedule. Teachers examine the hot spots and determine if preventive methods and strategies are in place and how they might be modified (Barnett et al., 1999; Crosser, 1992; Kaiser & Rasminsky, 1999; Lawry et al., 2000). When the behavior seems more generalized, the teacher looks for ways to adapt the environment to support the success of the individual child throughout the day. This is accomplished through ongoing observation, positive guidance techniques, and providing the child with appropriate choices to identify support strategies. If the challenging behavior persists or escalates, a collaborative team is formed and the process of further assessment and intervention begins. Identifying the hot spots, determining the factors present at these times, and developing a plan to address these environmental factors help the educator determine the next best intervention steps. The next subsections explore various points of the schedule during which problems may occur.

Transitions

It is important to note that each change in the child's day constitutes a transition. The simple act of coming to school is a significant transition for children (Gould & Sullivan, 1999). Often, challenging behaviors surface as children make transitions across points in the schedule or activities (Barnett et al., 1999; Sainato, 1990). During this shift of focus, some children are unable to maintain their sense of purpose and direction. Factors such as redirected teacher attention, increased classroom noise, changes in activity level, and/or inadequate warning or preparation for impending transitions frequently contribute to challenging behavior in these children (Davis, Reichle, & Southard, 2000; Sainato, 1990).

It is important to identify strategies that can be implemented or adapted to help children for whom transitions trigger challenging behaviors (Crosser, 1992). A successful method of preventing transition conflicts is maintaining a consistent classroom schedule. Children feel secure when they experience consistency and can predict their day (Bredekamp & Copple, 1997). Therefore, setting up a consistent schedule is a first step in preventing transition problems. Additional factors that the early childhood educator should assess are discussed next.

Determine the Reason for a Transition

It is important to consider the reason for each transition. For example, is the child leaving an activity at the teacher's request, as the result of a natural or logical consequence, or because he or she chose to go to another area? Determining the reason provides the teacher with information that can clarify the child's response during the transition. This distinction needs to be determined before putting a transition strategy into place.

Give Prior Notice

A child who has difficulty with transitions may not understand when transitions will occur. Or the child may have difficulty because he or she is unable to complete the current activity before changing to another. When making transitions is a hot spot, the teacher can evaluate the strategies that are in place to heighten the child's understanding. A highly successful strategy is giving the child prior notice before moving to another area or activity (Rosenkoetter & Fowler, 1986; Sainato, 1990). For example, the teacher might say, "In 5 minutes, it will be time to go outside." Telling each child individually demonstrates respect for his or her interests and emotional well-being and provides an opportunity for the teacher to acknowledge the child's play or work, to deter any arising conflicts, and, in turn, to facilitate the upcoming transition. In addition, this communication strategy enhances the child's ability to understand the message being sent. The use of songs can provide children with prior notice as well (Honig, 2001). Children who do not respond to teacher suggestion may make changes more successfully when songs are predictably associated with certain transition times. Using positive language to remind the child of classroom guidelines is another preventive strategy that assists children who have difficulty making transitions (Bredekamp & Copple, 1997; Cellitti, 1998; Katz & McClellan, 1997; Read, 1992).

Charts provide children with a concrete representation of upcoming transitions. Some examples of classroom charts that support children's following routines are 1) attendance charts, where the child can place his or her name card after entering the classroom; 2) gross motor area or playground charts, to which a child moves his or her name when it is his or her turn to leave the classroom and go to that area; and 3) waiting list charts, on which a child can choose to place his or her name in anticipation of moving to another activity or area.

Storyboards, picture schedules, and social stories also are helpful transition tools for some children. These are pictorial representations of the child's schedule or routine, presented in the form of a chart or a book. They can include photographs or line drawings that depict the choice time centers for the child who has difficulty making or maintaining a choice or that illustrate the day's sequence of events (Schmit, Alper, Raschke, & Ryndak, 2000). Social stories are books that can be used to help a child to understand the sequence of the classroom day or the sequence of an activity (Gray & Garand, 1993; Swaggart & Gagnon, 1995). For example, a child who is having difficulty with making the transition from lunch to naptime may be read a social story that clearly states the order of activities and predictably indicates what will happen next.

Examine Conflicts During Transitions

Conflicts can arise when a child chooses not to participate in a group transition. For example, a child resists the transition to outdoor play because she wants to continue playing inside. The teacher gives this child the choice of using her name tag to save her place at the activity. The child insists on staying inside, so the teacher then reminds her of the inviting choices outside: "Will you ride a scooter or climb on the climber with your friends?" The child replies, "I don't want to ride a scooter." The teacher responds, "Then what would you like to play with outside?" This method changes the child's focus from what she is playing with inside to the choices available on the playground. The teacher further encourages the child to go outside by offering to help her put on her jacket and acknowledging the child's disappointment in leaving her activity inside. It is important to remember to keep such interactions positive (Cellitti, 1998; Wittmer & Honig, 1994). The teacher should communicate an understanding of the child's feelings and remind her that it is possible to return to the activity later (Katz & McClellan, 1997; Kuebli, 1994).

The same challenge can arise when returning from the playground. One preventive strategy designed to increase the child's sense of predictability is to give a 5-minute warning. Once the teacher gives this notice, it is important that he or she follows through with the limit. If a child does not want to leave a certain outdoor play area, several things can facilitate the transition. Often, a child wants to climb the rope one more time or show that he or she can cross the monkey bars. It is best to simply let the child do this. Most of the time, he or she will be ready to go in after performing the task. Sometimes, a child may run in the opposite direction and refuse to come into the building. One way to redirect this behavior is to engage him or her as a play partner. The teacher can let the child be the guide and playfully redirect him or her, using the transition as a learning opportunity for the child by extending the play to an indoor activity (Wolery et al., 1998). If the child is determined to stay outside, the teacher can talk about the upcoming indoor activity. For instance, if the next transition is lunch, the teacher can talk to the child about that day's menu choices. The teacher also can facilitate the child's transition by suggesting alternative ways to move to the door (e.g., hopping, skipping, crawling) and empowering the child to choose still another idea—one of his or her own.

Evaluate the Transition Process

Moving young children in small groups is an effective way of determining whether a child has difficulty with the noisy disorganization of whole-group transitions or with the concept of the change itself. It often is helpful to have children sit on the floor while waiting to make a transition out of the classroom. This often reduces the general activity level (e.g., pushing) as children prepare to be more active and anticipation of the next activity mounts. The teacher can observe to see whether the resulting reduction of activity level and/or the moving of children in small groups supports the child who is experiencing difficulty. In addition, before returning to the classroom, teachers can facilitate a child's successful transition to the classroom by implementing individual support strategies. A transition song can be used to help the children gather into their small groups. As children return to the classroom, teachers can encourage each child to determine which of the offered activities he or she will choose. For some children, this process is too abstract. The teacher can assist by providing a concrete representation (e.g., a picture, a small object) that helps a child recall the choices in the classroom or shifts the child's focus away from the request to make the transition (Davis et al., 2000; Schmit et al., 2000). Providing each child with the necessary assistance to engage in an activity after returning to the classroom allows teachers to assess the factors contributing to an individual child's difficult reentry. Facilitating each child's reengagement in classroom activities should take place prior to having another small group of children make a transition.

Each strategy suggested in this chapter is intended to show respect for the individual child (Bredekamp & Copple, 1997; Katz & McClellan, 1997; Wittmer & Honig, 1994). Understanding that a child does not want to immediately tear down the block structure that he or she spent 20 minutes building or that a child wants to go down the slide just one more time communicates respect for his or her feelings (Kuebli, 1994). To understand the challenging behavior more clearly, the teacher must assess which preventive strategies are already in place and consider other preventive strategies that can be implemented. By establishing a relationship that shows respect, keeping a consistent and predictable schedule, and having transition methods and strategies in place, the early childhood educator can more accurately determine the need for further assessment. Some of these strategies are illustrated in the following vignette.

> Making transitions from the gross motor room is a challenge for a particular group of children. When it is almost time to leave the room, staff members individually give each child a 5-minute warning. This allows the children to finish what they are doing. If the children are building with large, hollow, unit blocks, they are given an amount of time to continue playing and then a reminder of when it is time to clean up. Teachers give the children choices of cleaning up by themselves or with adult help. When it is time to leave the activity area, the lead teacher sings a song that tells children to meet her at the door. The other teachers suggest that the children skip to the door. As the children line up at the door, the lead teacher prompts a discussion about what activities will occur back in their classroom. Snack time is next, so a conversation about the juice and crackers that will be served provides motivation for a successful transition.

CLASSROOM APPLICATION

What preventive strategies are in place to support children during transitions? Are they effective? Are the following actions utilized to improve transitions?

Suggest ways for the children to move from one place to another (e.g., crawl down the hall to the gross motor room to prevent running).

Help the children focus on the activity that will happen next.

Remind the children of guidelines before making transitions.

Use songs during transitions or as notification that a change is going to happen.

Use preplanned lists so the children will know when it will be their turn and/or use child-initiated waiting lists to facilitate waiting for a turn.

State guidelines in positive language.

Move the children in small groups rather than in large or whole groups.

Give children the opportunity to "save" their unfinished activities when they are required to move to the next point on the schedule.

Keep a consistent daily schedule.

Give the children prior notice of transitions.

Assist the children as needed to facilitate transition.

Use positive management strategies to calm activity levels. Provide concrete prompts.

What other adaptations and modifications can be implemented?

How does using preventive strategies contribute to better teacher understanding of challenges during transitions?

Group Time

Challenging behaviors may surface during group time (Gould & Sullivan, 1999). Strategically selecting the location of a particular child within the group-time seating arrangement can be a key element for success (Farver, 1996). The teacher can add structure to the group activity by 1) selecting the child's neighboring children, 2) providing carpet squares or mats to identify each child's space, and 3) seating the child in close proximity to a teacher or assistant. It is very important that the group activity is both individually and developmentally appropriate for each child within the group (Bredekamp & Copple, 1997). Children who have difficulty in large group activities may dislike feeling crowded or find the activity too challenging. Other factors to consider are the length of group time, the children's prior experiences with the group time activity, and the interest of the children in the chosen activity (Zeece & Corr, 1988). Activities that allow for each child's individual participation (e.g., choosing the movement for an activity song, choosing a fill-in for an interactive chart) can seem too long for some children. Tailoring the group time focus to the experience and interest levels of the children enhances opportunities for group time success.

Teachers must brainstorm to find strategies that help a child successfully participate in group time activities (Church, 1996; Hoyson, Jamieson, Strain, & Smith, 1998; Sainato & Strain, 1992). It can be effective to schedule group time between two larger blocks of time within the daily schedule (e.g., between choice time and outside play time). This scheduling provides for a more natural transition to and from group time. Children should have ample opportunity to complete their previous tasks before being expected to participate in a group activity. As with transitions, individually giving 5-minute warnings allows children to finish an activity before cleanup. When the teacher prepares the group area by setting out mats or materials, the children receive a visual cue that group time is approaching. Again, a transition song can be used to signal the actual time for cleanup and assembly in the group time area. As the teacher sings the cleanup song, he or she can provide individual support to children who especially need it and finish the song while moving to the group area. For example, while singing, the teacher might hand a few blocks to a child to facilitate the cleanup of the block area or assist with removing a paint smock as a child is finishing up in the art area.

Assess the Seating Plan

Children need some direction for seating during group time (Hoyson et al., 1998; Zeece & Corr, 1988). Individual mats help identify each space. Individual and whole group needs must be considered when determining mat placement. Some groups of children are able to choose their own mats. Others may need more structure and specific teacher direction. One effective strategy in structuring group time seating is placing name cards on the mats. This allows the teacher to select which children sit next to each other and to seat children in an accessible location for additional guidance and support from assistant teachers. Assistant teachers can model appropriate participation by engaging in movement activities and listening attentively to the stories being read. Sometimes, a child benefits from a permanent seat location, which gives the child practice in identifying his or her name. In addition, being permanently seated closer to the teacher ensures teacher opportunities for offering subtle verbal and nonverbal cues that facilitate better focus on the activities. Finally, careful attention to each child's ability to see and hear is important. The teacher should ask him- or herself, "Are others blocking this child's view?" "Is the child attending to what is being presented?" and "Does the child's medical history indicate that group time needs to be modified for him or her?"

Consider the Length of Group Time

Group time length and activities are important factors in implementing a successful experience. It is not developmentally appropriate to expect young children to attend to large-group activities for an extended period of time (Bredekamp & Copple, 1997). Again, the individual characteristics of the classroom group also must be considered. Some children may be able to attend for only 5 minutes, whereas others may be able to participate appropriately for as long as 15 minutes. Their attention span may be influenced by the actual activities planned and the degree to which these activities account for children's prior experiences, activity levels, and interests. One effective strategy is having two short group times in place of one longer one. Another is making group time optional for children. A child who chooses not to participate in group time on a given day may look at books while sitting in a quiet area or engage in an activity that does not distract the rest of the group. Often, children who choose this option actually attend to group time activities from their removed vantage point.

Evaluate the Selection and Sequence of Group Activities

The specific sequence of activities during group time must be carefully planned (Hoyson et al., 1998). A familiar opening activity is effective in gaining children's attention. This may take the form of a simple song that includes each child's name as a welcome to this part of the day. Alternating quiet and active activities also is effective in planning for a successful group time. For example, the teacher may read a short story, then follow with a movement activity. A closing or transition song is an effective tool for ending group time. This song may direct children to the next activity and can include each child's name, followed by a directive such as "Put your mat away and get your coat." With this approach, children leave the area in smaller groups, causing less confusion and activity and thereby reducing the possibility of challenging behavior. The final direction in the song typically provides information about the next planned activity.

Despite careful planning, teachers must be flexible with group time plans. They may need to shorten group time and exclude a previously planned activity because of declining child interest levels, distractions, or the activity level of the group as a whole.

Identify Factors Contributing to Distraction

Having effective strategies in place reduces distractions that can contribute to behavior challenges at group time. Nearby shelves may be covered, and materials may be removed from an area that is easily accessible to children during group time. Having all necessary group time materials prepared and in place prior to group time is imperative. Limiting movement by staff is helpful as well. With these preventive strategies in place, early childhood educators can determine more clearly when a child needs further intervention for successful group time participation. The following vignette illustrates some of the factors that may be addressed during group time challenges.

> Mike, in his second year of preschool, has recently been diagnosed as having ADHD. Because he has difficulty succeeding at school and is easily discouraged, Mike is reluctant to try new tasks. In addition, he often displays limited social skills when interacting with peers.
>
> Group time is particularly difficult for Mike. He has trouble finding the name card that identifies his mat, and distractions (e.g., nearby materials, other children) limit his ability to attend to the group time activity. To assist Mike, the teacher gives careful thought to his placement in the group. The mat closest to the teacher becomes his permanent spot. Mike can successfully find his name card because its location is consistent. The nearby storage shelf is covered to limit the likelihood of toys distracting him. His place close to the teacher reduces peer distraction and allows the teacher to give Mike cues and reinforcement to help him stay focused

on the activities. Because Mike is seated close to the teacher, she can help him without drawing unnecessary attention to her assistance.

CLASSROOM APPLICATION

What preventive strategies are in place to support the child during group time? Are they effective? Are the following actions utilized to improve group time participation?

Alternate quiet and active tasks.

Present new or difficult activities first.

Begin group time activities when most children are ready rather than wait for everyone.

Cover or remove distracting materials in the group time area.

Limit the length of group time to 5–10 minutes.

Shape group time activities to the ability, experience, and interests of the children.

Minimize wait time between activities.

Make sure that all children can see and hear.

Have two small groups instead of one large one.

Plan the seating. Use name cards or mats to identify each child's space.

Seat children who may need assistance in close proximity to an adult.

Give children story props to increase focus and attention.

Consider making group time an optional experience.

What other adaptations and modifications can be implemented?

How do preventive strategies contribute to better teacher understanding of group time challenges?

Naptime

Children who feel insecure in a situation often act out or resort to aggressive behavior to avoid participation in the activity. During naptime, a child must be able to lower his or her defenses. Depending on previous sleep experiences, some children will express more anxiety than others at naptime. When a child feels anxious for any reason in the naptime environment, behaviors will likely surface.

Many strategies can help provide a restful atmosphere and thereby reduce conflicts at naptime (York, 1997). First, from the initial day of school, it is imperative to establish a well-defined, consistent routine. In addition, it is difficult for many young children to change their focus too quickly from a higher activity level to the quiet time necessary for a restful nap period. Thus, the stage must be set for calm and quiet before naptime. Typically, naptime follows lunch. Dimming the lights, drawing the blinds, and playing soft music during lunch are effective environmental modifications that help facilitate this transition.

Arrange the Room for Naptime

The needs and strengths of each child must be considered when implementing the naptime routine. One way that this is accomplished is through careful placement of the cots within the room (York, 1997). Some children may need to be in dimly lit places, whereas others can sleep in brighter conditions. Possible external distractions must also be considered. A child who is easily distracted may rest better if his or her cot is far from high-traffic areas (e.g., the door). Cots also can be placed to avoid distractions from other children. Shelves and partitions serve as natural barriers to section the room into small nap areas of two or three children, although some children may benefit from sleeping in a solitary location. The teacher must be careful to place all cots in areas that are visible throughout the classroom. Although some children can successfully and appropriately regulate their own behavior, others need teacher facilitation. Still others require immediate and prolonged teacher attention. The placement of cots plays an important role in this facilitation. A child with greater needs can be placed next to a child who is able to model more appropriate behavior. Conversely, the teacher may place two children who need increased teacher facilitation next to each other. This allows the teacher to assist both children at the same time. Limiting the number of times that others enter and exit the room during naptime further reduces distractions.

Select and Sequence Naptime Activities

It is important to minimize the number of steps in the routine. Although toothbrushing can be a natural step in the transition from lunch to naptime, it also can be a high energy, stimulating activity. For this reason, the teacher may find it more successful to incorporate this task during morning choice time. Young children generally need to use the bathroom before settling down for a nap. This is a good first step in the transition from lunch to nap. Once children are on their cots, they need a quiet-focus activity. Providing a basket of naptime books to choose from helps facilitate this part of the routine. The books provided should be calming and reassuring. A collection of story bags (cloth bags containing a storybook and story props—i.e., concrete objects that help children retell the events of the story in their own words) also may be available to the children. Familiarity is important as well. Children may achieve comfort from the familiar feel or smell of a special pillow, blanket, or stuffed toy from home (York, 1997).

Allow Individual Time with the Teacher

Giving each child individual time with the teacher is important to establish and maintain a trusting child–teacher relationship. Maintaining consistent staff is necessary, and, if possible, the teacher who facilitates naptime for a child should be available when the child awakens. The teacher and classroom staff can circulate the room and read to each child the book that he or she chose for naptime. Looking at a book is a relaxing activity that may also mirror the child's home bedtime routine. In addition, looking at a book helps the child self-regulate while waiting for his or her special time with the teacher.

For children who have a particularly difficult time falling asleep, the teacher might consider extending this time by offering a backrub. This is an excellent way to help a child to relax physically; however, a child may not like having his or her back rubbed. Simply tucking in the child and telling him or her to have a good rest may be enough, although some children may need prolonged teacher attention to relax enough to fall asleep.

Communicate with the Family

The family's sleep routine and culture must be considered; it may be necessary to adjust the method in which the teacher uses to help a child relax (Lynch & Hanson, 1998). Communicating with the family is an excellent tool for sharing information about the methods in which a child best achieves relaxation, comfort, and security during naptime (Bredekamp & Copple, 1997). For example, a child may feel more secure if given the opportunity to sit on a teacher's lap while the teacher reads a book or rubs another child's back. Or a child may prefer being rocked on a teacher's lap. Flexibility within the routine is needed to accommodate special considerations for a particular child. The teacher should investigate whether the child takes a nap at home or in any other environment and, if so, what naptime guidelines and routines are used. The teacher should ask whether the child is accustomed to falling asleep alone or with a sibling or other family member. This routine differs significantly across families (Bhavnagri & Gonzalez-Mena, 1997; Gonzalez-Mena & Bhavnagri, 2001). Having information about the child's prior naptime experiences allows assessment of the child's ability to comply with the classroom naptime routine.

Consider Other Issues

Even with consistent routines and preventive measures in place, some children may be unable to understand and/or follow naptime expectations appropriately. They may no longer require a nap or may exhibit fears about resting at school. These children often exhibit disruptive and aggressive behaviors at naptime. Additional strategies can be put in place to help these children relax. Parental assistance may be especially helpful for a child experiencing anxiety about napping in the school environment. Having a parent come to read the child's book at naptime can be reassuring. An alternative environment can be provided for children who no longer require naps or have difficulty understanding naptime expectations. This environment may be another classroom, where the children can participate in quiet activities and still be given the opportunity to rest on a cot. There also may be a comfortable classroom space for a child and a teacher to spend additional nurturing or wind-down time.

Disruptive and aggressive behaviors can be the most challenging at naptime. In conjunction with simple adaptations to the environment, the teacher's attitude sets the stage for success (Lieber et al., 1998). The consistent routine provides predictability; soft music, muted lighting, and stuffed toys provide comfort (Field, 1999). Encouraging families to pick up their child for departure before or after naptime limits the number of naptime distractions. Finding what works best with each child and group of children takes patience and some trial and error, but starting with a well-defined and consistent routine is key. The following vignette illustrates typical strategies used during naptime.

> Jennifer, age 4, needs extra time to move around the room before being able to relax enough to lie quietly on her cot—an observation that was reinforced by talking with her mother. During this wind-down time, Jennifer often cleans the lunch tables with paper towels. On other days, she prefers to sit next to another child's cot and listen to the teacher read a story. Sometimes, she sits on the teacher's lap while the teacher rubs the back of the child who is lying on the cot. These activities allow Jennifer to relax, and they reinforce the expectation of calm and quiet. Frequently, after experiencing this period of activity, Jennifer is able to lie down quietly on her cot.

CLASSROOM APPLICATION

What preventive strategies are in place to support the child during naptime? Are they effective? Are the following actions utilized to improve naptime success?

Establish a consistent and concrete routine. Keep the routine's steps to a minimum.

Dim the lights and draw the blinds or curtains.

Play soothing music softly in the background.

Consider individual children's needs when arranging cots.

Provide a plan for children whose developmental progress indicates that they no longer require a nap (e.g., an alternative space).

Provide a selection of books from which the child may choose. Ensure that these books are calming, have limited text, and are short enough to permit time for reading to each child.

Provide consistent naptime caregivers, and limit movement in and out of the nap room/classroom. Prevent external distractions.

Encourage parents to pick up children before or after naptime.

Provide quiet activities to be used on the cot for children who do not sleep (e.g., story bags, dry erase boards).

Encourage use of transitional objects, such as a familiar blanket from home.

Interview the parents to obtain information on the child's sleep routine.

Provide individual attention to help the child to relax (e.g., backrubs).

What other adaptations and modifications can be implemented?

How does using preventive strategies contribute to better teacher understanding of naptime challenges?

Choice Time

Choice time naturally creates many opportunities for children to interact, express themselves, and problem solve (Bredekamp & Copple, 1997; Campbell, 1990; Katz & McClellan, 1997: Kelman, 1990; Odom & Diamond, 1998). Children with self-regulatory or sensory integration issues often experience difficulty during this part of their day. Lighting, noise level, the activity level of the other children, and individual classroom dynamics can contribute to problem situations. Other children demonstrate difficulty becoming engaged with an activity or maintaining engagement (McCormick, Noonan, & Heck, 1998; McWilliam, 1991; McWilliam, Trivette, & Dunst, 1985). Early childhood educators cannot assume that all children feel in control or safe in the choice time environment. For this reason, extensive effort in structuring the environment to support individual needs is important (Kontos & Wilcox-Herzog, 1997).

The teacher should ask, "Which existing strategies can be expanded or modified to help children with challenging behaviors participate more successfully in the choice time routine?" Developmentally appropriate activities and materials that are arranged in an appealing, convenient display help children become engaged and focus on the task. These activities and materials should be age appropriate, individually appropriate, and geared to each child's interests (Bagnato, Neisworth, & Munson, 1989; Bredekamp & Copple, 1997). Availability of materials, appropriateness, and cues for clean up should be determined by the characteristics of the children in the class (Elgas, Prendeville, Moomaw, & Kretschmer, 2002; Whaley & Bennett, 1991).

Provide Clear Limits

Many strategies and techniques prevent conflict situations and management issues from occurring in early childhood classrooms. Because young children are concrete thinkers, teachers must avoid abstract and vaguely stated rules (Bredekamp & Copple, 1997; Katz & McClellan, 1997). During choice time clear visual limits and boundaries should be set, based on observations of young children in general and/or a particular child in the class (Read, 1992). For example, as discussed in Chapter 4, self-correcting limits can be set in an activity area. Four chairs and four trays clearly indicate an art activity for four children. One chair is placed at the computer. These visual cues depict teacher expectations regarding the number of children who may participate in an activity. Occasionally, a child will pull up a chair or take a smock from another activity area. The teacher should restate the limit in a clear way—for example, "I see four chairs and four trays. It looks like there is only room for four children. You can put your name on the waiting list for the next group."

Waiting lists are another tool that can be used during choice time. Preprinted waiting lists might be labeled "special activity waiting list," "dramatic play waiting list," "easel waiting list," and "computer waiting list." Each list has a visual cue (e.g., a picture of a computer). Waiting lists, along with pencils attached by Velcro, can be placed on clipboards in the centers or on the wall of each appropriate area. When a child is reminded that an area or activity is full, the teacher may then point out the waiting list. This visual account of an upcoming turn helps children understand who has the next turn.

Another preventive measure is asking children to sit down as they work in the manipulative area. When the children stand as they play or work, the activity level and noise level is higher. If the children are sitting, they have their own spaces and are less likely to encroach on another child's space or work. It is important for teachers to use responsive rather than restrictive language when interacting with a child throughout the day.

Responsive language provides the child with information concerning what he or she can do. Restrictive language focuses on information concerning limits—specifically, what is not permitted (Stone, 1993). By responding to a child's individual needs, providing appropriate choices, and, when needed, limiting the choices to support a child's needs, the teacher is able to establish clear limits and document the child's behavior in response to them (Wilcox-Herzog & Kontos, 1997).

Arrange the Classroom for Choice Time

Classroom setup can play a major role in preventing challenging behavior (Crosser, 1992; Lawry et al., 2000). If the classroom is messy and chaotic, the children will reflect this disorganization. Therefore, classroom organization and aesthetics play a role in preventing management issues from occurring. Manipulative toys can be placed in attractive wicker baskets, creating a place for each item. Children should be encouraged (and expected) to clean up after themselves so the activity will be ready for another child. At the art shelf, each item should be in its own container, which is clearly labeled with words and pictures. The children also should have a sense of ownership in the classroom, as well as a sense of community (Bredekamp & Copple, 1997; Katz & McClellan, 1997). Recognizing that sharing is not typical behavior for preschool children, the teacher may provide duplicates of high-demand materials. Providing self-correcting activities (e.g., puzzles) and open-ended materials helps teachers to observe and document the progress and behavior of individual children (Elgas et al., 2002).

Identify Visual Boundaries

Teachers should ask, "Which visual boundaries are in place, and how does the child respond to them?" Each choice time area might have only one opening for entering and exiting—a strategy that prevents running. Play in the manipulatives and block areas can result in driving toy cars, flying toy airplanes, or building structures into the path of others. Teachers can use colored tape to create boundaries on the floor and instruct, "Stay on this side of the green tape." This strategy is much more effective than repeated redirection.

The placement of shelves and dividers can further define the use of space and prevent running and unsafe behavior. The placement of quiet areas next to noisy areas can result in distraction and frustration, and conflict may occur (Bredekamp & Copple, 1997).

If preventive planning is in place, it is significant when a child's behaviors require additional modifications. As a result, individual space may also be provided to children in the classroom (Katz & McClellan, 1997). This can be a small corner with one comfortable chair and a rug or an area with a curtained divider. It might include a small basket with board books and stuffed animals. Sometimes, the individual space is next to a window, has mirrors, or contains headphones for listening to soft music. The teacher should avoid using this area for punishment. Instead, it is a quiet place where children choose to go. The teacher may suggest that a child use this area when he or she expresses frustration or a desire to be alone. The teacher might explain, "There is room in this area for four children, but if you want to be alone, you can go sit in the quiet space." Children can then choose to use the space to calm themselves.

Create a Sense of Classroom Community

Often, when a child acts out, the sense of classroom community is at risk. Numerous prevention strategies promote a sense of belonging, which can help the teacher to determine the need for additional adaptations and modifications (Bredekamp & Copple, 1997). Children's artwork can be prominently displayed. Each child can have his or her own place to put personal belongings. Fresh flowers might be provided in the classroom and on the lunch tables each day. When the classroom is clean and attractive, children feel valued (Katz & McClellan, 1997). Children's ideas and interests can be valued and acted on, allowing children to be part of a community in which teachers learn alongside children. Projects can reflect what the children show or tell and may be based on their interests. Children can contribute what they know about a particular subject and discuss what they want to know. Children can go to the library and get books with their parents, or an expert (e.g., a veterinarian) can visit the classroom and answer the children's questions. The children's learning can be recorded on documentation panels that are displayed in the room and in portfolios (Edwards, Gandini, & Forman, 1998).

Children can play an active role in their learning, constructing knowledge based on interactions with materials, other children, and teachers. Teachers can ask questions to extend thinking without incessantly correcting children, providing appropriate models for respecting others and communicating acceptance of the children's mistakes (Cellitti, 1998; Edwards et al., 1998; Wittmer & Honig, 1994). It should be communicated that mistakes can be a part of learning. Children have to feel safe in order to make mistakes. When the classroom belongs to the children, they are more likely to feel safe and less likely to display destructive, challenging behaviors.

At times, even when preventive measures are in place, teacher suggestions and directions are not followed. Perhaps the child is unable to process the request, unable to control his or her movement, or unwilling to comply. Further observation and documentation can determine what occurs before, during, and after challenging behavior (see Chapter 7). Teacher strategies are illustrated in the following vignette.

> Choice time is difficult for 3-year-old Ethan. He has trouble choosing activities and staying focused until their completion. He forces himself into his peers' play, becoming disruptive and aggressive. He wanders around the room, spending short periods of time at many activity centers. To

improve Ethan's engagement, the teacher helps Ethan makes a picture board of things that he wants to do. This board helps him plan his day. The teacher also helps Ethan become engaged, sometimes acting as a play partner to model appropriate play. As Ethan accomplishes a task, he goes back to the picture board to find his next activity. If he gets off track, the teacher reminds him of what he has planned.

It is apparent that Ethan wants to play with others but does not know how to approach them. The teacher gives Ethan words for entering play and helps him interact appropriately. Wristbands are used for participation in certain areas with limited space; these areas provide a more manageable group with which Ethan can interact. Waiting lists also help Ethan to realize that he will get a turn. As he becomes more successful at waiting, it is hoped that his desire to rush into others' activities will lessen.

CLASSROOM APPLICATION

What preventive strategies are in place to support the child during choice time? Are they effective? Are the following actions utilized to improve the choice time experience?

Provide clear visual limits and boundaries.

Implement the use of waiting lists so that children can engage in other activities while they are waiting.

Encourage children to sit down when engaged in an activity.

Supply duplicates of certain materials so more than one child can play.

Give a child limited choices if he has difficulty engaging in play.

Provide a quiet space for children who need to retreat.

Organize materials to facilitate independent cleanup.

Provide self-correcting activities.

Recognize that sharing is not typical for preschool children.

Encourage children to ask about helping other children.

What other adaptations and modifications can be implemented?

How does using preventive strategies contribute to better teacher understanding of choice time challenges?

Gross Motor Time

Children should have a chance for gross motor activity every day (Bredekamp & Copple, 1997). Opportunities for indoor active play can occur in a separate gross motor room, where equipment and activities are available for children to extend physical development. Because children are more active in this area, chances for unsafe play and conflicts increase.

Careful planning of gross motor room setup can help keep children focused on appropriate play and reduce the need for adult intervention.

It is important to ask 1) "Which strategies can be added or modified to help a child for whom movement to the gross motor room stimulates challenging behavior?" and 2) "What can be done to help that child self-regulate his or her behavior?" A successful experience in the gross motor room depends in part on smooth transitions to and from the classroom. Children are usually anxious for their turn in the gross motor room. In a center with several classrooms, a small number of children from one class may be combined with small groups from other classes. This provides socialization experiences with other children and increases the sense of community within the center while children wait to go to the gross motor room.

There are several ways to select groupings. A gross motor room chart with a specific number of spaces allows children to reserve a place in a particular group. This type of waiting list allows children to know when they will be in the next group (Moomaw & Hieronymous, 2001) and to choose a time that fits around their other activities. Depending on the characteristics or behavioral issues in a specific class, however, it may be better to preselect the groups. This permits the teacher to consider the activity levels, interests, and social interactions of certain children (Farver, 1996). With this structured technique, children know when it will be their turn simply by looking at the list.

Sometimes, a blend of methods is more appropriate. The groups may be preselected, but children may be able to request that a friend join their group, or they may have the option of delaying their turn if they want to finish a classroom activity in which they are engaged. Allowing children to make requests provides opportunities for note writing or dictation. For example, a child who wants to continue an activity in the classroom may write his or her name on a note or dictate to the teacher a message reserving a space in the next group. By encouraging children to reserve their spaces in writing, the children experience meaningful interaction with print. Having choices also motivates children to display appropriate behavior. It also may be helpful to consider children from other classes and the social climate of the gross motor room during various times of the day. The teachers might plan to stagger the gross motor room time of two children who repeatedly experience conflicts while in the same group (Farver, 1996). Certain times in the gross motor room (e.g., when it is less crowded) may be better for a child who is easily excited or overwhelmed by high activity levels.

Examine the Arrangement of the Gross Motor Room

Thoughtful arrangement of the gross motor room activities and equipment can provide children with guidelines for appropriate play. Safety is a major consideration (Read, 1992). The floor surface should have proper padding to lessen the chance of injury if children fall while climbing. Running activities can be separated from climbing and other less active areas. There can be a variety of activities to meet the needs of children with both high and low activity levels. Children can have opportunities to run, climb, and jump; access to large building materials; chances for throwing and catching; and an area for playing games. Printed guidelines and suggestions to extend play accompanying activity setup allows teachers and children to focus on a visual cue rather than on repeated teacher reminders. For example, a beanbag target game might display a sign that says "Throw the beanbags at the target" to remind children of appropriate play. A line of tape on the floor can be a reminder of where the running area stops and children must walk.

Staff placement is vital to the safe management of this area. A teacher should be close to equipment where children are engaged in large muscle skills such as climbing or jumping. He or she can provide support, encouragement, and a safe presence, all of which extend the children's skills and comfort level. The teacher also facilitates the awareness of nearby children. As children engage in activities in the gross motor room, conflicts can and do arise. Careful attention to traffic patterns, activity levels, safety concerns, and appropriate use of equipment results in needed guidelines that communicate respect for children. In addition, teacher facilitation and the structuring of activities to support the success of children are key. This point is demonstrated in the next vignette about a child who has difficulty participating safely in a tumbling activity.

> Daron, age 3, entered the center halfway through the school year, and his teacher has concerns about his behavior. Daron's high activity level interferes with his ability to engage in activities with his peers. If not constantly supervised, he destroys others' projects and is physically aggressive with classmates. The unstructured nature of gross motor room time is especially difficult for Daron. A staff member is always aware of Daron's location and is ready to protect others and help Daron make safe choices.
>
> In the corner of the room, there is a wedge-shaped tumbling mat with flat mats extending from the end. Children are encouraged to start at the high end, tumble to the end of the mat, exit, and return to the start, where others are taking their turns. Daron enjoys the tumbling but keeps going back up the mat, an action that is unsafe for him and those coming down the mat. To help manage the flow of the activity, small carpet squares are placed on the floor starting at the end of the mat and moving up the side of the mats to the beginning. Small pieces of Velcro are stuck to the bottom of the carpet squares to keep them from slipping. Print is added to direct the path back to the beginning. Daron enjoys hopping from square to square, enabling him to get back to the beginning safely.

CLASSROOM APPLICATION

What preventive strategies are in place to support the child during gross motor time? Are they effective? Are the following actions utilized to improve the gross motor time experience?

Preselect groups, combining children on the basis of interests, level of interaction, and energy level.

Allow children to choose the members of their group to help them form relationships with peers. Remind them of that privilege if behavior becomes inappropriate.

Have a group list available so children can see when they will have a turn.

Ensure a variety of activities that are appropriate for the groups of children.

Use print or charts in the gross motor room to remind children of the guidelines for equipment use or to suggest ways to extend play.

If possible, be aware of the activity level and specific children already in the gross motor room when a group is sent.

Provide clear, concrete boundaries and limits.

Make sure that staffing is optimal and that staff are placed strategically throughout the room.

Give children prior notice before transitions occur (e.g., when leaving an activity, when returning to the classroom).

What other adaptations and modifications can be implemented?

How does using preventive strategies contribute to better teacher understanding of gross motor time challenges?

Outside Play

Going outside is an exciting time of the day for children. It provides chances to run, speak in loud voices, and gain gross motor experience. It also can be a time for more safety concerns. A well-planned outside area helps ensure that children will be engaged in appropriate activities that challenge and interest them (Vaughn, 1990). Thought should be given to the placement and quantity of materials available as well as to the assignment of sufficient personnel to provide supervision and extend thinking.

Outside facilities can vary greatly in size and available equipment. All climbing areas should have protected surfaces underneath to ensure children's safety. Strategic placement of materials or activities also can encourage a safe experience. Riding toys can be limited to a specific area, with one-way directional movement to help reduce collisions. Areas for riding should be separate from those for running, and areas for quieter activities should be more isolated. Consider the needs of the children playing outside. Some children are more vigorous in their play and need running areas and activities that use a lot of energy. Other children may choose quieter, more solitary activities. It is important to have a variety of activities available to meet the needs of all the children and to provide enough materials for a reasonable number of children to participate at one time (Read, 1992).

Consider Staffing on the Outdoor Playground

Staffing of the outside area is important. Teachers stay near areas with greater risk for accidents to provide guidance and support children in problem solving. Outside experiences can provide opportunities for children to solve conflicts, decide on rules of play, and extend their own limits. It may be necessary for teachers to facilitate these skills. Teachers must be aware of typical developmental motor accomplishments for the ages of the group so that they can provide necessary support when children are extending their skills. Teachers can provide proximity and physical assistance to help children problem-solve emerging motor skills and abilities (Read, 1992). Children who are successful will keep working on newfound skills and remain appropriately engaged. Teachers also can help children who engage in quieter activities by asking open-ended questions and making observations about their activities. This often results in extended play themes. The vignette that follows describes an outside play space with several of the characteristics described in this section.

> The center's outside area is divided up into activity areas. One end is the riding area for tricycles and scooters. Children travel in the same direction in a circular pattern around a cushioned surface, which is limited to small motion toys such as a rocking boat or sedentary toys placed on the ground such as a dollhouse. Dividers contain the riding toys and remind children engaged in running games to keep a safe distance from the riding toys. Another part of the outside area contains a sandbox that is large enough for several children and filled with numerous sand toys. There is a raised platform with a Plexiglas easel for quieter activities, a wooden gazebo for outside dramatic play activities, and a large climber with a padded ground covering. An outside water fountain eliminates requests to go inside for a drink.

CLASSROOM APPLICATION

What preventive strategies are in place to support the child during outside play? Are they effective? Are the following actions utilized to improve the outside play experience?

Provide enough appropriate activities to keep children engaged.

Provide a broad selection of high- and low-activity level choices to meet the needs of all children.

Separate quiet and active areas.

Set guidelines for the safe use of equipment.

Provide enough materials for a reasonable number of children to participate in an activity at one time.

Provide optimal staff for supervision and facilitation of problem-solving opportunities.

What other adaptations and modifications can be implemented?

How does using preventive strategies contribute to better teacher understanding outside play challenges?

Lunch and Snack Time

With certain strategies in place, lunch can be a relaxing and enjoyable part of the preschool day. It is a time for informal conversation and getting to know each other better (Bredekamp & Copple, 1997). This section reviews strategies that can increase the probability of successful lunch or snack time routines.

Make a Natural Transition to Lunch or Snack Time

Building a natural transition into the daily schedule, such as coming in from the playground, can be instrumental in facilitating a successful lunch or snack time. Individual and group needs must be considered. The number of steps in this transition can be especially challenging to some children (Murray, 2000), so keep steps to a minimum to allow for children's varying abilities in following multistep instructions. For some children, hand washing and going to the table may be all that should be expected. For others, independently getting lunch items to take to the table may be appropriate. The amount of waiting time is a strong factor for consideration. Whereas some children can wait until other children have been served, other children may need to have food served immediately. Careful thought must be given as well to the number of children making the transition at one time. Guiding children in small groups can be effective, and table groupings are a logical way to arrange the move from the previous activity to lunch.

Group Children During Lunch or Snack Time

Careful attention to the grouping of specific children for lunch or snack time also can contribute to a relaxing classroom atmosphere. Individual child needs and characteristics must be considered. Peer modeling can play a role in the seating arrangement. Pairing a skilled partner with a child who tends to have difficulty can reduce disruptions. In this manner, beneficial peer relationships can be fostered through careful seating arrangements. In addition, a child who frequently disrupts lunch or snack time can be seated next to the teacher. Children who may be in conflict with each other can be placed at separate tables (Farver, 1996). Consistency in seating arrangements may also be a factor because some children adapt more easily to change than others. The teacher may need to consider whether it is appropriate to maintain consistent table assignments for extended periods of time, yet he or she may choose to rotate seating on a weekly basis rather than moving the children around too frequently.

Arrange the Physical Space

A name card at each seat helps establish individual space and reduces confusion. The environment plays an important role at lunch as well. Soothing music and muted lighting can contribute to the relaxing atmosphere desired at this time (Wittmer & Honig, 1994). Small vases of flowers and tablecloths can transform a room to a more home-like setting (Katz & McClellan, 1997). The following vignette demonstrates that in addition to environmental considerations, it is important to consider the child's agenda and how individual expectations can be blended with the needs of the group and the needs of the center. It is important for teachers to be aware of the potential barriers to successful lunchtime experiences. These include a child not being hungry or being more concerned about a treasured activity or material. Also, writing a note to a friend a day in advance in anticipation of having lunch together can turn a challenging time of day into a valued social experience. The next vignette illustrates strategies for lunchtime success.

Lunch time is a required part of the program at Molly's child care center. Molly, age $3^1/2$, sometimes eats before coming to the center and is rarely interested in sitting down for lunch so soon after her arrival. As a result, she is defiant at lunch on many days. Her teachers have put strategies in place to help Molly successfully participate in lunchtime. When the teachers start singing the song that cues children to wash their hands and sit down, Molly is just getting involved in a puzzle activity. She is encouraged to save her work by putting her name card on the puzzle table, and she is assured that she can continue working after lunch. Molly's assigned seat is at a table located in a corner area of the room. The location of her chair facilitates her staying at the table for longer periods of time. Molly's friend can sit to her left, and the lead teacher sits to Molly's right to offer additional support. The teacher facilitates the conversation toward topics that interest Molly and the other children. The children are expected to sit for a reasonable amount of time, but not until every one is finished. Once Molly throws away her paper plate and juice box, she is able to return to her saved puzzle activity.

CLASSROOM APPLICATION

What preventive strategies are in place to support the child during lunch or snack? Are they effective? Are the following actions utilized to improve the lunch or snack time experience?

Preselect table groups according to group interaction and compliance.

Seat children with challenging behaviors in close proximity to the teacher.

Use furniture to help contain a child who has trouble sitting (e.g., have the child's chair straddle a table leg to encourage staying seated).

Use songs and conversation to help keep the children focused.

Be reasonable in expectations concerning how long children need to sit at the table.

Decide appropriate levels of independence for the group (i.e., plan how much children can do for themselves).

Consider dietary restrictions when grouping the children.

Play soothing music in the background and/or dim the lights.

Keep the routine's steps to a minimum.

> ### *What other adaptations and modifications can be implemented?*
> ### *How does using preventive strategies contribute to better teacher understanding of mealtime challenges?*

Summary

As each hot spot in the daily schedule is identified and preventive strategies are put in place, the challenge is more clearly defined. For some children, these and other preventive measures are the only interventions needed. For others, complying with the suggested limits is difficult, if not impossible. For those children, the assessment process continues with the formation of a collaborative team, and information gathering continues through planned observations, parent interviews, and ongoing team collaboration.

WHICH METHODS CAN BE USED TO COLLECT INFORMATION ABOUT CHALLENGING BEHAVIOR?

Efforts to determine the underlying cause of a challenging behavior include an examination of the physical and programmatic environments. Teachers can initiate change in each area, which, in turn, can prevent the targeted behavior (Barnett et al., 1999). Although it is important to know the underlying cause of a challenging behavior, the main challenge for teachers is how to change that behavior to a more positive or acceptable one. Through close observation and use of the following data collection techniques, teachers can contribute important information to the intervention planning process.

Decide What to Record

Often in preschool programs, teachers record behaviors as they occur before referring a child for intervention. Whenever a child demonstrates a behavior of concern, documentation is appropriate. It is possible such a behavior falls within the realm of typical development; however, as mentioned in Chapter 1, these behaviors are more frequent, of longer duration, or of greater intensity in some children than in their typically developing peers (Bell & Barnett, 1999; Hewitt, 1995). These challenging behaviors can constitute a pattern that should be carefully documented.

When documenting a child's behavior, it is important to state the information in objective terms. This indicates describing the behavior of concern as it happens, without using judgmental or subjective wording (Hewitt, 1995; Miltenberger, 2001). This initial documentation provides a baseline regarding when the behavior first surfaced, whether the behavior has continued over time, and if it has ceased to be a concern. When a challenging behavior continues, more in-depth information gathering is indicated.

Communicate with Parents Early in the Process

In the early stages of documentation, the teacher must inform the parents of behaviors of concern as they unfold (Barnett et al., 1999; Bredekamp & Copple, 1997). This is important for two reasons: 1) parents are identified as valued collaborators in their child's educational process and 2) if the behavior continues or escalates, parents are able to make informed choices when asked to give permission for further evaluation and intervention. The documentation of these behaviors often signals the need for further information gathering, collaboration, and intervention.

Choose Methods of Observation

There are various methods for observing the child's natural home and school environments (Brown, Odom, & Holcombe, 1996). The purpose of an initial observation is to gather information that helps determine the specific behavior(s) requiring intervention (Bauer & Shea, 1999). Once the behavior is identified, further observation is needed to collect more specific information related to the child's behavior of concern. These observation methods and strategies are designed to gather information about the behavior itself and about the setting in which the behavior takes place. It is important that the system of data collection is "reliable, viable, and useful" (Brault et al., 1999, p. 66). Observation planning is another important part of this process. The collaborative team needs to make decisions in terms of who will observe, what will be observed, when the observation will take place, where it will take place, and for how long the observation will last (Barnett, Bell, & Carey, 1999).

Anecdotal Record Keeping

Anecdotal notes provide documentation about a child's behavior and accomplishments. An accumulation of anecdotal notes identifies a child's strengths, areas that need support, and other factual information. An *anecdote* is a brief, objective description of a child's behavior on a specific date and in a specific area of the center or classroom. Anecdotes also may include other relevant information, such as whether a child is alone, with other children, or with an adult (B. Hieronymus, personal communication, 2000; MacDonald, 1997). Anecdotes refer to a child's performance in the cognitive, motor, communication, social-emotional, or self-help domains. They should not include teacher's judgments or perceptions. For example, anecdotes do not describe whether the child is happy, angry, bossy, in a bad mood, or having a bad day (B. Hieronymus, personal communication, 2000).

Anecdotes record information about a child's growth and development over an extended period of time rather than on a single day during an isolated testing situation. They provide information that guides teacher planning for the group as well as for individual children (B. Hieronymus, personal communication, 2000). Often, the anecdotal records remind teachers of the strengths of a child who exhibits challenging behaviors. Teachers should plan to document anecdotes on a daily basis. Sometimes, they may record several anecdotes for one child on a specific day; these can be documented collectively on one form.

Counting Specific Behaviors

Tallies of selected behaviors are helpful in determining heightened problem areas (Barnett, Bell, & Carey, 1999). This method of data collection allows the teacher to record the behaviors of an individual child while remaining responsive to the rest of the group. Keeping a small notebook to record pertinent information facilitates data collection. Frequency counts often take the form of a grid. The time of day is listed in one column, and the behaviors to be documented are listed across the top. Each time the child exhibits a specific behavior, a tally mark is recorded next to the corresponding time frame (Miltenberger, 2001). To further specify the behavior, this can be recorded by placing the letter *P* or *T* next to the tally mark to indicate whether peers or teachers were involved in the interaction.

Objective information can be documented and later recorded on center-designated forms, or teachers can develop daily or weekly data collection sheets that only require a plus (+) or minus (−) sign to indicate that the behavior was observed. Confidentiality is a critical part of this process. It is extremely important to refrain from discussing the details of data collection in the presence of the children in the classroom. All recording grids and data information sheets are confidential and must be treated accordingly. In most cases, a child is not aware that the teacher is recording data. However, when a child is aware, it is important to answer the child openly and honestly, giving only as much information as the child requires. For example, if a child notices that a teacher is writing down an anecdotal note and questions it, rather than ignoring the question, the teacher may reply, "I have some writing to do." If the child persists in wanting to know more, the teacher might add in a reassuring voice, "Sometimes I write down notes about the things we do at school." When information is given to children in this type of matter-of-fact manner, they usually accept it and move on.

Parent Interviews

It is important to identify factors from the home environment and to hear the parents' view of their child's development and progress (Bagnato et al., 1989). This step often can be accomplished by conducting a home visit and/or a parent interview. When preparing to meet with parents to discuss intervention plans, teachers should keep a few things in mind. First and foremost, the teacher should anticipate that the parents may experience various feelings—including anxiety, worry, defensiveness, stress, hesitancy, anger, confusion, guilt, or inadequacy—when discussing the behavioral concern (Hewitt, 1995).

A single parent may feel particularly overwhelmed by other stresses in his or her life, and hearing of the child's troubles at school might be the proverbial straw that breaks the camel's back. When a single parent faces daily concerns about money and perhaps the family's physical safety, it can be very difficult to take on additional worry about the child's behavior at school. This stress may manifest as avoidance. The parent may miss appointments, not answer the telephone, and seemingly show a lack of concern, although it is likely that the parent is very concerned. When approaching a single parent, the teacher should consider other factors that can contribute to stress, such as 1) family size, 2) parental age, 3) substance abuse issues, 4) parental levels of education and literacy, 5) cognitive impairments or mental illness, 6) guardianship issues, 7) available social support, 8) religious or cultural practices, 9) the level of parenting skills, and 10) the parent's current employment situation (Lynch & Hanson, 1998).

Discuss the Issue in a Sensitive Manner   Parent misgivings can be compounded when teachers or administrators share information in an insensitive way. This perception can surface if information is given in a seemingly blunt or, even worse, accusatory manner. Parents may feel vulnerable or as though they are being judged. Often, this results in their becoming upset, hostile, or inattentive. If a parent is overloaded with negative images of his or her child, he or she may simply reject any additional messages perceived as negative. Therefore, the main objective when interacting with parents is keeping that line of communication open. The success of any subsequent intervention weighs heavily on gaining trust and cooperation from parents, and that may require a great deal of delicacy and finesse on the interviewer's part. The best option is to use techniques that empower parents to generate their own ideas and solutions to the problems at hand. When parent input is considered part of the solution, parents will be more invested in the process. In addition, as mentioned in Chapter 3, teachers should be aware that parents may have had negative experiences with teachers, administrators, and social workers prior to their involvement with the early childhood program. Thus, it is important to show parents respect and kindness. The following suggestions are recommended when interviewing parents:

1. Create an inviting atmosphere when interviewing the parent at the school or center. The room should appear as friendly as possible.

2. Strive to make the parent feel comfortable. This may be accomplished by offering the parent water, tea, or coffee. Even if the parent refuses, the offer indicates a welcoming atmosphere (Lynch & Hanson, 1998).

3. Ask the parent how he or she prefers to be addressed to demonstrate respect.

4. Take time to explain the reason for the meeting, allowing the parent to ask questions to gain a further understanding. During this time, be particularly aware of personal feelings and biases. If keeping feelings and biases in check is going to be difficult, another teacher or staff member should introduce the purpose of the meeting.

5. Use open-ended questions. This gives the parent control over the information shared and can stimulate thoughtful replies.

6. Thoroughly explain any classroom or home intervention strategies.

7. Be aware of additional information conveyed through nonverbal cues (e.g., body language, eye contact). These cues can be used to regulate the flow of the interview. In return, teachers should be aware of their own nonverbal cues (Lynch & Hanson, 1998).

8. Most important, be persistent and encouraging. Remember that a seed has been planted with this initial parent meeting, and it may not sprout right away.

Maintain a Goals and Strengths Approach   There are many ways to gain input and support from a parent, without putting him or her on the defensive. By first identifying some of the child's strengths, the teacher can encourage the parent to think positively; then, the teacher can switch the focus to goals (i.e., areas that need improvement) (Berg, 1994; DeJong & Miller, 1995; De Shazer, 1985; Hewitt, 1995; Saleeby, 1992). This technique is even more effective when the parent takes part in outlining these goals.

A nonthreatening way to get started is to use a simple scale of 1 to 10. The teacher must start by acknowledging the parents as the true experts regarding their child, and anything that they can share about the child or his or her environment is helpful. The teacher then asks the parent to complete the scale to reflect his or her opinions on specific issues. It is a good idea to explain that the scale uses positive, solution-focused terminology (i.e., a rating of 1 or 2 indicates a serious or urgent concern; a rating of 9 or 10 is a strength or an area of no concern) and is not a typical scale that ranges from *poor* to *excellent* (Berg, 1994; DeJong & Miller, 1995). The teacher should then ask questions about the parent's perception of the child's cognitive development, social capabilities, emotional well-being, and kindergarten readiness (if appropriate). The key is that the parent is doing the assessment instead of being assessed.

If factors in the home environment may be contributing to the child's challenging behaviors, the teacher can ask a few scaling questions, such as "On a scale of 1 to 10, how do you feel about your current housing situation?" or "How do you feel about your family's support system?" This technique allows the interviewer to ask the toughest, most provocative questions—such as those about parental depression, inadequate parenting skills, and domestic violence—without seeming too invasive. Once the interviewer and the parent have assessed the situation together, the parent may be more open to receiving additional information and available support (Greene, Kamps, Wyble, & Ellis, 1999).

The following vignette illustrates several of the previously discussed information-gathering methods.

> Four-year-old Bob likes preschool but has difficulty engaging in activities and playing appropriately. Because typical behavior management techniques have few positive results, more in-depth observation and intervention is necessary.
>
> Anecdotal notes indicate that Bob rarely chooses manipulative activities, even when encouraged by an adult. When Bob does enter the manipulatives area, he gets easily frustrated, asks an adult to finish the project for him, and is reluctant to clean up. He prefers open-ended activities, such as dramatic play or sensory activities involving water or sand; however, he often wanders around the room, refusing to choose an activity and sometimes interfering with others' play. He particularly has difficulty engaging in an activity after returning from the gross motor room. Anecdotes indicate aggressive, disruptive behavior when a teacher tries to engage him in an appropriate activity at that time. Bob lies down on the floor and cries, refusing assistance. He also becomes verbally and physically abusive to adults, kicking, spitting, and using inappropriate language.
>
> Bob's mother is a single parent who is expecting a second child. Early in her pregnancy, she had to be hospitalized, so Bob stayed with a neighborhood family that has no children Bob's age, only older boys. Bob's mother says that Bob is very active at home but usually complies with her requests. He has few playmates and spends much of his time playing alone or watching television. Although Bob's behavior at home is not a concern for her, after observing him in the classroom, she acknowledges a need for a school intervention.

Journaling

Journaling is a solution-focused communication link between parents and teachers that offers detailed descriptions of the child's progress and of strategies used in the classroom.

Journal entries are typically made on a daily basis and are designed to provide a daily "conversation" with a child's parent. The journal itself may be as simple as a stenographer's notebook that is placed in the child's cubby. Parents are sometimes asked to sign off upon reading each entry, and they are encouraged to respond.

This method provides the opportunity for the teacher to highlight a child's small achievements and successes daily. At the same time, parents have the opportunity to receive the information in an informal fashion and the option to respond in writing and/or to acknowledge the child's progress. In addition, parents can use the journal to provide information, ask questions, confirm processes, and validate the child's progress. Through the process of journaling, parents are more informed and involved. When an intervention is in place, keeping a daily journal provides the opportunity for early childhood staff to highlight a child's small achievements and successes each day to the parents.

Determine the Journal's Content   Each journal entry should include information about the child's day at school, beginning and ending with a positive comment about the child. It can also include daily information on progress toward goals, which is especially helpful when parents request daily input from or have daily input for the teacher. The journal should not include judgmental remarks, daily lists of the child's shortcomings, or unsolicited suggestions for parental changes. Rather, it provides parents with confidential, honest communication. The following is an example of a journal exchange:

> 5/8/03
> Dear Emma,
> Raymond has had a better day today than yesterday. It was easier to redirect him. He spent a long time using the computer this morning with Chris and was able to play appropriately for the most part. Raymond is still having great difficulty engaging in and focusing on activities. This leaves time to wander around, which tends to lead to challenging behaviors. As a member of Raymond's team, you are aware that we are meeting tomorrow afternoon to discuss some new strategies to help Raymond become more engaged in classroom activities.
> Ann
>
> Ann,
> Please list specific behaviors that are inappropriate so I can better address them with Raymond.
> Emma

Videotape Recording

Videotaping can further communication and understanding (Brown et al., 1996). This method of recording behavior is particularly effective when working with limited staff and resources or when it is difficult for parents to observe during the program day. In turn, this method allows parents to observe their child's behavior prior to a parent–teacher conference (Borgia, 1992). Howlin, Baron-Cohen, and Hadwin (1999) recommended analyzing videotaped observation sessions to document the play of children with autism, for example. As children with autism are engaged in specific types of play, the level of play is observed, identified, and recorded (Brown & Murray, 2001).

Videotaping does not capture the full stream of action when used for observation purposes, however; behaviors outside of the scope of the camera are not observed and recorded. This can result in the observer's missing important information (Barnett, Bell, & Carey, 1999). Many cautions apply to videotaping as an observation tool. It is essential that permission to videotape is obtained from the parents of all children in the play session. Some families may object to the videotaping for cultural, religious, or legal reasons. Videotapes should be treated as confidential and protected from review by unauthorized individuals.

CONCLUSION

If established positive behavior support strategies are ineffective, it is important to develop an action plan that is specific to a child's needs. This is best accomplished through the assessment process of collaboration, observation, documentation, problem solving, and, finally, developing a plan of action. The first portion of this chapter has discussed strategies that a teacher may use to structure the classroom arrangement, activities, and routines to prevent problem situations. The second portion of the chapter has suggested methods for documenting problem situations prior to formal assessment and intervention design.

Observation, documentation, collaboration and problem solving, and the development of an action plan are basic tools that the classroom teacher uses to determine effective strategies to individualize for young children. By gathering information (observation and documentation) that addresses what is happening before, during, and after a behavior occurs, the classroom teacher can effectively develop a plan to support both the child and the classroom. Collaboration and problem solving help the classroom team (including the child's parents) to know what works for the child and what does not work in terms of effective strategies. An action plan takes into consideration the child, the classroom community, and the teacher by blending the individual needs with the needs of the group and the needs of the center to support the child's success.

Chapter 6

Determining the Teacher's Role in Further Assessment and Intervention

Susan Hart Bell, Amy Clancy, and Erin N. Gaddes

The classroom teacher is the architect of child success in the early childhood setting. Although the teacher cannot directly change children's choices about how they behave, he or she can affect their behavior indirectly through changes in the situations and people that surround them. This chapter builds on the assessment process begun in Chapter 5, which highlights ongoing assessment of classroom effectiveness for a given group of children and for the child with behavioral challenges (Bredekamp & Copple, 1997). The classroom teacher has the means to facilitate learning in young children through 1) creating an effective physical arrangement in the classroom, 2) planning developmentally appropriate curricular activities that are tailored to child interests, 3) providing clear and consistent classroom limits and routines, 4) using developmentally appropriate and specific language to outline acceptable behavioral choices, and 5) facilitating child skills using empirically supported instructional strategies. Following a brief discussion of positive guidance, this chapter introduces the concept of functional assessment and examines each of the noted teacher strategies.

Much of the research reviewed in this chapter concerns the instruction and support of children with identified disabilities in inclusive settings. According to Wolery and

Wilbers (1994), the benefits of inclusion in early childhood settings include interaction with socially competent peers, exposure to skilled communicative partners, imitation of peer models for self-help skills, and promotion of friendships through reduced stereotyping of children with disabilities. Children with challenging behaviors also can benefit from interventions designed to promote these goals, regardless of whether their challenging behaviors co-occur with identified disabilities. For this reason, research on children whose developmental delays include difficulties in language, social interaction, and classroom behavior are applicable to the design of interventions for typically developing children who face similar challenges.

HOW CAN POSITIVE GUIDANCE HELP WITH CHALLENGING BEHAVIOR IN THE CLASSROOM?

The National Association for the Education of Young Children developed guidelines for best practices in early childhood settings (Bredekamp & Copple, 1997). Child care environments that follow these guidelines have been identified as the most beneficial for the education and care of young children, regardless of whether they have identified disabilities (Wolery & McWilliam, 1998). Developmentally appropriate practice guidelines advise the use of basic strategies to address challenging behaviors in the classroom, such as redirecting the child from inappropriate to acceptable classroom choices, setting clear expectations and limits for classroom behavior, and providing consequences for unacceptable and unsafe behavior (Bredekamp & Copple, 1997).

Guidance approaches have been suggested as additional strategies for teachers in developmentally appropriate practice settings. These practices encourage the teacher to approach challenging behaviors as learning experiences for young children—framing "misbehaviors" as "mistaken behaviors," or errors in learning (Gartrell, 1995, 1997). Guidance is provided within the classroom through creating a positive atmosphere for learning, coaching children to talk through problems, and providing interpretations of expressed or inferred feelings (Bryant, Vizzard, Willoughby, & Kupersmidt, 1999). The teacher is encouraged to decrease levels of mistaken behavior by reducing wait times, offering choices, adjusting classroom schedules and room arrangements, providing clear expectations of classroom behavior, and providing corrective feedback (Gartrell, 1997). The following vignette illustrates positive guidance procedures.

> Tyler runs joyfully into the gross motor room, straight to the tire swing. He skids to a stop when, disappointed, he sees that three other children are spinning and swinging under the teacher's watchful eye. Tyler impatiently rocks from side to side while watching the children on the swing. After a moment, he yells, "Hey, I want a turn!" Ignored by the children, he grabs the rope and pulls it toward him. The children on the swing shriek as they are shifted to one side. The teacher approaches Tyler, gently removes his hand from the rope, and repositions the children in the swing. She then crouches down to look directly at Tyler's face. "Tyler, that's not safe. The children might fall if you jerk the rope that way. I can't let anyone pull on the rope while children are swinging. How do you think that made

these children feel?" Tyler looks sadly at the floor and begins to cry. "It's my turn to swing." The teacher nods and says, "I understand that you are really excited about getting to swing. Thank you for using words. These children were really scared when you pulled on the rope. You can have a turn in 3 minutes."

Although guidance approaches are necessary in designing an optimal learning environment, they are often insufficient for addressing the needs of children whose behaviors pose frequent and severe challenges. With respect for the guidance tradition, this chapter suggests an expanded repertoire of interventions to meet the previously stated goals, calling on interventions from the long-established behavioral literature. The individual teacher may choose strategies with which he or she is comfortable, taking into account his or her personal teaching philosophy and agency policy. The teacher is free to tailor the strategy's directiveness to the severity and disruptiveness of the problem situation.

HOW CAN THE PROBLEM SITUATION BE ASSESSED?

Antecedent-behavior-consequence (A-B-C) analysis, functional assessment, and functional analysis are used to address challenging behavior. Each approach is detailed in the following subsections.

Antecedent-Behavior-Consequence (A-B-C) Analysis

A-B-C analysis has been suggested as an abbreviated method for identifying important variables contributing to the maintenance of challenging behaviors (Bijou, Peterson, & Ault, 1968). Kazdin (2001) identified antecedents (A) and consequences (C) as variables that increase or decrease the likelihood that a specific challenging behavior (B) will continue. Antecedents can include factors related to the child (e.g., tiredness, hunger, illness, pain), the teacher (e.g., language, instruction, proximity), or the situation (e.g., room temperature, crowding, activity demands, schedule changes). Consequences may include teacher or peer responses to the child's disruptive behavior (e.g., removing the child from a nonpreferred activity, obtaining positive reinforcement from peer attention). It also is possible that these observed variables have no impact on the behavior selected for intervention. Examining these factors through direct observations throughout the day and through interviews with other staff members who interact closely with the child can help to clarify the problem situation.

Different formats have been employed for recording results from A-B-C analyses. The most simple is a four-column data sheet with 1) the date and time, 2) a description of antecedent events (i.e., the events occurring before the behavior of concern), 3) a description of the behavior (i.e., a vivid and specific picture of the child's actions and language), and 4) a description of consequences (i.e., child, teacher, and peer behaviors occurring just after the behavior of concern) (Barnett, Bell, & Carey, 1999; Miltenberger, 2001). A user-friendly checklist format allows the recorder to write in typical behaviors, suspected antecedents, and possible consequences at the top of each column. During a classroom observation, the teacher simply and quickly places a mark in the corresponding column as the variable is observed. Additional columns are provided for noting unexpected variables (Miltenberger, 2001). This assessment strategy is illustrated in the next vignette.

> The teacher flips the lights on and off and begins singing the clean-up song: "Clean up, clean up, everybody clean up." Maria, age 4, frowns as she looks at the large pile of interlocking blocks left on the ground in the manipulatives area. She has a big mess to clean up before group time. Maria begins scooping up the blocks and throwing them into the bin. This takes several seconds, and Maria is one of the last children to finish. She moves eagerly to the group area, running to get her carpet square and place it in the circle. She sees her friend, Julie, sitting between Anna and Eric. Maria quickly squeezes her carpet square between Julie and Anna, squishing Anna's fingers as she plops down on the square. Anna screams and pushes at Maria, "Move, I was sitting here!" Julie yelps and says, "You can't sit here—there's not enough room!" Maria shoves at Anna, "Scoot over. I always sit here." The teacher assistant gently lifts Maria and her carpet square to a spot near the teacher. Maria protests, kicking and screaming, "I want to sit by Julie! That's not fair!" She continues to cry and hit the assistant. The assistant then decides to move Maria to a seat near the door, where the assistant talks quietly and Maria continues to cry. The assistant returns Maria to the group, asks Eric to scoot over, and places Maria's carpet square on Julie's other side. Maria smiles happily at Julie and begins to listen to the story. Later, the assistant creates this A-B-C analysis for Maria's behavior:

Date	Antecedent	Behavior	Consequence
Monday, April 22 10:15 A.M.	The teacher sings the cleanup song a few seconds before group time begins.	To sit in her preferred spot, Maria squeezes between two children, invading their space and hurting them.	The teacher assistant physically moves Maria to another spot.
Monday, April 22 10:17 A.M.	The assistant places Maria in a spot near the teacher.	Maria kicks and hits the assistant, screams and protests the move, and falls on the floor in front of the teacher.	The assistant physically moves Maria to a quiet spot near the classroom door and talks with Maria about her feelings.
Monday, April 22 10:20 A.M.	The assistant leads Maria back to the group, helping settle her next to Julie.	Maria stops crying and smiles at Julie, then begins to listen to the story.	Maria listens quietly and participates appropriately during the remainder of group time.

This A-B-C analysis allows the teacher to determine that staff may have inadvertently maintained the disruptive behavior by not requiring Maria to calm down before returning her to the group and by rewarding her crying with the seat next to Julie.

The A-B-C analysis has been criticized because of its lack of specificity in identifying pertinent variables in complex settings (Barnett, Bell, & Carey, 1999). For this reason, attention has shifted to the application of the principles of functional analysis and functional assessment to unravel the factors that affect challenging behaviors of young children.

Functional Assessment

Challenging behaviors in young children have been characterized as efforts to communicate with adults and peers (Feldman & Griffiths, 1997). It is incumbent on the early childhood teacher to interpret this communication and to make appropriate changes (e.g., to curricular activities, the order and length of daily routines, or instructional strategies) that encourage the development of alternative, more acceptable behaviors for achieving the same ends. Although disturbances in each component of the instructional environment may contribute to the occurrence of challenging behaviors, only a comprehensive functional assessment can identify the most relevant factors (Doggett, Edwards, Moore, Tingstrom, & Wilczynski, 2001; Gresham et al., 2001). For this reason, a necessary first step is to conduct an assessment of contributing factors (e.g., situational elements, teacher strategies, peer actions). Several methods guide the teacher through this process.

The rather inclusive term *functional assessment* describes a range of procedures to identify the antecedents and consequences that maintain an undesirable child behavior (Gresham et al., 2001; VanDerHeyden, Witt, & Gatti, 2001). These assessment procedures may include interviews with parents, teachers, and other staff members; direct observations of child behavior in the classroom (i.e., recording the exact nature, frequency, duration, and intensity or severity of the behaviors of concern); A-B-C analyses; and the examination of products such as artwork (Doggett et al., 2001; Gresham et al., 2001).

For example, Galensky, Miltenberger, Stricker, Garlinghouse, and Koegel (2001) used functional assessment to examine problematic home mealtime behaviors for three preschool children. Interviews with caregivers and initial observations identified escape, access to preferred food, and adult attention as possible maintaining variables for food refusal and running away from the table. Attention was then provided for appropriate mealtime behavior (e.g., sitting in the chair, refraining from play behaviors during mealtime, eating), and preferred foods were used as positive reinforcement for bites of nonpreferred foods. Physical redirection of running away and play behaviors prevented escape from eating. One family withdrew their child from the study, but the remaining children increased their overall bites per minute and consumption of nonpreferred foods as well as decreased their levels of play and running away during mealtimes.

Functional Analysis

The terms *functional analysis* and *functional assessment* are used broadly throughout the intervention literature. Each procedure seeks to identify the purpose that an isolated behavior serves for an individual child (e.g., to gain teacher or peer attention, to communicate boredom or frustration, or to escape from a nonpreferred activity or difficult task) (Gresham et al., 2001). Because these procedures are time intensive, the research literature has focused on their use with behaviors that are severely disruptive or dangerous to the child or his or her peers. In these cases, significant teacher time and energy already are being focused on daily classroom management, so the time spent on a functional assessment can be viewed as a worthwhile investment.

Functional analysis refers more narrowly to an experimental investigation of environmental variables under highly controlled conditions (Kazdin, 2001). Arndorfer and Miltenberger (1993) identified three objectives of a functional analysis: 1) to extinguish a challenging behavior by eliminating its reinforcement, 2) to reinforce more acceptable alternative behaviors that serve the same function as the challenging behavior, and 3) to alter aspects of the environment or the problem situation that are related to the behavior of concern.

Sterling-Turner, Robinson, and Wilczynski (2001) developed a four-step process for carrying out a functional analysis within a classroom:

1. Collect information about the behavior of concern and the environmental antecedents and consequences that may be maintaining this behavior.

2. Interpret the data from the previous step and develop theories about the function of the targeted behavior.

3. Verify the proposed function by manipulating environmental variables and observing accompanying changes in the targeted behavior.

4. Develop and implement an intervention plan that addresses the behavior of concern.

Once the function of a particular behavior or set of behaviors is proposed, classroom instructional strategies and contingencies can be arranged to teach more acceptable alternative behaviors and to reward their use (Dyer & Larrson, 1997).

Several research examples further illustrate this process. Umbreit (1996) used functional analysis within a kindergarten classroom to identify variables maintaining disruptive and noncompliant behaviors in a young child with mild mental retardation. Manipulating these identified variables (i.e., the difficulty of curricular activities and the availability of assistance during instructional tasks) resulted in a complete resolution of the problem behaviors. Umbreit further emphasized that the intervention took little time and could be implemented by classroom staff.

Boyajian, DuPaul, Handler, Eckert, and McGoey (2001) utilized brief functional analysis to identify relevant variables for three preschool boys with aggressive and noncompliant behaviors. Antecedents apparently precipitating the behaviors of concern were teacher reminders and requests. Consequences were escape from compliance with teacher requests, provision of teacher attention, and access to preferred toys and activities. Planned manipulation of these variables resulted in behavioral improvement for all three children.

A more ambitious project applies the functional analysis methodology to the entire classroom during activities in which children are particularly disruptive. VanDerHeyden and colleagues (2001) conducted functional analyses of child behavior during morning and afternoon circle time activities in a preschool program for children with autism. Direct observation revealed that teacher attention was maintaining these disruptive behaviors. Three changes seemed to be indicated: 1) ignoring minor inappropriate behaviors, 2) increasing positive teacher attention for appropriate behaviors during group time, and 3) providing opportunities for active participation by the children in the group activities.

These strategies produced reductions in disruptive behaviors. The researchers emphasized that the total amount of teacher attention provided to the children during group time did not vary; the attention was simply redirected toward affirmations for positive child behaviors and away from reprimands and physical redirection for disruptive and non-compliant behaviors. The next sections provide examples of antecedent variables that the teacher can identify as contributors to the problem situation, expanding on the information provided in Chapters 4 and 5.

CLASSROOM APPLICATION

Is there an accurate picture of the problem situation?

What are the behaviors of greatest concern (i.e., the behaviors that are most disruptive to the child's participation in the daily classroom activities)?

At which time(s) of day is the child most likely to exhibit those behaviors?

Which other staff members should be interviewed about their views of the problem situation?

Have the frequency, duration, and intensity of the challenging behaviors been specifically observed to establish baseline (preintervention) levels?

Are there antecedents that elicit these behaviors (e.g., difficulty of classroom activities, noise level in the room, crowding, limited access to preferred activities, inadequate child language skills)?

Are there consequences that reinforce and maintain these behaviors (e.g., teacher attention, peer attention, access to preferred activities, escape from a boring or difficult task)?

WHICH ELEMENTS OF THE CLASSROOM MIGHT NEED TO BE MODIFIED?

Classroom Arrangement

As discussed in Chapters 4 and 5, the physical arrangement of the classroom sets the stage for daily activities, establishing expectations for child behavior and highlighting the availability of positively reinforcing events (Feldman & Griffiths, 1997). The classroom activity centers should be arranged to facilitate ease of movement between areas and to allow visual monitoring by the classroom teacher (Paine et al., 1983; Stainback, Stainback, & Froyen, 1987). Limiting long, open spaces by the positioning of bookshelves and tables can decrease running within the classroom (Lawry et al., 2000). Crowding or even low levels of classroom noise can increase aggressive behaviors in young children (Feldman & Griffiths, 1997). Efforts to separate quiet and noisy play areas, limit numbers of children in confined spaces, and reduce group sizes during high traffic times of the day can help. Using "closed" signs or symbols to reduce access to play areas, facilitating ease of teacher monitoring, and limiting choices to reasonable numbers of toys and play materials can effectively decrease disruptive and noncompliant behaviors (Lawry et al., 2000).

Classroom Activities

Wolery and Winterling described a *curriculum* as "an organized description of a body of content, assessment procedures for selecting goals for instruction, and methods for teaching selected skills" (1997, p. 88). Some children respond with challenging behaviors when curricula are developmentally inappropriate (e.g., too difficult or complex), uninteresting, or involve limited classroom instructional materials (Feldman & Griffiths, 1997; Wolery & Winterling, 1997). Rotating classroom materials and incorporating theme-based activities (e.g., a day at the beach, a trip to the pet store) can be a powerful method for decreasing off-task and disruptive behaviors during free play (Lawry et al., 2000; Peters, 1995). Daily opportunities for participation in engaging and developmentally appropriate activities set the stage for child behavioral change, such as increased social responsiveness, prosocial (helping) behaviors, and decreased negative mood (Dunst et al., 2001).

Activity Engagement Level

The level of activity engagement has been described as one of the important indicators of quality child care. A useful definition of activity engagement is the amount of time that a child spends interacting with adults, peers, and classroom activities in a developmentally and contextually appropriate manner (McWilliam & Bailey, 1995). Classroom activities that are carefully chosen to fit the individual interests and abilities of a particular group of young children should result in high levels of classroom engagement and low levels of disruptive and problematic behaviors (Lawry et al., 2000; Wolery & Winterling, 1997). The following activities increase targeted child engagement and social interaction when coupled with peer-mediated interventions: math and literacy games, feeding and care of the classroom pet, snack time setup, art activities, small group science and cooking activities, and activity-related helper jobs during classroom routines (e.g., transitions, circle time) (Kohler & Strain, 1999).

As discussed in Chapter 5, group or circle time activities are often cited as hot spots for disruptive and inattentive behavior. Lawry and colleagues (2000) provided the following suggestions to increase child engagement during circle or group activities:

1. Limit structured group times to a maximum of 15 minutes.
2. Include opportunities for child interaction (e.g., allow participation through motor movement or verbal responses).
3. Provide objects that relate to the theme or the story, and allow the children to take turns holding the objects.
4. Use props that augment the lesson through visual, auditory, and tactile stimulation.

5. Use an enthusiastic narrative, varying the voice intonation and style as indicated by the activity.

Such strategies are utilized in the following vignette.

> It is Monday morning group time during "I live on a farm" week. Each child brings a farm-related picture, book, or toy to the group. The children place the objects in a laundry basket sitting in front of the teacher and return to their carpet squares. The teacher begins group time with an active farm song, during which the children imitate the noises and movements of different farm animals. The teacher then pulls each child's name from a deck of index cards. This provides individual opportunities for the children to lift their offerings from the basket and briefly discuss them. The group ends with an interactive reading from a book about farms and a quick review of the farm-related play centers available in the classroom.

Play Materials

Specific toys (e.g., modeling materials; interlocking construction toys; brightly colored, realistic dramatic play materials) elicit higher levels of play involvement and social interaction (McCabe, Jenkins, Mills, Dale, & Cole, 1999). Kohler, Anthony, Steighner, and Hoyson (2001) incorporated novel and preferred toys (e.g., cartoon characters, bubbles) into typical classroom activities and thereby increased the engagement of children with autism. Ivory and McCollum (1999) examined how social (e.g., blocks, dolls, puppets) and isolate (e.g., paints, playdough, puzzles) toys affected the social interaction levels of preschool children with identified disabilities. They found that although parallel play remained the most often-observed form of play for all children, the availability of social toys significantly increased levels of cooperative play. Conversely, isolate toys intensified the tendency toward parallel rather than cooperative play.

Curriculum-based assessment procedures give the teacher an idea of the child's ability to perform routine classroom activities, the child's rate of progress through the classroom curriculum, and child or classroom variables that might interfere with this progress (Barnett, Bell, & Carey, 1999). This can be accomplished by observing the child's skills as he or she moves through the daily routine—noting activities that are avoided and tasks that prove difficult or frustrating (e.g., cutting with scissors, connecting blocks, completing interlocking puzzles). Careful selection of developmentally appropriate activities affects behavior in the next vignette.

> Josh, a 3-year-old with limited language skills, is having difficulty participating successfully during free play in a classroom of 3- and 4-year-olds. He moves through the room, dumping baskets of interlocking blocks, spilling puzzles, and pulling books from shelves. He actively resists the teacher's efforts to assist him in putting the blocks together, completing a puzzle, or looking at pictures in a book. He easily participates in gross motor activities, scaling the climbing structure and pedaling the tricycle effortlessly. He laughs as he joins in a chase game on the playground. The teachers assess the gap between his cognitive, language, and fine

motor skills and the activities available in the classroom. They decide to introduce some simple cause-and-effect toys for toddlers. These toys have few pieces, large knobs and buttons, and are easy to activate. Josh happily approaches these toys, remaining engaged for several minutes at a time, and other children gather around to enjoy the toys with him.

Daily Schedule

As mentioned previously, it is important for daily classroom schedules to provide young children with the comfort of predictability (Lawry et al., 2000; Wolery & Fleming, 1992). Inconsistencies in the daily schedule can provoke disruptive or aggressive behavior (Feldman & Griffiths, 1997). Changes in routine can be announced ahead of time, easing the anxiety and raising enthusiasm for unusual play experiences (e.g., trips to a pumpkin farm or bakery, arrival of a visitor to demonstrate weaving). For some children with identified disabilities, predictability of routine becomes essential. Schedules that are tailored to the needs of an individual child can be constructed to increase independence in following the classroom routines and to ease behavior problems during transitions (Mesibov, Browder, & Kirkland, 2002). As described in Chapter 5, these schedules can use drawings or photographs to depict classroom settings and activities, and the teacher can use a variety of prompting strategies to encourage the child to move to the next activity.

Transitions between activities often have been identified as particularly difficult times for children with behavior problems. Incorporating a clear signal at the beginning of transitions (e.g., flicking the lights, singing a cleanup song, starting a familiar tape or CD, issuing "beat-the-timer" cleanup challenges) can improve the smoothness of the transition (Lawry et al., 2000). Transition-based teaching is a particularly clever method for embedding instruction and teacher support within the daily routine's hot spots. In one example, Wolery and colleagues (1998) selected four children with mild disabilities and identified eight learning objectives for transition-based teaching. Four teachers implemented an intervention involving securing the child's attention, showing the child one of the targeted learning objectives, asking a task-related question, and providing praise for correct answers and a model for incorrect or missed responses (after a 4-second time delay). This method increased accomplishment of learning objectives without increasing the length of transitions. A subsequent study found that individual learning objectives could be embedded into circle times as well (Wolery, Anthony, Caldwell, Snyder, & Morgante, 2002).

Child Groupings

Teachers often have created specific peer groupings to facilitate social interaction and engagement. Researchers have noted that children who display the highest number of aggressive behaviors tend to spend more time interacting with other children who also are more likely to be aggressive (Farver, 1996). This finding indicates the need to separate individuals for whom this behavioral effect is evident or to design group interventions to address aggressive behaviors (Siemoens, 2001). This strategy is implemented in the following vignette.

> Jamal, age 5, sits quietly with Laura and Rochelle in the book area. Rochelle plays teacher as she "reads" the book to Jamal and Laura, asking them to look at the pictures. It is early in the morning and only a few children have arrived in the full-day classroom. Jamal looks up excitedly as there is a sound at the classroom door. Cody has arrived and his mother is helping him take off his coat. Jamal rushes to the door, asking Cody if he wants to play in the block area. Jamal and Cody move to the block area and join two other children, Dustin and Lakeisha. These two children already have built a bridge and a highway from the large wooden blocks. They are busily constructing a city with the remaining blocks. Jamal yells, "We want to play!" and moves to the shelf. "Watch out!" Dustin yells, leaping to protect the bridge. The bridge topples as Jamal drags three heavy blocks from the shelf. Dustin protests and Jamal and Cody laugh, kicking down the rest of the blocks making up the buildings in the city. The teacher comes over to announce the first group to go to the indoor gross motor room. Jamal jumps up excitedly, "We want to go! Me 'n Cody!" The teacher looks at her list and announces that Jamal is in the first group but Cody will be in the next group to go to the gross motor room. Jamal runs to the door, and Cody begins helping Dustin and Lakeisha rebuild the block city.

CLASSROOM APPLICATION

Is the classroom environment safe and engaging?

Does the physical layout of the room(s) work?

Can the children move easily into and between activity areas?

Are boundaries defined between activity areas (i.e., does the arrangement of the play area facilitate engagement and containment of materials within the activity area)?

Which centers have the highest occurrence of aggressive or disruptive behaviors?

Can teachers easily monitor children playing in each activity area?

Are the toys and activity areas developmentally appropriate and interesting?

Does the order of the daily schedule work for this group of children?

Is the amount of time devoted to each activity appropriate?

Are there children for whom the content, length, or order of activities seems challenging? How can these special needs be accommodated?

Are there children whose aggressive or disruptive behaviors escalate when they play together for extended periods of time?

WHICH STRATEGIES CAN
EFFECTIVELY PREVENT THE PROBLEM SITUATION?

Interactions with teachers can powerfully affect child behaviors (Singh, 1997). Teacher behaviors include instructional techniques that exemplify best practices in early childhood education and encourage the growth of all children. They also include techniques specifically chosen to nudge child choices in a desirable direction to maximize learning and skill development. This section examines a continuum of teacher behaviors that may be necessary to influence child behavior.

Classroom Limits

Failure by teachers to establish firm and consistent classroom limits and to provide consequences based on violation of these limits is associated with increased levels of classroom misbehavior (Arnold, McWilliams, & Arnold, 1998). Some children push until they bump up against the comfort and security of classroom limits. For this reason, it is imperative for the teacher to establish clearly delineated boundaries for acceptable behavior. By convention, these are few in number and worded positively to emphasize acceptable behavior.

Teachers should ensure that regular and temporary staff members are aware of the classroom language used to convey common limits. Examples include

- "I can't let you do that. That's not safe."
- "We can only build towers as tall as our waist. Where's your waist?"
- "Let's use our inside voices."
- "We don't play that game at school. What else can you make with the blocks?"

Each early childhood center finds a language that is consistent with its teaching philosophy and classroom culture. The language of teachers in early childhood settings also varies by the type of activity and the ages of the children in individual groups (Girolametto, Weitzman, Lieshout, & Duff, 2000).

Teachers should use similar words and phrases each time children violate situational limits. This allows children to begin internalizing those phrases to regulate their own behavior and that of peers in conflict situations. For children who consistently violate classroom limits, more directive teacher language may be necessary. This technique may include approaching a child and using his or her name to secure his or her attention before delivering the limit appropriate to the violation (e.g., "Jennifer, it is time to clean up. You were playing with the rainbow puzzle. Put the puzzle back on the shelf.") These brief directives should be delivered in a firm but pleasant tone of voice and use developmentally appropriate language (Forehand & McMahon, 1981). Suggestions or questions can be confusing, indicating that the child has a choice to disregard the limit (e.g., "Jennifer, will you pick up the puzzle before you come to snack time?"). Directions requiring several actions also can confuse the child, who may choose to follow the last direction in the sequence (e.g., "Jennifer, finish the puzzle, put it on the shelf, wash your hands, and come to snack time"). The child who follows only the last step then may be distressed at being redirected to pick up the puzzle, clearly believing that he or she is complying with the teacher's request.

As mentioned in Chapters 4 and 5, expressions of classroom limits can take forms other than verbal reminders. Pictures or photographs can be posted to remind children of acceptable ways to engage in classroom activities (e.g., a picture of a child wearing a smock at the water table). Limits for activity centers can be established using symbols (e.g., pictures of four place settings indicate that only four children can be in the housekeeping center at one time), placemats or trays of art or modeling materials (e.g., four trays of sponges, paint and paper or four trays with cookie cutters and playdough), or other badges or items indicating that a child is engaged in a certain center (e.g., four sets of scrubs for children in the doctor's office activity center). The use of proscribed numbers of materials to define expectations is illustrated in the following vignette.

> Richie, age 3, approaches the art area, then hangs over the chair of a seated child. He reaches over to touch the bright blue paint on a flower-shaped sponge. Soon he is sharing a chair with Robin, who is busily stamping red and blue flowers on her light green paper. The teacher looks up from helping Cheryl stamp her paper. "Oh, Richie, you need a smock and a tray to be in this area. I'll write your name on the waiting list so you can play here next. Find another place to play until I call you."

Naturalistic Teaching Strategies

An important indicator of effective teaching is the degree to which an adult stays in close proximity to the children, facilitating without interrupting or unduly directing their play. Teachers can choose from a variety of strategies to sustain child engagement and prevent conflict, thereby reducing inappropriate child behaviors (Bredekamp & Copple, 1997). The instructional strategies chosen by the classroom teacher should ensure that children acquire knowledge and skills and apply them in daily interactions with teachers and peers (Wolery & Winterling, 1997). Naturalistic teaching strategies are effective in increasing social interaction and classroom engagement with children who have identified disabilities. Kohler and colleagues (2001) 1) incorporated novel materials into daily classroom routines, 2) used verbal and physical scaffolding of the child's play to improve levels of engagement, 3) offered choices, 4) commented on child play activities, 5) elaborated on child language, and 6) capitalized on environmental barriers to increase engagement and social interaction (e.g., removed the serving spoon for a preferred food so the child would communicate with peers and teachers to get a serving). Additional scaffolding behaviors—such as directing the child's attention to play materials, verbally suggesting and physically modeling actions that the child might take with the materials, and verbally prompting the child to attempt to imitate the teacher's actions—increase levels of engagement (Malmskog & McDonnell, 1999).

Limited Choices

McCormick and colleagues (1998) found that children with and without identified disabilities were more likely to be actively and appropriately engaged with classroom activities when teachers used redirection and facilitation rather than firm and direct assistance. Effective monitoring strategies allow the classroom staff to redirect off-task and non-compliant behaviors before they escalate to disruptive levels (Lawry et al., 2000). A careful assessment of a child's more and less preferred activities can help the teacher to introduce limited choices, which will guide the child toward increased levels of compliance and decreased levels of challenging behaviors (Harding et al., 1999). Scaffolding with redirection and facilitation is highlighted in the next vignette.

> Anthony, age 3, moves to the sensory area, standing near three other children who are scooping water from a table lined with small landscaping stones. He watches as Jacob pours water into a funnel and lets it flow back into the table. The teacher moves to help Anthony join the fun. She says, "You need a smock if you play at the water table, Anthony." She takes the smock from the yellow plastic hook and helps him pull it over his head. She moves with him to the table, reaching for a red plastic scoop and placing it in his hand. Anthony then uses the scoop, filling it with rocks and water and pouring them into the funnel. Anthony smiles and looks at the teacher, holding the funnel and looking at the bottom. The teacher says, "Look at Anthony. He put rocks in his funnel and the water won't come out." Soon the other children begin experimenting with the sifters and funnels, using the rocks to block the openings. The teacher moves away to a nearby play area. Anthony continues to scoop and pour rocks and water into the funnels and sifters.

Assistance with Play Skills

Another variable that may precipitate challenging behaviors is a lack of success in social interaction with peers (Feldman & Griffiths, 1997; Wolery & Winterling, 1997). This may be linked to limited experience in peer interaction and the size of the child's social network outside the classroom setting (e.g., parents, extended family, friends) (Franco & Levitt, 1997). Disruptive or aggressive behaviors during play also may be linked with a fundamental lack of knowledge and understanding of the various skills required for successful peer interaction. This reciprocity of play—the ability to initiate activities and respond easily to the social bids of other children—is a key ingredient for successful social interaction. Children with disabilities tend to make and receive fewer social initiations to and from peers in preschool settings (Brown et al., 1999). For this reason, peer-related social competence has been identified as a critical foundation skill for further development (Odom et al, 1999).

Kohler and Strain (1997) highlighted a number of events that are observed during reciprocal peer interactions:

1. Statements or actions that function as play organizers (e.g., suggestions for play themes or activities)
2. Offers of or requests for play items
3. Requests for assistance or help from another child
4. Compliments that offer praise for another's actions or ideas

5. Verbal or physical expressions of affection
6. General statements or behaviors that are not readily categorized; negative behaviors (e.g., grabbing materials, hitting) also may be observed

Roberts and colleagues (1996) observed the behaviors of children with and without hearing impairments who attempted to gain entry into pretend play activities with typically developing peers. The researchers identified numerous direct strategies used by children to enter play, including verbal or nonverbal requests to play and joining ongoing play with words or actions. They also observed indirect play entries such as waiting just outside the play area and watching the activity, commenting on peer play, verbally suggesting a possible play action, requesting adult intervention, or stating a classroom rule or limit regarding play. Indirect play entry behaviors were found to be the most preferred by other children and the most successful.

Assisting the development of social skills is paramount because children who lack these skills may be continually rejected as they clumsily attempt to enter cooperative play interactions. This situation sets the stage for increasing adjustment problems because the children often respond by becoming more aggressive or withdrawn. These undesirable behaviors, in turn, increase the likelihood that the children will continue to be rejected (Repetti, McGrath, & Ishikawa, 1999).

Scaffolded Play Entry

Odom and colleagues (1999) created three major categories of teacher-directed strategies for improving the social competence of preschool children. The first is environmental arrangement, in which children who are less competent are paired with socially skilled peers in small group activities that include substantial teacher direction for child roles and actions. The second is instructional activities, during which educators teach specific social skills in small group settings, providing prompts and reinforcement throughout the classroom day as those skills are exhibited in other classroom routines. The third is peer-mediated interventions, during which peers with social competence are selected and trained to engage and instruct their peers with fewer skills under diminishing levels of teacher supervision. All of these strategies are effective in increasing the frequency and efficacy of child social interaction. Higher levels of general teacher–child interactions are associated with increased frequencies of conversational initiations in toddlers and preschoolers (McCartney et al., 1997).

Partnering

After observing 112 preschoolers—some typically developing, some with identified disabilities—who were enrolled in preschools across 16 states, Brown, Odom, and colleagues (1999) highlighted the importance of teacher support for successful engagement and social interaction. Teachers may have to support a child's play entry through partnering and modeling effective social interaction strategies (Roberts et al., 1996). This approach may involve instruction of successful direct and indirect strategies and encouragement to repeat attempts to gain entry following initial rejection by the group members. Stimulation of child conversations during play also can be accomplished by direct teacher involvement. Filla, Wolery, and Anthony (1999) found that teachers using modeling and direct prompting to facilitate conversations increased the overall number of conversational turns and the rate of verbal interaction. The prompts included redirections of child conversations from teachers to peers, direct and general prompts suggesting that the children talk with each other, and modeling of phrases that a child might use for social interaction. Play partnering to facilitate interaction is described in the following vignette.

> Jacinda, a 4-year-old with a severe visual impairment, sits alone, rocking on a beanbag in the book area. She hears two of the children playing with cars and a ramp that they have built in the block area. Jacinda says, "Laura" and continues to rock, smiling as she listens to the children's play. The teacher approaches Jacinda, greeting her, "Hi, Jacinda. Are you listening to Laura and Hope? Let's go play with them." Using minimal guidance, the teacher places her hand under Jacinda's elbow, exerting a slight pressure and physically prompting her to stand and move to the block area. As they enter the area, the teacher says, "Jacinda is smiling because you are having so much fun with the cars and the ramps. Is there a car for Jacinda?" Hope picks up a truck and places it in Jacinda's hand. The teacher says, "You have a fire truck, Jacinda. You can make it roll down the short ramp." The teacher guides Jacinda's hand to the top of the ramp. The children yell, "Ready, set, go!" and the teacher helps Jacinda release her truck to race down the ramp parallel to Hope's car. Jacinda sits down close to Hope and reaches into the bucket of cars, lifting her hand to place a yellow school bus on the top of the short ramp. Laura says, "No, Jacinda, wait. It's my turn. You can go again in a minute." Jacinda lowers the bus to her lap and listens as Hope and Laura race their cars. The teacher moves away as Jacinda smiles at the "thump" of the cars hitting the bottom of the ramps and Hope and Laura's laughter. Jacinda reaches to place the bus at the top of the short ramp.

Peer Modeling

Teaching peers who are socially competent to engage and interact with children who have interaction difficulties is highly effective (Odom et al., 1999). Kohler and Strain (1999) suggested factors that teachers should consider when determining the need for peer-mediated interventions to increase engagement and social interaction of preschool children. The interventions should be implemented across classroom routines and activities, provide multiple opportunities for practicing targeted skills, be feasible in terms of the resources invested (i.e., personnel, materials, and time), and produce clear changes in the skill level of the targeted child.

Classwide Social Skills Training

Kohler and Strain (1997) suggested that teachers can improve social interactions in early childhood settings through the implementation of a structured training program. With their recommended program, social skills training takes place in daily 15-minute sessions, in which small groups of children (typically three children per group) are introduced to the following social interaction skills: 1) organizing play, 2) sharing, 3) assisting others, 4) giving compliments, and 5) using appropriate expressions of affection. During these structured teaching sessions, the adult models each skill, in turn, and children are given opportunities to practice the skill with corrective feedback and positive reinforcement. Children are taught to offer and respond to social initiations from others. The entire curriculum is usually completed within 15 classroom days.[3]

HOW SHOULD TEACHERS RESPOND TO CHALLENGING BEHAVIOR?

The literature has examined the effectiveness and appropriateness of certain approaches to addressing challenging behavior. Several are discussed in the following subsections.

Rewards for Acceptable Classroom Behavior

The goal of differential positive reinforcement is to decrease the occurrence of challenging behaviors by selectively attending to or rewarding the child for displaying more acceptable behaviors (Kazdin, 2001). Teachers are often less attentive to the times when children who exhibit aggressive or noncompliant child behaviors are cooperative, appropriately engaged, and enjoying play. For this reason, observation can identify times when teachers can highlight and encourage these positive behaviors. This assessment should include a careful analysis of the types of encouragement, praise, or tangible rewards to which a particular child is most responsive. Social reinforcers can include sincere praise tailored to the immediate situation, including hugs, smiles, thumbs-up gestures, and other celebrations of the good choices that the child has made. Tangible reinforcers can include stickers, stamps, positive notes to parents, or privileges such as extra minutes for computer time or outside play. These reinforcers can be provided for the child's use of appropriate alternative behaviors (e.g., asking for a teacher's help instead of throwing materials when frustrated), incompatible behaviors (e.g., staying on one's own carpet square during group time instead of leaning into the neighboring child), or reduced levels of disruptive or aggressive behaviors (e.g., engaging in only one incident of unfriendly talk as opposed to the usual five incidents per day) (Kazdin, 2001; Matson & Duncan, 1997). As always, strategies should be consistent with an early childhood center's philosophy and practice. The following vignette demonstrates rewards for good behavior during group time.

> Daniel, age 5, sits close to the classroom assistant as the teacher assembles the class for group time. Today's book is about airplanes, and Daniel's attention wanders almost as soon as the teacher begins to read. Daniel turns around on his carpet square and leans out of the circle. The assistant

---

[3]Several social skills programs are available in prepackaged instructional formats, including Shure's (2001) *I Can Problem Solve* and the *Skillstreaming* curriculum by McGinnis and Goldstein (1990).

places an index card with five empty squares directly in Daniel's sight. She brings it to Daniel's lap as he turns back to the circle and looks at the teacher's book. The assistant whispers soothingly in Daniel's ear as she comments on the pictures in the book. After 1 minute, she selects a sticker of a large fuzzy caterpillar and peels it off the paper backing. Daniel presses it to the first empty spot on the card. He looks back at the teacher and the reading continues. The teacher pushes a button on the cassette player and the children get up to act out a song. Daniel rises with minimal assistance and the next minute goes by. The teacher selects a picture of a bumblebee and Daniel presses it to the second square. This process continues for the remainder of group time. After 5 successful minutes of engagement, the squares of the card are full, and the assistant teacher leads Daniel to the book area where they share Daniel's favorite insect book. He eagerly leans into the assistant as she reads the book to him. The rest of the children finish group and line up for outside play. Daniel joins them at the door with a large plastic magnifying glass in hand, ready to scour the grass for bugs.

Effective Reinforcers

The Premack principle (1959) established that a child is more likely to engage in nonpreferred activities (e.g., working at the writing table) when he or she is reinforced with the opportunity to spend extra time doing preferred activities in which he engages with relatively high frequency (e.g., building in the block area). Umbreit and Blair (1997) used a similar procedure with a 4-year-old boy who engaged in noncompliant and aggressive behaviors when asked to come in from the playground and when it was time for the afternoon nap. A functional analysis revealed that this child particularly enjoyed helping the staff set up materials for the next activity. At naptime, he had asked for a top and bottom sheet on his cot and to be allowed to have his stuffed whale from the beginning of naptime. These preferred activities were embedded into the problematic transitions with success. The noncompliant and aggressive behavior virtually disappeared during naptime and indoor transitions, and the effects generalized to his behavior throughout the day.

Say-Do Correspondence

Say-do correspondence involves instructing children to give appropriate responses when questioned about their intended behavior or plans in a given classroom activity and then reinforcing them for following through. Luciano, Herruzo, and Barnes-Holmes (2001) examined the effects of generalizing say-do correspondence training to similar but untaught behaviors in preschool children. They found that children were able to maintain say-do correspondence when reinforcement was reduced and when the adults gave less frequent prompting about the need to verbalize intentions. A teacher who chooses this strategy should identify a child's often violated limit and remind the child before the situation in which it usually occurs. Kazdin (2001) defined *feedback* as the knowledge of how well one has performed a particular task or activity. Feedback in the absence of other positively reinforcing activities, privileges, or events has been shown to influence behavior. Transition strategies are utilized in the next vignette.

> Brandon, age 4, bumps into Jared and Leah as he excitedly lines up for the trip to the indoor playroom. The teacher approaches him and reminds him that he sometimes has trouble walking down the hallway. She says, "How are you going to walk down the hall to the playroom?" Brandon says, "I'm going to use my 'walking feet.'" The teacher then scans the line, sees that all of the children in this group are ready to leave, and opens the door. Brandon looks down at his feet, walking carefully down the hall. At the door to the playroom, the teacher smiles at Brandon, gives him a thumbs-up sign, and says, "You said you were going to walk, and you did."

Punishment for Unsafe Behavior

Although teachers and staff in early childhood settings are reluctant to institute punishment procedures, severe behavioral disruptions may indicate the appropriateness of selecting these strategies in a crisis situation or on an individual child basis. Matson and Duncan (1997) described *punishment* as the removal of an activity or privilege that is positively reinforcing to the child (i.e., response–cost) or the presentation of aversive stimulation (e.g., appropriate physical restraint) following aggressive, unsafe, or destructive behavior. In any event, effective punishment should be delivered immediately, consistently, and in a manner that is commensurate in form and severity with the rule violation (i.e., the punishment should fit the crime). In addition, efforts should be made to avoid any unintended side effects of punishment, including positive reinforcement through the provision of teacher attention or escape from nonpreferred activities (Kazdin, 2001).

Reprimands

The verbal reprimand is one of the most frequently used punishing responses. This may or may not include feedback about the desired alternative behavior or instructions to apologize or comfort a victim. Reprimands may be only temporarily effective, and children are unlikely to attend to them unless teachers deliver the verbal punishment while standing nearby and follow through with a loss of privileges for repeated infractions (Kazdin, 2001).

Response–Cost

Response–cost may enforce a penalty when a child engages in an undesirable behavior. For example, the teacher may have a plan that involves losing a turn in a classroom activity (e.g., block building, playing in the housekeeping area) after repeated aggressive or disruptive behaviors. The teacher should establish clear guidelines for the administration of a behavioral plan involving positive reinforcement and response–cost. In other words, the loss of privileges is ineffective in modifying a child's behavior in the absence of sensitive, responsive, and positive caregiving. The child, in turn, should understand clearly the parameters for earning, maintaining, and losing classroom privileges (Kazdin, 2001). Response–cost is used in the following vignette.

> Nicole, age 4, stands at the sensory table, scooping the sand and placing it in a bowl. From time to time, she looks toward the teacher, takes a scoop of sand, and pours it between the table and the wall. The teacher watches this, deciding to ignore this minor behavior instead of giving attention to it. Nicole stops when she catches the teacher's eye and returns to scooping sand into her bowl. The teacher looks away to watch a child in another center. She looks back just as Nicole deliberately spills more sand between the table and the wall. The teacher decides that she needs to interrupt this behavior. She approaches Nicole, touching her shoulder and saying, "Nicole, please keep the sand in the table." Nicole returns to scooping until the teacher is called away to help a child put on his smock. Then, she fills a scoop with sand and inserts it between the table and the wall, starting to pour the sand into the space. The teacher returns to Nicole and says, "Nicole, the sand needs to stay in the table. You have lost your turn at the sand table for today." The teacher helps Nicole to take off the smock and directs her to the art table. "There's an empty space at the art table. You can play at the sand table again tomorrow."

Time-Out

Time-out is somewhat controversial, but it is a highly effective intervention strategy when used appropriately (Sterling-Turner & Watson, 1999). Time-out involves removing a child from a reinforcing event or activity for a brief period of time following the expression of inappropriate or undesirable behaviors (Kazdin, 2001; Matson & Duncan, 1997). It is agreed that time-out should be very brief (i.e., a few seconds to a few minutes for a preschool child) and that the strategy works best when "time-in" is highly reinforcing (Kazdin, 2001). There is some disagreement regarding the effectiveness of using warnings prior to time-out. Olmi, Sevier, and Nastasi (1997) instituted a verbal warning followed by a 5-second waiting period for child compliance. When a child failed to change the disruptive or noncompliant behavior, he or she immediately was taken to an adjacent time-out spot, where he or she remained for several seconds. Upon quiet compliance (i.e., sitting quietly in the time-out chair), the child was retained for 3–5 additional seconds before being released from time-out. He or she was returned to the previous activity and allowed to participate. This time-out procedure was effective in reducing object throwing behaviors, noncompliance to teacher requests, running away, and aggression.

Time-out can be described as falling on a continuum from partial to complete removal of the child from the activity. Time-out has been described as nonexclusionary (i.e., time spent in an area adjacent to the activity in which the challenging behavior occurred) and exclusionary (i.e., time spent in an area out of sight and sound of the activity in which the challenging behavior occurred) (Miltenberger, 2001). Less punitive contingent observation procedures remove the child briefly but allow him or her to watch the ongoing activities without directly participating in them (Porterfield, Herbert-Jackson, & Risley, 1976).

Miltenberger (2001) provided several questions that teachers should ask to determine the appropriateness of time-out as an intervention choice:

- Does the child use time-out to escape from a nonpreferred classroom activity?
- Due to limitations in classroom personnel, is the child unsupervised or partially supervised during the time-out procedure? Can he or she leave the time-out area? Is adequate staffing available to end the time-out appropriately?
- Does the time-out area provide additional opportunities for reinforcement of the disruptive behavior (e.g., individual teacher attention)?
- Is the use of time-out acceptable to teachers, staff, and parents?

If time-out is chosen as an intervention strategy, Sterling-Turner and Watson (1999) suggested that classroom staff or center administrators develop consistent time-out policies, including

1. Developmentally appropriate explanations for the use of time-out
2. Descriptions and models of appropriate child behaviors while in time-out
3. Identification of safe and effective areas of the classroom for the implementation of time out
4. Methods to determine the length of time-out and the conditions under which the child will be allowed to return to the previous activity
5. The manner in which warnings or explanations will be given to the child regarding future expectations for behavior

Time-out procedures are illustrated in the next vignette.

> Lamont, age 4, is carefully arranging a pile of long wooden blocks. He places them in a crisscross pattern, building them to eye level. Madison and Jahid run cars across blocks that are arranged end to end on the ground, pausing to glance up anxiously at the hovering tower. The teacher approaches and reminds Lamont of the waist-high rule. She helps him select places on the ground for the blocks that she removes and then walks away. Lamont rebuilds the tower to its previous height while the teacher is helping a child in the bathroom. A precariously placed block begins to wobble as the teacher emerges from the bathroom. The tower collapses on top of Madison and Jahid. The assistant moves to comfort the children and assess their injuries. The teacher takes Lamont to a quiet area near the door and places him in a child-size "thinking" chair. "The blocks were too high. You're in time-out." The teacher stays near Lamont, twisting the knob on a plastic timer decorated with pictures of baby animals. The timer shows 1 minute. Lamont shuffles his feet and looks sad, but sits quietly in the chair. When the timer rings, the teacher approaches Lamont and says, "You can have another turn in the block area. Remember the waist-high rule. If you don't follow the rule, you will lose your turn in this area for today."

Overcorrection

Overcorrection, another punishment strategy that may be used for seriously disruptive or dangerous behaviors, includes restitution (i.e., restoring the environment to the original condition) and positive practice (i.e., repeated opportunities to practice an acceptable alternative to the unsafe or disruptive behavior) (Kazdin, 2001; Matson & Duncan, 1997). For example, when a child *intentionally* tips a full glass of milk onto a neighboring child's plate, causing milk to run across the table and drip to the floor, restitution would involve the child's wiping the spilled milk from the table and helping clean the floor with a mop or damp cloth. Positive practice might involve helping clean up the entire snack area after the other children leave, pouring half-empty glasses and pitchers of milk into the sink, and wiping all of the tables.

Contingent Restraint

Restraint is used almost reflexively in response to physically aggressive or dangerous behaviors in the early childhood classroom (Matson & Duncan, 1997). For this reason, a strong possibility exists that this strategy will be overused by an early childhood setting that has not examined the effectiveness of less invasive procedures (Singh, 1997). Teachers are strongly encouraged to consider the less restrictive procedures outlined in this chapter before physically holding a child in response to aggressive or noncompliant behavior. Although it is frequently necessary to guide or hold a child briefly to prevent injury, the frequent use of restraint signals the need for a more thorough assessment of the problem situation. A-B-C analyses or functional assessments may reveal maintaining factors for these disruptive behaviors, and classroom practices can be adjusted accordingly. Center administrators may consider the development of specific policies for using physical restraint (e.g., informing and involving parents, training staff how to prevent injury, planning to prevent further severe aggressive behaviors) a worthwhile time investment.

CLASSROOM APPLICATION

Should alternative strategies be considered to modify severely aggressive or disruptive behaviors?

Does the consistent use of naturalistic teaching methods and guidance strategies effectively manage problem situations?

Would this group of children benefit from a classwide social skills training program?

How much time does classroom staff spend physically restraining or moving children in response to aggressive or noncompliant behaviors?

Does the administration and staff consider the use of differential reinforcements and/or punishment procedures acceptable?

Which strategies are acceptable at this early childhood center, and are there consistent guidelines for their use?

Do parents and administrators collaborate with teachers in developing individual child plans involving the ongoing use of extraordinary measures (i.e., tangible reinforcers, punishment procedures)?

Is there a quiet and easily monitored area for time-out interventions?

Are there consistent guidelines for brief child-friendly response–cost and time-out strategies?

CONCLUSION

Building on the discussions in Chapters 4 and 5, this chapter has addressed the role of the early childhood teacher in crafting an appropriate fit between the classroom environment and the specific group of children enrolled at any given time. This chapter has included an examination of positive guidance procedures and the need for additional, more directive teacher strategies for severe and repeated problem situations. The chapter has introduced A-B-C analysis and functional assessment as vehicles for analyzing factors related to the challenging behavior, including environmental arrangement, curricular activities, limits and routines, teacher language and instructional strategies, and reinforcement and punishment strategies. Chapter 7 addresses the collaborative development of individualized behavior plans for children whose challenging behaviors are not immediately responsive to the strategies outlined in this chapter.

Implementing Individualized Behavior Plans

Susan Hart Bell and Victoria Carr

An early childhood teacher attempts to provide an orderly, engaging classroom environment for a group of children with diverse temperaments, skills, and experiences. Some children rush into the classroom with tales of weekend activities, excitedly sharing their stories with peers and teachers. Others trail in sadly, scolded by parents who are late for work, seeking the comfort of a warm lap and a good book. Still others experience cyclical changes in their moods and behavior and may be forced to adapt to the fluctuating expectations and daily schedules of divorced parents with joint custody. In turn, the classroom climate changes daily, mirroring the moods and activities of the children. As suggested previously, the early childhood teacher routinely assesses the goodness-of-fit among the classroom schedule, the physical arrangement, the curricular offerings, and the needs of the children, making changes as problems arise. These changes, although usually discussed with assistant teachers and staff, are informal and subject to revision. The teacher uses "gut feeling" in determining how the modifications contribute to the smoothness of the classroom routines.

As discussed in Chapters 5 and 6, an experienced classroom teacher follows this same process when addressing behavior that results in a marked disruption of classroom activities. The teacher begins to step up his or her involvement with the child, closely scrutinizing the child's behavior and providing more support during tough times of the day. The educator looks for patterns in the child's behavior, which serve as warning signs, and begins to group the child with different children or to modify his or her daily schedule. These strategies are followed intuitively but informally—almost on an experimental basis. When the teacher finds a strategy (or combination of strategies) that seems to resolve the problem, he or she can turn to other concerns.

However, when the teacher is faced with a child whose behavior 1) is resistant to these informal strategies, 2) appears to escalate or become more frequent despite accommodations and increased support, and/or 3) occurs apparently without warning, the time spent attending to the daily management of the child's behavior justifies further investment in the development of an individualized and formal intervention plan. Jackson and Panyan (2002) described *behavioral intervention* as a deliberate rearrangement of environmental conditions. This plan is based on a general understanding of the factors influencing the behavior to promote the child's growth and learning. The eventual goal of any behavioral intervention is to enhance the comfort of the child and those around him or her. This chapter highlights the factors that the classroom teacher should examine in planning for behavioral intervention: strategies for deciding when formal intervention is necessary, methods for convening an intervention team, techniques for gathering information related to the problem situation, and components of a successful intervention plan.

WHEN IS FORMAL INTERVENTION NECESSARY?

The following subsections examine possible indicators of the need for a formal intervention plan.

Factors Beyond the Teacher's Control

As part of initial intervention planning, the classroom teacher should determine whether the challenging behaviors stem from medical conditions or characteristics of the home environment that are difficult to address with classroom interventions (Barnett, Bell, & Carey, 1999). If health conditions are present, then the appropriate response is to refer the child to a medical practitioner. If home characteristics are an issue, then the plan must effectively target parent consultation rather than individual child behaviors. Additional factors that may require involvement of other professionals (e.g., psychologists, physicians, social workers) have been addressed more thoroughly in Chapter 1. Parent factors are highlighted in the following vignette.

> Jamie, age 4, yawns as he turns the pages in the book. He is slumped in the beanbag chair in the book area, his eyes drooping. As the teacher begins singing the cleanup song and encourages the children to wash their hands for snack, Jamie's eyes finally close. The teacher approaches him gently, touching his shoulder and repeating, "Jamie, it is time for you to put the book away and get ready for snack time." Jamie only snuggles more deeply into the beanbag chair and asks the teacher for his blanket, saying that he is sleepy. The teacher insists, "Jamie, it's time for snack. I'll help you put the book away." Jamie begins to sob, and the teacher holds him as he quickly falls back to sleep.

Concerned that Jamie is ill, the teacher leaves him in the care of an assistant and calls Jamie's mother at work. Jamie's mother tells the teacher that Jamie did not go to sleep until after midnight the night before. She confides that it is hard to get Jamie to bed, so she usually gives in and lets him stay up with her while she watches television. Jamie's mother works long hours, and early evening is the only time that she and Jamie have together during the week. She reveals frustration with the nightly bedtime battle and regrets that this is causing Jamie to be sleepy at school. The teacher suggests a parent–teacher conference to discuss some bedtime suggestions, and Jamie's mother immediately agrees.

Disruption of Daily Activities

Another factor to consider in deciding whether to develop a formal intervention is the degree to which the daily classroom activities are disrupted by the child's behavior. Jackson and Panyan (2002) described *challenging behaviors* as falling on a continuum from mildly inattentive and disruptive to severely disruptive and dangerous. Mild noncompliance (e.g., frequently leaving one's carpet square to sit near the teacher during group time) and ill-timed self-expression (e.g., responding enthusiastically and loudly to every teacher question during group time) may be supported with increased teacher proximity, quiet reminders (e.g., "It's Jeffrey's turn to talk now"), redirection, and the institution of logical consequences (e.g., "You left the art table, so you lost your turn at sponge painting"). Depending on the frequency of the minor disruptions, the teacher might consider the need for collaboration with classroom staff to develop a time-limited and simple behavioral intervention. When the child's behavior falls further along the continuum, involving severe and frequent disruptions to the classroom day and interfering with other children's learning experiences, the teacher should consider a more intensive assessment and formal intervention plan. The same is true for dangerous behaviors, regardless of how infrequently they occur.

Behavior that Differs from that of Peers

Another deciding factor is the degree to which the child's behavior departs from that of other children in the classroom. The teacher can directly observe during a classroom activity (e.g., free play) to assess whether the child's behavior of concern (e.g., hitting) occurs with greater frequency, duration, or intensity than that of his or her classmates. Peer micronorms are one way in which this can be determined. The teacher can define the behavior of concern, identify "average" children in the classroom of the same gender and age, and conduct a focused observation of the child and his or her classmates to document the occurrence of the targeted behavior during a specified time interval (e.g., 30 minutes of free play) (Bell & Barnett, 1999). If the teacher finds that all of the children are equally likely to display the inappropriate behavior, then he or she might consider implementing a classwide intervention (Siemoens, 2001). Classwide problems with the naptime routine are illustrated in the next vignette.

The teacher presses the button on the tape player, and the naptime song begins to play. She quietly calls the remaining children in the book area to their cots. Fifteen cots line the walls of the nap room, and children sit or lie on or near them. The song continues to play as assistant teachers move toward the children who have the most difficulty falling asleep. The teacher turns down the volume of the song and picks a naptime book to read. The children wait attentively as the teacher opens the book. The story is lively, full of animal sounds and actions, and soon Marquis has moved to stand on his cot. He bounces excitedly as the story continues. Ellen sees Marquis, and soon she is jumping, too, as the story builds in tension. Rachel begins to pull her cot closer to the teacher to better see the pictures in the book. The teacher notices that Marquis, Ellen, and Rachel are not lying on their cots. She stops reading, closes the book, and reprimands them by saying, "I'm not going to read unless you're lying on your cot." The three children lie down briefly, but soon are up again, joined by Lauren, Tommy, and Jacob. The children move to sit or lie on the floor at the teacher's feet. The teacher abruptly stops the story, closes the book, and says, "I can't read if you are not on your cots. I'll try this again tomorrow."

Severity of the Behavior

Finally, the teacher should determine whether the challenging behaviors are serious enough to require an individualized behavior plan. Running away can endanger the child's safety, and one occasion can persuade the teacher of an immediate need for intervention. Tantrums that last more than a few minutes and cause damage to classroom materials or physical harm to teachers or children warrant individualized planning as well. Durand (1990) suggested that the teacher ask the following questions to determine the severity of a behavior:

1. Is the challenging behavior life-threatening, or does it pose a health risk?
2. Will the behavior seriously interfere with future learning?
3. Is the challenging behavior resistant to routine classroom strategies, or is it getting worse despite consistent efforts to intervene?
4. Does the behavior hurt other children or staff or damage materials?
5. Does the behavior significantly interfere with acceptance in community settings?

Answering yes to even one of these questions indicates the need to develop a comprehensive behavioral intervention plan.

CLASSROOM APPLICATION

Is an individualized behavior plan needed for this child?

Are the current classroom strategies effective with this child?

Does the child's behavior disrupt the flow of the classroom day?

Does the child's behavior differ significantly from that of his or her class-mates?

Does the child's behavior result in harm to self, staff, peers, or classroom materials?

Does the child's behavior seem to be intensifying or increasing in frequency?

Should any other factors be considered?

HOW SHOULD THE INTERVENTION TEAM BE CONFIGURED?

If a behavioral intervention plan is deemed necessary, an intervention team must be formed. The ensuing subsections detail various aspects of forming the team.

Team Members

The classroom teacher is the individual who is most familiar with the major stakeholders in the child's life. For this reason, he or she is the logical person to determine when the team should be convened and how to select members who will provide relevant assessment information and assist in the development and implementation of the intervention plan (Jackson & Panyan, 2002). Diverse representation on the problem-solving team is important (Epps & Jackson, 2000). Team members may include the teacher, the assistant teacher or classroom aide, the center director or classroom coordinator, and the parents. Related services personnel such as speech-language therapists, physical therapists, occupational therapists, or psychologists also may be involved. When possible, team members should have a knowledge of early childhood classroom principles. Specialized service providers may be trained to work autonomously within their own fields and may be unfamiliar with the philosophy and practices of the early childhood setting (Bruder, 1994; Hinojosa et al., 2001). Therefore, outside consultants may provide invaluable suggestions, but they may not understand the importance of adapting these strategies to the unique needs of preschool settings and may suggest interventions that are neither feasible nor comfortable given best practices guidelines and the resources available to the center (Fox, Little, & Dunlap, 2001). For early childhood educators and consulting professionals to work together in an effective manner, there must be a mutual respect and shared under-standing of the guiding theories and recommended best practices of their respective disciplines. In addition, during all phases of the intervention development process, team members must follow agency guidelines to secure appropriate permission for observation and intervention from parents (or guardians) and the teachers who will participate in the process (Barnett, Bell, & Carey, 1999).

Team Problem Solving

Collaborative problem solving involves two or more people whose goal is the development of an effective plan to address a child-related problem (Bruder, 1994; Pugach & Johnson,

1995). Although each team member may have a unique view of the problem situation, it is important that he or she realize that in true collaboration, there are no hierarchical relationships. Each team member has valuable information to contribute and an important role as the intervention strategies are put into place (Hinojosa et al., 2001).

Partnerships with Parents

The relationship between the early childhood staff and the child's parents should be defined by warmth, empathy, respect for cultural differences, and predictability of interactions (Bruder, 1994; Epps & Jackson, 2000). This partnership is built on frequent two-way communication between the teacher and the parents. As members of an intervention team, parents contribute knowledge about the child's skills and behaviors in community settings, insight into cultural practices and family values, and information about individual child preferences and interests (Barnett, Bell, & Carey, 1999; Bricker, Pretti-Frontczak, & McComas, 1998). Parents differ in their interest in and availability for active participation in the problem-solving process, so it is important to question parents about their preferences for involvement (Bailey, 1994; Brotherson & Goldstein, 1992). In research conducted by Bell (1997), parents identified several factors that facilitate their participation during educational planning: 1) parent–professional partnerships characterized by respect, information exchange, shared decision making, and mutual support, 2) access to the professional information base as a prerequisite to successful decision making, 3) validation of the efficacy of child advocacy efforts, and 4) help in tailoring strategies that will be effective in the home environment. Family members also may require specific information regarding the significance of their child's challenging behaviors and the resources that are available to address these behaviors (Bailey, 1994).

Effective Group Process

Small group development literature (Tuckman, 1965; Tuckman & Jensen, 1977) describes five stages of collaborative teaming:

1. *Forming* is the time spent developing initial rules to guide the scheduling and structure of team meetings and the manner in which decision making will occur. During this time, an understanding develops regarding the relationships among team members, the team's power structure, and the guidelines for communication.

2. *Storming* is the stage during which each member shares his or her own perspective, establishing his or her position on the team. Conflict may be observed at this time because each individual strives to present his or her view of the problem situation.

3. *Norming* is the point when the team begins to divide tasks, allocating decision-making power. Members begin to experience a sense of cohesion, however, as the team develops a unified purpose. There is an increase in the trust level and openness of communication among team members.

4. *Performing* occurs when team members develop a sense of common purpose, truly collaborating, sharing information and expertise, and establishing a working relationship to further progress toward a common goal.

5. *Adjourning* is the final stage, during which group tasks are completed and group member relationships are redefined.

Roles of the Group Facilitator

The facilitator is critical to the team's overall functioning. He or she is responsible for maintaining a positive atmosphere and conducting a productive meeting. The facilitator is an active participant, assuming a meaningful role as the group problem solves, guiding the group toward collaboratively defined goals and supporting the accomplishment of group tasks (Abelson & Woodman, 1983; Margolis & Shapiro, 1988). Pugach and Johnson (1995) asserted that the facilitator must 1) foster a comfortable atmosphere for all participants, 2) include a diverse group of individuals from a variety of professional disciplines and ethnic and socioeconomic backgrounds, 3) assume the perspectives of others while projecting a sense of unity for all group members, 4) arbitrate and resolve conflicts that arise to maintain group cohesion, and 5) engender a humility of spirit among members to reduce competition among individual member needs.

The facilitator must be able to change roles as the stages of group functioning evolve. For example, the facilitator begins as a guide and administrator and later becomes less directive, shifting to a mediator role among group members (Pugach & Johnson, 1995). In essence, the facilitator's primary responsibility is to assume leadership for the team, communicating goals and mediating conflicts throughout all stages of teaming and summarizing the degree to which group tasks are accomplished once the team is adjourned.

Time for Planning

As mentioned in Chapter 2, the availability of formally scheduled, administration-supported time is a key element in effective collaboration (Hinojosa et al., 2001; Sandall, 1997b). This refers to time that is available for the team to meet during the work day, free from distractions and for a long enough period to process assessment information and develop intervention strategies. Administrative personnel can highlight the importance of collaborative problem solving by providing additional staff for supervision of the classroom, thereby allowing teachers and assistants to meet with parents and related services personnel. Particularly when the behavioral intervention may involve partnering with outside agencies or garnering additional resources (e.g., hiring additional staff), it is essential for the administration to maintain active involvement in the intervention development process (Fox et al., 2001).

Professional Development and Staff Training

Training should be an ongoing part of successful intervention for children with challenging behaviors (Bruder, 1994; Epps & Jackson, 2000). Dole-Kwan, Chen, and Hughes (2001) surveyed individuals who provided early intervention to children with visual impairments. These individuals indicated a need for ongoing professional development in forming partnerships with families from diverse cultures and in techniques for participation in early intervention teams. Administrative personnel should support classroom teachers and staff as they seek opportunities to become better informed regarding issues that are important to children and families served by the early childhood program.

CLASSROOM APPLICATION

Is the intervention team effective?

Who are the key stakeholders in the child's life? Are they part of the problem-solving team? How can they be directly involved in the planning process?

Does everyone have an equal "voice" during problem-solving meetings? If not, how can this be changed?

Has a group facilitator been identified?

Are meetings scheduled during times that are convenient for all members? Do they accommodate the schedules of teachers and parents?

Is there sufficient time to plan the intervention? Can the center administration provide classroom coverage while teachers plan so that all staff can attend the meetings?

Do the teachers and other classroom staff need professional development to address behavior problems more effectively? Can the center administration make this training available?

WHICH FACTORS CONTRIBUTE TO TEAM DECISION MAKING?

The team needs to base decisions on specific behavioral factors, which are explored in the following subsections.

Typical Problem-Solving Process

Several steps are common to collaborative intervention development (Barnett et al., 1999). A typical sequence is

1. Defining and clarifying the behaviors of concern as well as the factors that contribute to the problem situation (e.g., conducting a functional assessment of the problem situation and developing a behavioral hypothesis about the maintaining factors)

2. Collaboratively developing an intervention plan for the targeted behaviors

3. Implementing the plan, observing the consistency and fidelity with which the plan is carried out, and reviewing the initial effectiveness of the plan as well as the comfort level of those directly involved

4. Revising elements as necessary

5. Fading the intervention plan as the challenging behaviors diminish

Definition of the Problem Situation

A first step in determining the most effective intervention strategies is to describe the behavior of concern in specific, clear language (Durand, 1990; Kazdin, 2001; Miltenberger, 2001). This step involves defining the boundaries of what is included in and excluded from the definition of the behavior of concern. This ability to translate a complex problem situation into observable and measurable component behaviors is the key to developing an intervention plan for which effectiveness can be directly evaluated (Bricker et al., 1998). Miltenberger (2001) advocated using active verbs to describe the child behaviors (e.g., pushes, shoves, hits, bites). This language avoids references to internal states that cannot be observed (e.g., anxiety, low self-esteem, resentment, jealousy) and from which inferences are drawn.

Conditions Contributing to the Challenging Behavior

It also is important to specify exactly when and under which circumstances the behavior occurs (Durand, 1990; Kazdin, 2001). In one example from the research literature, Dooley, Wilczenski, and Torem (2001) completed a functional assessment for a 3-year-old boy with pervasive developmental disorder who engaged in severe tantrums and displayed aggressive and noncompliant behaviors. The functional assessment identified that transitions were the most problematic times of day for the child. This discovery led to the development of a pictorial schedule that eased transitions, giving the child visual cues for the next activity. Identifying these specific times of day that prove especially difficult can provide further information regarding possible intervention strategies. The intervention development process is exemplified by the team's work with Tricia, discussed in vignettes throughout this chapter and in Chapter 8.

> The classroom teacher, the assistant teacher, and the classroom coordinator meet to discuss 4-year-old Tricia's challenging behavior. The classroom teacher says, "The most troublesome behavior is her aggressiveness toward the other children, especially during free play. She pushes her way into the block or dramatic play areas, bulldozing over the other children. She grabs their play materials and begins to boss the other children around." The assistant teacher contributes, "Tricia sometimes hits children who won't give up their toys. Then we have to get involved and convince her to give them back." The team identifies hitting, shoving, and grabbing toys as the behaviors of concern. They decide to observe Tricia more closely during free play and determine the number of times per day that these behaviors occur.

Other Contributing Factors

A functional assessment can contribute important information regarding the factors maintaining the disruptive or ineffective behaviors, as discussed more thoroughly in

Chapter 6 (Fox et al., 2001). Chapter 1 provided a beginning list of child, classroom, and home characteristics that contribute to problem situations and can function as starting points for intervention strategies. In developing an intervention plan, however, it is most helpful to ask, "What is affecting the problem situation right now?" A systematic functional assessment can identify situational factors that most effectively influence the behavior(s) of concern in a systematic fashion (Kazdin, 2001; Miltenberger, 2001).

As a part of the functional assessment, the problem-solving team might select a semistructured interview format to guide the team through the daily activities of the child and to identify the routines during which the child has the most difficulty. Barnett and colleagues (1994, 1997) suggested using the Waking Day (and Sleep) Interview to examine the child's behaviors as he or she moves through the day. The interview examines activities such as the manner in which the child enters the classroom, the skill with which he or she organizes materials, his or her behavior during individual and group activities, and his or her actions during the transitions between those activities.

Baseline Observations

To gauge the effectiveness of the intervention plan, it is critical for the classroom teacher to have a clear understanding of the problem situation before any planned intervention is in place (Jackson & Panyan, 2002). Baseline establishment is usually accomplished by direct observation of the child within the classroom setting. The teacher strives to record important characteristics of the child behaviors, including frequency (i.e., the number of times the behavior is observed during a specific time period), duration (i.e., the length of time the child engages in the problematic behavior), intensity (i.e., the amount of force the child uses or the energy displayed during the expression of the challenging behavior), latency (i.e., time after the occurrence of some antecedent variable until the onset of the behavior), the variability with which the child displays the behaviors on different days, and a clear trend toward increasing or decreasing levels of problem behaviors (Kazdin, 2001; Miltenberger, 2001). Establishing a baseline for each selected child behavior prior to initiating an intervention plan can help the teacher determine whether the subsequent strategies are effective, as shown in the continued vignette about Tricia.

The classroom teacher and assistant teacher decide to note Tricia's hitting, grabbing play materials, and shoving during the 90 minutes of morning free play. The teachers define *hitting* as Tricia's using her hand to strike a child with enough force to cause injury or discomfort. They define *grabbing* as Tricia's taking by force toys or materials currently in use by another child. *Shoving* is defined as Tricia's use of her body to move another child away from desired play materials. The teachers decide to alternate responsibility for observing Tricia every half hour. An index card is kept on the teacher shelf with columns for recording each incident. The teacher and assistant teacher record the following information.

Tricia's challenging behaviors during free play

Date	Hits	Shoves	Grabbing materials
Monday, May 22	///// (5)	0	///// (5)
Tuesday, May 23	// (2)	/ (1)	/ (1)
Wednesday, May 24	///// (5)	0	///// / (6)
Thursday, May 25	//// (4)	0	//// (4)
Average	4	.25	4

CLASSROOM APPLICATION

Does the team have enough information to develop a plan?

Have the child's behaviors been defined in measurable, observable terms? Do the team members agree on these definitions?

Has the team identified the times of day that are most difficult for the child?

Are there other contributing factors that should be considered?

Do the team members have enough information to describe the problem completely? Are they confident that they know the typical frequency, intensity, and duration with which the behaviors occur?

What else does the team need to know?

HOW CAN THE TEAM DEVELOP AN EFFECTIVE INTERVENTION PLAN?

The team's next step is forming the actual intervention plan. The ensuing discussions detail the needed elements for creating an effective plan.

Determine Which Behaviors Cause the Most Concern

Several criteria exist for selecting the behaviors that are of most concern to the classroom teacher. The safety of the child, the teacher, and the other children is, of course, a primary consideration (Barnet, Bell, & Carey, 1999). Kazdin (2001) prioritized behaviors in terms of those that 1) interfere with the child's daily functioning, 2) result in frequent rule breaking and disruptions of classroom activities, and 3) cause great concern among important individuals in the child's life (e.g., parents, teachers, peers). Selected variables should have maximum potential to affect other areas of the child's life (e.g., those that serve as prerequisite or foundation skills for other behaviors). Barnett, Bauer, Ehrhardt, Lentz, and Stollar (1996) described these as *keystone variables.* Compliance with teacher requests, following a daily schedule, communication skills, and play entry behaviors fall into this category. Skills to be targeted with an individualized behavior plan should be functional for the child, generalize across educational and community settings, and require instructional strategies and supports that are outside the classroom's general curriculum (Bricker et al., 1998). This step is illustrated by Tricia's case.

> Tricia's teacher and assistant teacher meet briefly on Friday morning with the classroom coordinator. After reviewing the teachers' baseline observations of Tricia's behavior during free play, they decide to focus on Tricia's hitting and grabbing materials. Tricia's shoving seems less frequent and, therefore, of less concern. The other two behaviors are important to target because they frequently disrupt free play in the classroom and result in the discomfort and occasional injury of classmates.

Select Effective Intervention Strategies

The planning team should consider the following variables from Barnett, Bell, and Carey (1999) when choosing an intervention strategy:

- The current classroom setting and the behaviors of the teachers and children within that setting
- Developmentally appropriate practice guidelines
- Research-based strategies that facilitate the inclusion of children with challenging behaviors
- Suggestions emerging from collaborative problem solving with teachers, family members, and administrators

Changes may involve manipulating the antecedents or consequences that surround the behaviors of concern. It is important to consider the feasibility and scope of intervention strategies. Highly complex interventions involving many steps and decision points may be difficult to remember and implement consistently. The team also should take into account available resources (e.g., support staff, extended space).

Present Appropriate Alternate Behaviors

Kazdin (2001) identified "positive opposites"—that is, prosocial replacements for achieving the ends that the challenging behaviors are designed to achieve. Durand (1990) advised the team to examine whether the alternative behavior will be easy to teach, is an age-appropriate response, uses materials and activities that are available in the natural environment, contributes to increased independence and self-regulation, and prepares the child with the skills that will generalize to other settings. This approach is shown in the continuation of Tricia's story.

> The teachers decide that improving Tricia's play entry and communication skills will decrease her physical aggression and allow her to enjoy play.

They decide to help Tricia learn to comment on the play of the children already involved in the activity before entering the play area and to request teacher assistance in getting a turn with preferred toys.

Create a Consistent and Specific Intervention Plan

The proposed intervention should be a detailed action plan specifying changes in the classroom environment and teacher strategies. Barnett and colleagues (1996) referred to these plans as *scripts* and emphasized the importance of using typical staff language and actions to increase the probability that the plan will be followed in a consistent, faithful manner. Following the results of the functional assessment, the plan should include changes in conditions prior to the occurrence of the behavior of concern (e.g., teacher warnings, rearrangement of the schedule, availability of play materials) as well as modifications to teacher responses when the behaviors are exhibited.

Address Antecedents and Practices

Specific antecedents that assist the child in performing acceptable behaviors include teacher instructions, cues, modeling, and physical guidance. These are referred to as *prompts* for socially desirable behaviors and can be verbal (e.g., "Remember to sign in if you want a turn"), visual (e.g., photographs of children seated on carpet squares with arms and legs folded during group time), or physical (e.g., hand over hand assistance in tracing the letters in a child's name) (Kazdin, 2001). The intervention plan can specify gradually decreasing these prompts as the child moves toward self-regulation of behavior.

A verbal prompt may take the form of a request or direction. High-probability requests (e.g., "Johnnie, please line up to go to the playground") concern behaviors that the child is very likely to do without teacher reminders or assistance. Low-probability requests (e.g., "Johnnie, please throw your snack plate away") concern activities that the child is less likely to complete immediately (Kazdin, 2001). Teacher requests can capitalize on behavioral momentum by combining these high- and low-probability requests (e.g., "It's time to line up for the playground; please throw away your snack plate and get in line") (Mace et al., 1988). To be most effective, these requests should be clear, simple, and directed to the individual child, as shown in Tricia's case.

Tricia's teachers determine that the availability of preferred toys and activities is an important factor in precipitating her aggression. They raid the toy closets for more materials and structure free play activities in which plenty of materials are available. The teachers have already stepped up their physical proximity to Tricia during free play. They note that most of the aggressive behaviors occur during the first few minutes of her entering a new activity area. They now decide to structure her transitions carefully, shadowing her as she moves to a new area. The teachers develop scripted language for the transition, which the team members decide to include in Tricia's intervention plan: "Tricia, I see that you are interested in playing in the block area. Jonathon and Maria are already building an airport.

There is room for you and there are plenty of <u>blocks</u>. What would you like to build?"

Establish Consequences

The classroom teacher is interested in increasing the probability that these alternative, effective behaviors will occur. (Positive reinforcement and punishment procedures are discussed at length in Chapter 6; see also Kazdin, 2001.) The teacher can choose consequences that highlight and reward the use of the alternative behavior and decrease the occurrence of the challenging behaviors, as shown in the example involving Tricia.

> To finalize the intervention plan, the members of Tricia's intervention team develop a script for differentially responding to her behaviors. They decide to respond to Tricia's successful play entries (i.e., entering the play area appropriately, choosing available materials, and playing cooperatively with children already engaged in the area) with encouragement and scaffolding for more successful play engagement. They design the language for encouragement and play entry as follows: "Tricia, you are really working hard on your <u>building</u>. Do you think <u>Jonathon and Maria</u> would like to help you build <u>a road from your building to the airport?"</u>
>
> The team members also plan for a consistent response to Tricia's hitting and grabbing for materials. They determine that Tricia really enjoys playing in the block area and dramatic play. Thus, the time in these activity centers is very important to her. They decide to institute a warning and response–cost procedure following aggressive behaviors. The team members build this into the script as well. Upon the first occurrence of aggressive behavior after this part of the script is formed, the teacher says, "Tricia, I can't let you <u>take those blocks from Jonathon</u>. You have <u>blocks</u> over here. Please <u>ask for help if you need it</u>." Upon observing a second incident of aggressive behavior, the teacher and the assistant decide to physically remove Tricia from the area and offer her another choice, shadowing her to the next area and repeating the process for helping her to engage in the play activity. They also use language created specifically for the situation: "Tricia, it's not okay to <u>hit Maria</u>. You have lost your turn in <u>blocks</u>. We'll see if you can share the toys in <u>blocks</u> tomorrow. Where else would you like to play?"

CLASSROOM APPLICATION

Is the intervention plan specific?

> Which behaviors are most disruptive to the daily schedule? Have these been defined in observable, measurable terms?
>
> Which alternative behaviors can serve as positive replacements for the behaviors of concern?

Which proactive strategies can alter the child's daily experience, making the behaviors less likely to occur? Are these strategies feasible, given the resources in the classroom? Is everyone comfortable with these changes in daily activities?

Which strategies can be used in response to the child's behaviors of concern? Is everyone comfortable with these strategies? Are the needed resources available to follow through with these strategies?

Have these strategies been translated into a scripted plan of teacher language and actions that promote consistency and ease of intervention? Is the plan simple to follow? Is everyone comfortable with the plan's language?

Does everyone have a copy of the intervention plan?

Which other factors should be considered as the plan is put into place?

Prepare for Crises

The intervention plan prepares the teachers and administration for the manner in which routine behaviors will be addressed, but it is important to develop a crisis plan as well. This type of plan is particularly relevant for children who frequently require physical restraint or removal from the classroom. It can be broad in scope and is applicable for any seriously aggressive or disruptive problem situation. Jackson and Panyan (2002) suggested developing centerwide criteria for identifying the behaviors that require a crisis plan. In addition, this plan should specify the procedures that are followed (e.g., physical restraint, time-out) during crisis situations to ensure the safety of the children and staff and the preservation of classroom materials. The plan also may identify a place to be used for protective restraint or removal from the classroom activities. The crisis plan should be developed through collaboration with parents and administrative personnel and should allow the classroom staff to confidently address crises in a preapproved manner.

Expect Plan Revisions

As the agreed-on plan is implemented, immediate changes may be needed. For example, a well-planned intervention for toileting requires immediate revision when a child flushes the necklace that she is given to remind her to use the restroom. In addition to responding to unforeseen child behaviors, plan revision should be guided by an evaluation of the data collected during the baseline and intervention phases and should account for the teacher's comfort with the language and actions specified in the plan (Barnett et al., 1999). See Chapter 8 for a detailed discussion of plan revision.

Recognize the Commitment of Team Members

Successful inclusion of a child with challenging behaviors is difficult and time consuming. Often, the classroom teacher who devotes extraordinary planning and effort to the integration process is rewarded with the enrollment of additional children who have learning and behavioral difficulties. The administration of the early childhood center should provide professional development opportunities to build the capacity of all of the classroom teachers to address challenging behaviors. In turn, the center should build in opportunities for recognizing intervention efforts and celebrating success (Epps & Jackson, 2000).

CONCLUSION

In this chapter, the teacher has been asked to identify strategies for deciding when formal intervention is necessary, methods for convening an intervention team, techniques for gathering information related to the problem situation, and components of a successful intervention plan. Chapter 8 suggests issues for consideration when evaluating the acceptability and effectiveness of an intervention plan.

Chapter 8

Evaluating and Revising Intervention Plans

Susan Hart Bell
and Christine M. Gilkey

Once the team has agreed on the most important child behaviors and the intervention plan's essential components, it must determine the plan's acceptability and effectiveness. This step is often missed in intervention design. As administrators, teachers, and parents become increasingly oriented toward accountability, however, it is essential to document an intervention plan's educational benefits (Schwartz & Olswang, 1996). This chapter discusses the elements of plan evaluation that must be in place to determine that the problem situation is being addressed appropriately. Just as collaboration is important during the plan's development, communication is essential during the evaluation and possible revision of that same plan. Several questions must be considered by the intervention team following implementation of the intervention:

1. Have the most important behaviors for intervention been identified?
2. Are the steps for intervention clearly specified, and is the plan easy to understand and follow?
3. Do all members of the intervention team consistently and carefully implement the plan?
4. Is the plan acceptable to all stakeholders?
5. Is the plan improving the targeted behavior (i.e., is the plan effective)?
6. Can this plan be carried forward, and is it cost-effective?

7. Does the plan need further revision?
8. Which procedures are specified for fading or discontinuing the plan?
9. What is the team's next step?

HAVE THE MOST IMPORTANT BEHAVIORS FOR INTERVENTION BEEN IDENTIFIED?

Once the team implements a plan, it is important to evaluate whether the selected behaviors remain the most pressing intervention concerns (Barnett, Bell, & Carey, 1999). Modifying one or more elements of the environment (e.g., classroom arrangement, classroom schedule, teacher instructional strategies) means that more dangerous or problematic child behaviors may emerge. For this reason, the intervention team should reconvene within a short time period to consider whether the identified behaviors are still the most important and whether changes in the previously selected targeted behaviors would likely lead to important current and future child outcomes (e.g., increased peer acceptance; compliance with teacher requests, leading to increased probability for future academic success). In this way, intervention planning is viewed as an ongoing, dynamic process. Although the team should guard against changing a carefully developed plan on the basis of the child's initial reactions, collateral plans may need to be developed to respond to escalating or emerging behaviors. Continuing Tricia's story, which began in Chapter 7, the intervention evaluation process involves a careful involves collection and analysis of data.

> Tricia's team members meet to evaluate the first week of implementing her intervention plan. The plan addresses her hitting and grabbing materials, which occur during Tricia's first few minutes of entering a classroom activity area. The team members have developed an intervention that consists of 1) modeling play entry behaviors, 2) play partnering and making suggestions for play entry, 3) increasing the availability of preferred toys, 4) providing warnings of response–cost for aggressive behaviors, and 5) removing Tricia from the play area after a second incident of aggressive behavior. The teacher and assistant teacher have observed that during the first week, Tricia's aggressive behaviors escalated during group and snack times. The teachers have noted that Tricia hit children who sat close to her during these times and that she grabbed food during snack time. The team members decide that the intervention should be revised to appropriately include snack and group times. The assistant teacher also scaffolds Tricia's transitions to these activities, giving suggestions for appropriate participation and warnings for aggressive behaviors.

ARE THE STEPS FOR INTERVENTION CLEARLY SPECIFIED, AND IS THE PLAN EASY TO UNDERSTAND AND FOLLOW?

In the first postintervention meeting, it is critical to review whether the plan specifies simple, easily understood steps. Each team member should be asked whether he or she encountered any confusion regarding the plan's steps. Team members are encouraged to suggest necessary modifications that have become evident upon the plan's initial implementation. This process allows individuals involved with implementing the plan to compare experiences and suggest revisions. Such clarification gives individuals directly charged with the plan's implementation the opportunity to use consistent language and behavior when interacting with the child.

The streamlined plan may take the form of a detailed intervention script. The scripted intervention can be written as a sequence of steps and duplicated and distributed to all stakeholders involved in the intervention. Barnett, Bell, and Carey (1999) described many advantages to using scripted interventions:

- Detailed understanding of the problem situation
- Ease of incorporating research-based intervention strategies
- The instructional value of teaching caregivers to respond in new ways to familiar problem situations
- The development of self-regulation as the child adopts the intervention's language and strategies
- Improved technical adequacy of intervention design, including the reliability with which the plan is implemented

In addition, peers may become familiar with the intervention script, adopting conventional ways to respond to the child as he or she exhibits the targeted behaviors. Revision and specification is illustrated in Tricia's continuing vignette.

> Tricia's teachers decide to generalize her plan to snack and group times. As a result, the intervention team develops a general action plan that is scripted to include all of the day's transitions and activity periods:
>
> 1. Prepare Tricia for each transition by providing an individual warning (e.g., "Tricia, it's almost snack time; please begin to clean up your play area").
> 2. Approach Tricia at each transition time, and accompany her to the next activity. Model appropriate words and actions to enter the situation (e.g., "I see your name tag between Robert's and Amy's seats at the snack table; let's go see what we're eating today").
> 3. Suggest appropriate play actions and language that Tricia can use during the activity (e.g., "Tricia, Robert has a shirt with a dog on it; tell us about your dog at home").
> 4. Ensure that there are adequate materials to allow access to preferred activities and to reduce waiting time (e.g., delay Tricia's transition to snack time until the table is set and the food is ready to be served).
> 5. Give a warning when Tricia exhibits inappropriate grabbing or hitting behaviors (e.g., "Tricia, I can't let you take food from Amy's plate; if you want more grapes, you can ask for them").

6. Remove Tricia from the activity area upon the second incident of inappropriate behavior (e.g., "Tricia, I can't let you sit at the table when you continue to take food from Amy's plate; you have to sit with the teacher at the next table for the rest of today's snack time").

DO ALL MEMBERS OF THE INTERVENTION TEAM CONSISTENTLY AND CAREFULLY IMPLEMENT THE PLAN?

Carefully developing a scripted intervention plan allows the team members to determine whether the plan is being implemented as originally intended and whether it is being carried out in a consistent and faithful manner across settings and caregivers. This approach has been described as intervention or treatment integrity (Gresham, 1989). Intervention plans that are too complex (i.e., numerous or illogically sequenced steps), or too costly (i.e., require additional personnel, time, or material resources) may be agreed on during the consultation meeting but often are implemented incompletely or infrequently.

Several strategies can increase the probability that the team members will carry out the agreed-on plan. Of greatest importance is collaboration during intervention development. As discussed in Chapter 7, it is critical that all team members have an equal voice in the plan's development. Encouraging stakeholders to contribute their observations and opinions fosters understanding and ownership of the plan's individual components. As a result, they are much more likely to consistently carry out the plan. In addition, involving all individuals in the plan's initial development allows a first check of suggested language and strategies. When the staff members who are responsible for implementing the plan get to read initial drafts, they can rule out words or actions that are artificial or inconsistent with usual instructional strategies and center philosophy.

A second strategy is to ensure that the plan's steps or elements are described in specific, observable, and measurable terms (i.e., operationally defined) (Gresham, MacMillan, Beebe-Frankenberger, & Bocian, 2000). Scheduling a trial run of the intervention plan and reconvening the team for evaluation can allow further planning for glitches that may occur. Once the team has assessed the plan's workability, it is important to continue assessing intervention integrity. Gresham and colleagues suggested counting the number of treatment elements that are implemented and dividing that sum by the total number of elements necessary in a given interaction. For example, Tricia's plan has six elements. If the teacher fails to remove Tricia from the play area after a second incident of aggression but implements the other five components of Tricia's plan, then the plan has 83% (5/6 = 0.83) intervention integrity. The percentage of intervention integrity can be compared with any changes in the child's performance of the targeted variables. This information can simply be checked off on a signed and dated form as often as the plan is implemented.

As an alternative, the teacher and other staff members can use a form to reflect on the classroom day, assessing the implementation of the intervention across the day and the number of steps used. In this manner, the team can assess the level of integrity when determining whether further revisions of the scripted intervention are necessary. In some cases, the teacher, parent, or administrator may choose to observe the manner in which other caregivers implement the plan and then bring these observations to the first evaluation meeting. Assessment of intervention integrity is illustrated in the continuing vignette about Tricia.

> Tricia's teacher is interested in monitoring the progress of the intervention plan. She is particularly interested in knowing whether all of the intervention steps are being used consistently by all staff members and across classroom activities. This information will be used to determine whether changes to the script are necessary. The teacher develops a simple checklist that includes the steps of the intervention with lines for each staff member to check as necessary. The sheet has a place for the staff member to indicate the date and activity during which the intervention strategies are used and the signature or initials of the person interacting with the child. The teacher designates the bottom of the form as a notes section, where the staff member should include anecdotal information about Tricia's behaviors, staff and peer reactions, and any unusual situations that arise. Tricia's teacher clips the checklists to a clipboard, which she then covers and places on a shelf above the children's cubbies. She asks the staff members to note their use of the scripted intervention at each activity period, and she uses these sheets to measure intervention integrity and changes in the targeted behaviors.

Implementing the Steps in Tricia's Plan

Check off the steps used:

1. Prepare Tricia for each transition with an individual warning. _____

2. Accompany Tricia to the next activity during transitions. _____

3. Model appropriate words and actions to enter the next activity, and suggest appropriate play actions and language. _____

4. Ensure that there are adequate materials to allow access to preferred activities and to reduce waiting time. _____

If necessary,

1. Give a warning when Tricia exhibits inappropriate grabbing or hitting. _____

2. Remove Tricia from the activity area upon the second incident of inappropriate behavior. _____

Date: _____   Activity: _____
Team member signature: _____
Steps needed: ____   Steps actually implemented: ____

Notes (briefly describe the situation):

CLASSROOM APPLICATION

Is the intervention plan feasible?

Did all the staff members have input during the plan's creation?

Are any revisions necessary after the first week of intervention?

Are the previously selected target behaviors still the most appropriate choices?

Have the problem situations been clearly defined?

Are the plan's steps operationally defined and arranged logically?

Can steps be deleted if they are not being used because the child's behavior is improving?

Do all team members understand how to implement the agreed-on strategies?

Are all elements being implemented, as necessary, on a consistent basis?

Are all staff members recording data on the plan's use and information about child behaviors to facilitate evaluation of the efficacy of the plan?

IS THE PLAN ACCEPTABLE TO ALL STAKEHOLDERS?

For staff members and parents who are involved directly with the child, the question of acceptability should have been addressed during initial team meetings. As a part of the collaborative intervention planning, the facilitator can informally poll the individual team members regarding the acceptability of the plan's individual elements. This can be accomplished verbally or through the use of a Likert-type questionnaire (Fawcett, 1991) with ratings from 1 to 5 evaluating the team member's comfort with the plan's individual components (e.g., How comfortable are you with this step? How easy is it to carry out this step?).

Caregiver opinions about the appropriateness or acceptability of the plan may change once it is actually put into place. Wolf (1978) discussed the importance of assessing the social validity of any intervention plan by interviewing the stakeholders involved in its implementation. He described the process of evaluating social validity as 1) identifying the value of intervention goals, 2) assessing the social appropriateness of intervention strategies, and 3) measuring the significance of changes resulting from intervention plans. Schwartz and Baer (1991) further described social validity in relation to the acceptability or viability of an intervention plan. Interconnected with intervention integrity, social validity may determine the extent to which caregivers and other stakeholders "buy into" the plan and consistently carry it out. Plans that are too costly in terms of effort, time, or comfort level and familiarity with strategies may be deemed unacceptable, thereby reducing intervention integrity. Unexpected caregiver behaviors also may indicate that the goals or instructional strategies are unacceptable. Schwartz and Baer stated that these behaviors may include complaints to other staff members outside team meetings, poor attendance or persistent tardiness, negative mood or attitude, and a general lack of expressed enthusiasm for the intervention plan and the overall program.

Schwartz (1999) suggested that team members question the clarity, significance, and general acceptability of the intervention's goals and objectives, strategies, and outcomes. The team should have come to a consensus on the changes that are expected in child behavior in response to the intervention plan. As the scripted plan is initiated and child behavior changes are monitored, the team has a chance to reevaluate the importance and acceptability of these goals and objectives.

Similarly, as the plan is put into place, teachers and other caregivers have an opportunity to evaluate the acceptability of the strategies that are being used (Wolery & Winterling, 1997). Caregivers may discover that the plan calls for skills that the child does not possess or relies on consequences that are not reinforcing for the child (Feldman & Griffiths, 1997). Kazdin (2001) described several factors that affect the acceptability of the strategies used: 1) the exact manner in which the strategy is applied; 2) the individual caregiver using the strategy; 3) the severity of the problem behavior that the strategy targets; 4) the number of strategies that have been previously attempted and proven ineffective in addressing the problem situation; 5) the effectiveness of the strategy in changing the problem situation; and 6) the sensitivity with which the team considers the interests, values, and lifestyles of all stakeholders. In addition, possible side effects of the intervention should be analyzed (Barnett, Bell, & Carey, 1999; Reimers, Wacker, & Koeppl, 1987).

Finally, teachers and caregivers can evaluate the significance of the plan's actual outcomes, not only for the child but also for the child's peers, the teachers and staff, and the parents. Kazdin (2001) referred to the importance of these outcomes as *clinical significance,* or the extent to which all stakeholders agree that the results are meaningful and have made a difference in the child's daily life. The assessment of social validity is described as an interactive process, one in which the scripted plan is continually evaluated and revised based on caregiver feedback (Finney, 1991). The overall goal is to design the most cost-effective and least restrictive procedure that will accomplish change in an acceptable manner (Barnett, Bell, & Carey, 1999; Kazdin, 2001).

It is possible for many individuals in the early childhood setting to be affected by implementation of a scripted intervention plan. Peers in the child's classroom, peers in nearby classrooms, teachers who are not directly involved with the child, administrative personnel, and the parents of children enrolled in the child's classroom or surrounding classrooms may have an opportunity to observe the plan's implementation. The intervention team should devote time to developing an explanation of the special circumstances necessitating the use of the scripted plan. This explanation should balance the obvious need for confidentiality surrounding individual child situations with the need for other teachers, staff, children, and the parents of other children (i.e., those individuals not specifically involved in intervention planning) to understand a staff member's use of extraordinary instructional strategies (e.g., time-out, physical restraint). A general explanation of the center's policy around planning to meet the unique needs of individual children should suffice. Tricia's story illustrates methods for handling intervention acceptability or social validity.

Tricia's lead teacher acts as the team facilitator. She makes an effort to talk with every staff member who has implemented the intervention plan regarding the continuing acceptability of its steps. She telephones Tricia's parents weekly with updates about Tricia's response to the plan, asking questions about their continued comfort with the intervention strategies.

Tricia's teacher also wants to make sure that everyone understands the purpose of the scripted intervention plan and is comfortable with the plan's individual components. She approaches the center administrator to ask whether there is a section in the parent handbook dealing with individual interventions. As there is no such section, the center administrator determines that it would be important to add pages on this topic. The administrator selects several teachers and parents and asks if they would like to write this new section of the handbook. In the meantime, Tricia's teacher and the other intervention team members decide to respond to questions about Tricia's plan with the following explanation: "We are doing this to help Tricia learn to be a better friend while she is in our classroom."

CLASSROOM APPLICATION

Is the intervention plan acceptable?

Did the facilitator poll the team members regarding the acceptability of the goals and objectives as well as of the individual instructional strategies?

Following initial implementation of the plan, do the goals and strategies remain acceptable to all stakeholders?

Are the changes in child behaviors important?

Are there any unintended side effects for the child, the child's parents, other children, or staff members involved in the intervention?

Regarding the use of extraordinary instructional strategies, does the team have an agreed-on explanation for individuals who are not directly involved in the intervention (e.g., the parents and teachers of other children at the center)?

IS THE PLAN IMPROVING THE TARGETED BEHAVIOR?

Intervention decision making should be driven by data—that is, specific information regarding the identified behaviors, which is collected in an organized fashion (Barnett, Bell, & Carey, 1999; Jackson & Panyan, 2002). Initiating a functional assessment of antecedent and consequential classroom characteristics; collecting baseline information on the severity, intensity, or duration of identified child behaviors; and continuing to collect information following the implementation of the intervention plan allow the team members to assess intervention strategy effectiveness. One way to depict data visually is to use a graph of the information collected during the assessment period (baseline) and compare it with changes that occur after the intervention has been implemented.

Miltenberger (2001) described the use of a graph to depict changes in behavior over time. He identified six graph components that can be used to summarize important aspects of the intervention process:

1. The *Y* (vertical) axis is used to label the observed characteristics of the identified behavior.

2. The *X* (horizontal) axis is the measurement of time and, by convention, is approximately twice as long as the *Y* axis.

3. Data points indicate the intersection of the measurement of the identified behavior and the time observed.

4. Numbers placed along the *Y* axis indicate the specific type of measurement used (e.g., frequency, rate, percentage).

5. Phase lines separate data collected during the baseline and subsequent intervention phase(s).

6. Phase labels mark the important elements of each phase (i.e., baseline, intervention, revised intervention).

After capturing important information on the intervention graph, the team can determine whether the scripted plan is as effective as anticipated. This can be assessed by comparing characteristics of the child's behaviors during baseline with those of the initial and subsequent intervention phases. Kazdin (2001) suggested calculating means or averages of measurements during the baseline and intervention phases to observe differences or visually inspecting changes in the slope or level of the line connecting the data points within and between phases (i.e., one line is drawn to connect the data points in each phase). If changes are not obvious during the first intervention phase, this phase can serve as a new baseline for subsequent intervention revisions (Barnett, Bell, & Carey, 1999). Measures of intervention integrity and social validity can be co-plotted with changes in the identified child behaviors (Ehrhardt, Barnett, Lentz, Stollar, & Reifen, 1996). Visual depiction of baseline and intervention data is illustrated in Tricia's story.

> Tricia's teacher wants to summarize the information from the baseline phase, the first intervention phase, and the revised intervention phase (extended to snack and group times). She collects the data sheets that the teachers have completed, then chooses to graph Tricia's hitting and grabbing of materials during the baseline and intervention phases. The teacher plans to supplement the group discussion during the next intervention team meeting with a visual image of Tricia's behavior during the previous 3 weeks. The graph plots a frequency count of Tricia's hitting and grabbing across the three phases.

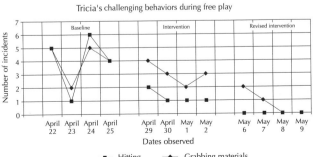

CLASSROOM APPLICATION

Is the intervention plan effective?

Was information about the identified child behaviors collected during the baseline and intervention phases?

Has this information been summarized in a manner that will allow decision making by the intervention team?

Has the average occurrence (arithmetic mean) of measured behaviors been calculated during the baseline and intervention phases, and have these data been compared?

OR

Have the observed behaviors been graphed across phases, and have the slope and level of the lines connecting the data points been compared within and between phases? Has the intervention integrity data been co-plotted?

CAN THE PLAN BE CARRIED FORWARD, AND IS IT COST-EFFECTIVE?

As mentioned previously, some plans may be very effective but too costly for the intervention team to continue. Plans that necessitate additional staff coverage, require extraordinary material resources, or tax the classroom teacher's time may be too complex to maintain over a long period of time. The intervention team should examine ways to manipulate available resources (e.g., change classroom schedules to accommodate the use of "floater" staff members in classrooms) and assess the intervention plan's most effective elements, thereby allowing the team to cut costly, less important components.

DOES THE PLAN NEED FURTHER REVISION?

The answer to this question is almost always "yes." In addition to revisions for cost-effectiveness (i.e., trimming the plan to its essential components), the team may be interested in extending the scripted intervention to other child behaviors or settings. The team may modify the plan yet again when examining intervention integrity or acceptability information. Teachers, parents, or administrators may determine that the strategies, although effective, are too emotionally costly to the child or to the staff members implementing the plan. Finally, as the problem situation shifts in response to intervention strategies, the team may determine that it is necessary to target other problem situations, necessitating a complete reassessment and script development.

WHICH PROCEDURES ARE SPECIFIED FOR FADING OR DISCONTINUING THE PLAN?

Whether revisions are made on the basis of acceptability, integrity, or effectiveness issues, the team must develop procedures for fading (i.e., gradually using fewer components of the plan or using it less frequently) and eventually discontinuing the intervention plan. As mentioned in Chapter 1, the eventual goal is for the child to regulate his or her own behavior. This goal requires specific planning for revisions of intervention scripts to intentionally teach the child how to monitor and modify his or her behavior. The teacher might introduce a correspondence training or say-do element, whereby the child plans what to do in a specific activity center and then reviews his or her behavior in the area with the teacher during transitions (Baer, Williams, Osnes, & Stokes, 1985). The teacher might also scaffold reinforcement opportunities for the child to reward appropriate choices. Again, this requires the intervention team to determine when teacher support has brought the child's behavior to peer levels (Bell & Barnett, 1999) and when a plan revision, including measures for self-monitoring and self-regulation, is indicated. Another possibility to increase expectations of appropriate child behavior is to change the criterion for success (Kazdin, 2001). The intervention team might require increasing levels of appropriate behavior (e.g., raising the criterion for reinforcement from 5 minutes to 8 minutes of rule-governed and appropriate participation during group time).

WHAT IS THE TEAM'S NEXT STEP?

In some situations, the intervention team must face that the intervention plan, as specified, has no demonstrable effect on the child's behavior within the classroom. In this case, the intervention team should reconvene to take another look at the problem situation. This examination might identify elements left unaddressed by the previous intervention. Perhaps the challenges are far beyond the knowledge base and expertise of the center's administration, teachers, and staff. At this point, the intervention team should determine the need for further evaluation and support and be prepared to provide the parents with information regarding appropriate community resources. These resources might provide fresh insight and additional personnel to conduct more complex interventions within the current early childhood setting (see Chapter 10 for more details). When the team members exhaust all available resources, they sometimes have to make the difficult decision that the child might be better served in another early childhood setting. This decision must be predicated on an assessment of the safety and well-being of all the children enrolled in the program, including the child with challenging behaviors. In any event, it is incumbent on the intervention team to provide referral and support information to parents of any child whose program enrollment is terminated.

CONCLUSION

The purpose of this chapter has been to discuss methods for assessing intervention plan effectiveness. The chapter has introduced strategies for evaluating the impact of the intervention on identified child behaviors and for using this information to revise, fade, or discontinue the intervention. The team facilitator is encouraged to assess the acceptability of the intervention strategies and the integrity with which the plan is implemented (i.e., the consistency and fidelity with which the steps are used) before abandoning the plan and starting anew. The intervention team may be able to fine-tune the strategies and make a good plan even better—and more likely to be carried out with enthusiasm.

Chapter 9

Planning for Crises

Victoria Carr, Helene Arbouet Harte,
and Louise R. Phillips

The creation of a comprehensive crisis response system has become critical since the September 11, 2001, terrorist attacks on the United States. The intensity of that disaster puts classroom crises in perspective; however, smaller crises occur far more frequently and must not be overlooked. Daily stressors can wear down staff enough that they may react inappropriately to both internal and external crises. Examples of such stressors include having an irate adult enter the classroom and disrupt the classroom activity, participating in an unexpected fire drill, or—even worse—actually experiencing a fire or other real-life disaster.

Miller (1996) wrote a manual for early childhood teachers facing classroom crises as well as other difficult situations in the lives of young children. Miller asserted that situations involving illness, divorce, child abuse, poverty, homelessness, prejudice, and natural disasters are all crises that parallel behavior management crises in terms of demanding an immediate, although carefully considered, teacher response. Early childhood centers must have policies and procedures in place to address such crises. In addition, these policies should address predictable daily events that place undue stress on a classroom. Whereas some events are unprecedented, teachers are keenly aware that children who exhibit challenging behaviors often instigate frequent, somewhat predictable crises. Continued stress from daily occurrences of behavioral challenges can lead to teacher burnout and feelings of incompetence (Miller, 1996).

Helping children build coping skills that reduce incidents of inappropriate behavior is the primary goal for teachers who use positive guidance (Gartrell, 1997). Yet, guidance is important for the center staff, too, as staff members address situations that constitute crises in the classroom. This chapter explores the tenets of a centerwide crisis intervention plan within the context of assisting children develop the self-regulatory skills needed for success in the early childhood classroom environment. The chapter discusses how to guide children objectively, promote self-regulation, and plan for and adapt to crises—including ways to address child behavior and engage parents. An appendix at the end of the chapter presents a particular program's behavior management policy to illustrate planning for crises that involve challenging behaviors.

HOW CAN TEACHERS GUIDE CHILDREN OBJECTIVELY AND PROMOTE SELF-REGULATION?

Many children engage in challenging behaviors at some point during their development. As discussed in previous chapters, most children's behaviors can be addressed by using positive guidance strategies, but some children do not respond to strategies typically associated with early childhood education settings. The Division for Early Childhood (DEC) concept paper on challenging behaviors stated that adults must explore their own beliefs and emotions regarding behaviors such as cursing or hurting others and respond to these behaviors objectively (Brault et al., 1999). Developing a centerwide plan for crisis response and intervention is critical for addressing these behaviors objectively. Otherwise, adults may get caught up in the emotional moment and respond to children without objective regard to the reason for (i.e., the form and function of) the exhibited behavior. In addition, even when a specific intervention plan is in place, children with challenging behaviors can present safety concerns for themselves and others. Realistically, even with great vigilance by adults, children can and often do hurt themselves and others.

In the preschool years, children begin to use language to control action and thought (Berk & Winsler, 1995; Luria, 1961; Vygotsky, 1962). They are much more capable of controlling their behavior than when they were toddlers and are increasingly expected to regulate their emotions and behaviors appropriately as they develop clear and conscious goals (Bronson, 2000). Therefore, as discussed in previous chapters, teachers must attend to the form and function of a challenging behavior to deal with a problem situation effectively (Neilsen, Olive, Donovan, & McEvoy, 1999; Reichle & Wacker, 1993). Considering that the function generally falls into one of two general areas—obtaining something desirable or avoiding something undesirable—teachers must be aware of the intended purpose of a child's behavior to react appropriately. For example, Neilsen and colleagues suggested that throwing an object (form) may be a purposeful strategy for hearing the sound it makes (one possible function) or for expressing anger (another possible function). A functional analysis (described in Chapter 6) helps determine the specific function of the behavior, but the teacher's response can keep the behavior from escalating into a crisis. Consequently, whenever a child risks hurting him- or herself or another person, a crisis is imminent.

When a child has language and communication skills typical for his or her age, teachers are better able to address crisis situations. For a child who has language and communication delays, additional techniques or adaptations must be used to help the child understand which behaviors are appropriate. Furthermore, when a child is frustrated, upset, or crying, the sound of an adult's voice is generally just noise. Self-control may be out of the question at that moment. Yet, self-regulation is the teaching and intervention goal, even in a crisis situation.

Bronson (2000) asserted that emotional regulation and the ability to use specific social skills or strategies effectively requires 1) the inhibition of inappropriate behaviors and 2) a positive self-directed approach to the selection and use of appropriate behaviors. Teachers and parents support this journey for children through modeling and using authoritative methods of guidance (Baumrind, 1967; Katz & McClellan, 1997). In essence, authoritative teachers or parents demand that children follow set rules and limits that are developmentally appropriate but respond respectfully to children, communicating appropriate reasons for these rules and limits. Adults also must model the desired behaviors, as children observe and imitate both appropriate and inappropriate behavior. Social learning theorists argue that adults must reinforce children's appropriate responses (Bandura, 1977), whereas cognitive-developmental theorists assume that children construct knowledge about appropriate behaviors by attending to and interrelating multiple aspects of situations in which social conflicts arise (Berk, 1997). Both perspectives attribute the following to the learning of self-regulation: 1) the exhibition of prosocial behavior, 2) the mastery of skills needed to successfully interact with others in a social environment, and 3) the acquisition of adult desired behaviors within specific community settings, including the early childhood classroom. Children with challenging behaviors may not have constructed this understanding desired by community members. The balanced use of teacher strategies within the classroom setting (i.e., authentic encouragement and reinforcement) promotes a community of learners that supports children who have challenging behaviors. Therefore, it is appropriate for teachers to note for children incidents of successful interactions and conflict resolution as well as to use reinforcement for prosocial behaviors in the classroom (Bredekamp & Copple, 1997).

Early childhood educators must be cognizant of their interaction styles, their abilities to implement an interesting integrative curriculum, the appropriateness of their guidance strategies, and their understanding of child development theory. In the early childhood years, children shift toward self-regulation within an environment that provides choices and limits, so prevention in terms of routine and a prepared environment (detailed in Chapters 4 and 5) is critical to the development of self-regulation. Most children will be successful within such an environment, particularly if teachers have modeled appropriate behaviors, encouraged prosocial behavior among the children, and authentically reinforced desired behaviors within the classroom. Nevertheless, the disruption of the environment due to challenging behaviors constitutes a crisis.

CLASSROOM APPLICATION

Are the following areas addressed to guide children objectively and foster self-regulation?

Is the classroom curriculum well defined?

Is self-regulation inherent and emphasized in the curriculum?

|| Are children encouraged to problem-solve, or does the teacher solve their problems for them?

|| Does the teacher understand how to scaffold prosocial development?

HOW CAN EDUCATORS PLAN AHEAD OR ADAPT PLANS FOR CRISES?

Teachers are typically hired in accordance with licensing laws, particularly with regard to teacher–child ratios. As discussed in Chapter 2, early childhood program directors must recognize that to fully include children with challenging behaviors, additional staff may be needed. When teachers are developing a curriculum and planning for its implementation, they must consider these staffing ratios. It is possible to plan a richer curriculum when staffing ratios are conducive to facilitating children's development and alleviating the undue stress caused by the behaviors of one or two children. Teachers and administrators must consider this point when planning curriculum to meet federal and state outcome mandates.

Following the assignment of assistants and additional staff to individual classrooms, and thereby guided by the number of adults in the classroom, teachers should plan curricular activities that lead to positive outcomes for children. One of the greatest mistakes teachers make, often precipitating crises in the classroom, is failing to modify the lesson plan when expected staff members are absent. If activities and/or specific children require the assistance of three adults and only two staff members are present, an alternate plan of action must be implemented. This prevents loss of control due to a lack of supervision for activities and/or children. Otherwise, the original curricular activity, carefully planned by the teacher, may go awry. For example, on days when a staff member is absent, teachers should provide materials that require little adult management (e.g., playdough). The following teacher strategies may prevent a crisis:

- Restructuring the lesson plan to minimize transitions
- Reducing the need to prepare materials for an activity
- Closing off areas of the classroom
- Positioning staff for extra supervision

Certainly, even with such proactive strategies in place, a child can punch, bite, kick, or pull the hair of another child before an adult can intervene. Yet, if planning has not occurred for a staff member's absence, the adults are less prepared to address these disruptive and hurtful behaviors. Thus, planning ahead for known staffing patterns and adapting for unexpected absences creates a less stressful environment for teaching staff. Although adequate prevention is the key to avoiding crises, situations do arise, and a plan of action should be in place for meeting the challenge of a crisis in the classroom.

Develop a Crisis Management Plan

Early childhood program staff and administration must agree on a plan for addressing behaviors that challenge classroom integrity or harm the child or others. A team of teachers and administrators should dedicate a sufficient amount of time to discussing the program's strengths and weaknesses before creating a plan. It is up to teachers and administrators to supply information that is guided by theory and based on research translated into practice. Discussion of the following issues is of paramount importance: appropriate proactive guidance strategies, reactive strategies, policies on child restraint, and information about working collaboratively with parents and other staff members. Often, however, situation-specific crises that occur within programs need individualized plans.

Barnett (1999) suggested that a crisis intervention plan should address three issues: 1) the teacher's immediate actions with the child (or children), 2) ways to contact and engage parents, and 3) the center's policies regarding the use of child restraint. It also is important to develop a system for obtaining help in the classroom should a crisis occur. The following vignette illustrates a crisis situation precipitated by challenging behavior.

> Zoe, age 4, recently enrolled in Fanny's preschool classroom. During Fanny's home visit before Zoe's first day of class, Zoe sits on her mother's lap and watches television while her mother talks to Fanny. Her mother directs Zoe to speak to Fanny, but Zoe is glued to the television and she does not comply with her mother's directives. She then squirms off her mother's lap and sits closer to the television for the rest of the visit.
>
> Even though Zoe's mother says that Zoe sometimes "gets wild," Zoe is quiet and seemingly observant the first day she attends preschool. Fanny attempts to engage her in activities throughout the day. On the second day, Zoe successfully participates in the dramatic play area, which is set up as a post office. Fanny facilitates positive interactions between Zoe and Janelle while they are "writing" post cards to their parents. After Fanny moves across the room to assist another child, Zoe screams, "Get off my letter!" and pushes Janelle into the post office letter slots, knocking over the counter where she and Janelle are writing. Apparently, Zoe dropped her post card and Janelle stepped on it by accident. Zoe begins yelling, "I hate you!" to Janelle, who is crying and holding her head in pain.

Although the actions in the previous scenario may not exactly match incidents in every classroom, similar incidents occur in many early childhood settings. Panic frequently sets in, and the teachers hurry across the classroom to comfort and talk to the children. Too often, teachers attend to the perpetrator (e.g., Zoe) while the hurt child (e.g., Janelle) stands by crying and perhaps feeling ignored. It is important to address the hurt child first. Surely, the entire room has been disrupted and teacher levels of anxiety have been raised. However, planning for a crisis includes learning to remain calm externally even if one is feeling anxiety. Teachers must model composure for children and assist children through each crisis.

Follow the Initial Plan for Addressing a Crisis

A procedure for initially addressing a situation should include the following steps:

1. Ensure that the hurt child does not need medical attention. Obtain medical attention if necessary.

2. Use developmentally appropriate language to ask about the injury while assessing it.

3. Comfort the hurt child by remaining close and using a warm tone of voice. Encircle the child with one arm while keeping the perpetrator in the general vicinity through the use of verbal requests or a gentle hold. When two staff members are present (i.e., the best case scenario), one staff member can attend to the victim while the other addresses the perpetrator. However, it is important for the perpetrator to realize that another child has been hurt. The initial conversation should be limited, just acknowledging that the victim is upset and that the incident will be discussed as soon as he or she is calm.

4. Use conflict resolution strategies as soon as both children are calm.

Steps for Conflict Resolution

In a similar fashion, Wittmer and Honig (1994) suggested five basic steps for conflict resolution:

1. *Initiate mediation:* After stopping the aggressive behavior and ensuring that the victim does not need medical attention, maintain neutrality and make a statement about what occurred.

2. *Define the problem:* Restate or paraphrase what the children say has happened and/or help them identify their feelings. Facilitate agreement on the problem between the two children.

3. *Generate alternative solutions:* Facilitate suggestions for resolving the problem in a different manner. Observers can sometimes be included in this part of the resolution process.

4. *Agree on a solution:* Work with the children individually to reach an agreement on how to resolve the problem. Restate the solution that each child accepts.

5. *Follow through:* Observe each child carefully to ensure he or she is participating in the agreed-on solution. Teachers can bring closure to the incident by acknowledging that the problem has been resolved.

Sometimes, conflict resolution happens rather quickly. In the previously described vignette, if Zoe accepts that Janelle did not step on her letter intentionally, she may agree to use more appropriate strategies in the future (e.g., ask someone to step off her work without pushing or shoving). However, it is possible that the scenario would not be resolved in this manner, particularly because Zoe is a new child in the classroom. For this type of problem-solving process to be successful, 1) children need to trust the facilitator; 2) time needs to be taken to work through the situation without rushing; 3) all stakeholders in the problem-solving process must be able to engage in the process without being too upset, sick, tired, or hungry; and 4) participants must possess the basic communication skills that are necessary for working through the issue (Daigre, Johnson, Bauer, & Anania Smith, 1998). If this process is not effective, then the teacher must implement an alternative plan.

Follow Alternative Steps for Addressing a Crisis

When the previously described suggestions are not effective in defusing the crisis, an alternate plan should be specified as standard practice. If Janelle needs medical attention, for instance, this takes precedence over conflict resolution. The teacher needs to ensure that immediate medical intervention is provided, either in the classroom or in the office of a designated individual (e.g., school nurse). Thus, a plan for obtaining help must be predetermined by teaching staff and administrators. Optimally, more than one teacher is in the room. This allows the other teacher to assume sole responsibility for the class until the teacher who is attending to the hurt child returns or until someone else can assist in the room. However, the teacher may need to seek help from a colleague, particularly if the child with challenging behavior cannot calm down—a situation that contributes to a continuing sense of crisis. In this event, changing the adult who is attending to that child sometimes helps to calm the child.

Communication and Availability of Help

An alternative plan for conflict resolution assumes the availability of additional staff. The teacher must be able to summon someone to assist immediately. The installation of intercoms, telephones, cellular phones, or some other form of electronic communication is critical in emergency situations. Without such devices, teachers feel isolated, more at risk, and less able to handle a crisis situation effectively. In a pinch, another child can be sent with a request for help to teachers in adjacent classrooms. This is not an optimal solution, however, because it places a child unattended in the hallway and thereby presents another opportunity for potential problems. Thus, if there are not multiple staff members in the classroom, the alternative must contain procedures for obtaining help from someone outside the classroom. The center-designated method must be made known to all staff. These procedures must be reviewed each school year so that teachers know that they have a plan for summoning help. This plan should be as simple as possible and may include a few code words if necessary.

Child Restraint

After assessing injury and summoning help, if needed, the alternative plan addresses the child behaviors related to the crisis. If the child continues to express his or her anger physically (e.g., pushing over shelves, slamming items), the teacher must address these inappropriate behaviors in a way that ensures the safety of everyone in the classroom—including the child. This part of the plan may include restraint so the child does not hurt him- or herself, the teacher and staff, or other children. Programs must have written policies on restraining children and a rationale for when restraint might be used. The plan should state clearly that when restraint is part of an intervention, parental permission (i.e., informed consent) must be obtained. Furthermore, teachers must participate in training sessions to learn appropriate restraint techniques. Teachers who use child restraint should do so to help the child calm down, using a soothing voice and a gentle, firm hold and letting the crisis pass so that conflict resolution strategies may proceed. It is critical to help the child return to a point of classroom participation where he or she once again has choices and control over his or her environment. Parents should be notified any time that restraint is used, and teachers should document the events that occur before, during, and after the incident requiring restraint. (See the appendix at the end of this chapter for an example policy with further references to restraining children.)

Contact the Child's Parents

Policies for contacting parents should be part of the center procedures manual for managing challenging behaviors in the classroom. Program administration and teachers first must decide who will contact parents and in which situations they should be contacted. Often, the teacher is the first to share details about a crisis with the parents. Most parents do not want to hear negative news about their children, so the contact person should take care not to project blame but, rather, to emphasize the center's interest in creating a plan to solve the problem together. Therefore, engaging parents as partners in the educational process is parallel to engaging parents as partners in solving classroom challenges. In the vignette about Zoe, the teacher (Fanny) had just completed a home visit, during which Zoe's mother mentioned how wild her daughter could be. This certainly provides an opening for Fanny when approaching Zoe's mother. For example, Fanny might say, "You had mentioned that Zoe can get wild sometimes. In the classroom today, I observed the behaviors that might be what you were talking about." This opening might raise some anxiety, but it is clearly communicating that Fanny respects the mother's view of the behaviors that Zoe exhibits, thereby linking the situation to information from the home visit and using the mother's words. Fanny can elaborate from that point, describing the incident in the classroom, how it was handled, and how Zoe responded. Fanny and Zoe's mother can then plan future contact or meetings to discuss the development of an intervention plan, if warranted.

Most parents want to cooperate, but some present challenges. For example, when teachers describe inappropriate behaviors in the classroom, parents may say that the child does not engage in that behavior at home. It certainly may be true that those behaviors are not observed at home but only when children must vie for toys and share adult attention. However, indications of challenging behaviors frequently do occur within the home. As discussed in Chapter 3, collaborating with parents to develop strategies that move the child toward self-regulation works very well when relationships are established and communication is generally positive.

CLASSROOM APPLICATION

Have the following steps been taken to plan ahead or adapt plans for crises?

Has a basic crisis management plan been developed? Does this plan include steps for conflict resolution and address communication issues and the availability of help?

Have alternative steps been formulated for times when the initial plan is unsuccessful?

Are guidelines for using child restraint included?

Have plans been made for when and how to contact parents regarding a crisis situation?

CONCLUSION

An initial crisis plan provides direction for dealing with a crisis situation in the classroom. An alternative plan provides direction for obtaining outside help and/or calming a child who is unable to exhibit self-control to the extent that safety is jeopardized. The more specific the center-developed plans are, the more competent teachers feel about their abilities to handle crises. It also is critical that parents are made aware of challenging situations that have or have not been resolved. As discussed in Chapters 3 and 7, partnering with parents is the first step in developing an intervention plan.

To summarize and provide additional information about planning for crises, a written plan is included in the appendix to this chapter. It is an example of how one early childhood program collaborated with stakeholders—including parents, teachers, mental health and disabilities staff, university personnel, and other health professionals—to develop a behavior management policy that assisted in planning for crises and coping with challenging behaviors in the early childhood setting. It is an excellent example of how various aspects of positive child guidance are emphasized to facilitate a hierarchy of responses beginning with the least restrictive intervention.

Chapter 9 Appendix

Example Policy
for Guidance
on Behavior Issues

Cincinnati-Hamilton County Community
Action Agency (C-HCCAA) Head Start

C-HCCAA Head Start recognizes that Positive Guidance is an essential component of early childhood education. Classroom environments will incorporate positive guidance into day-to-day practice to promote child development while assuring safety and support. In the classroom setting, behavioral challenges need proactive responses provided by qualified, capable adults. Individualized strategies will be created with input from the child/family and interdisciplinary educational team. Positive guidance practices will assure a hierarchy of responses, which start with the *least restrictive intervention*. Efforts will focus on reinforcing desirable behaviors and extinguishing undesirable behaviors. Special attention will be given to protect the rights of the individual, foster appropriate expression of feelings and meet the unique needs of each child.

Child guidance techniques are an important tool for the teacher of preschool children. Many developmental tasks in this stage of development are linked to behavior and impulse control issues. Therefore, a primary task of caregivers is to assist the children in learning how to appropriately express feelings and get needs met in an acceptable manner. At

---

From Cincinnati-Hamilton County Community Action Agency Head Start. (2000). *Positive guidance policy.* Cincinnati, OH: Author; reprinted by permission. (These guidelines were based on Vanderwert, M., & Carlson, A. [1997]. *Child guidance task force: Ramsey Action Programs, Inc.—Head Start child guidance policies and procedures.* St. Louis: Ramsey Actions Programs, Inc.)

C-HCCAA Head Start our goal is to model, encourage and guide the behavior of children within the classroom. An additional goal is enabling them to develop healthy peer relationships, an internal set of behavior controls and to support parents in their role as primary teachers of their children.

The following policies and procedures have been developed by a task force of Head Start staff and parents and are intended to serve as a guide and resource to all C-HCCAA Head Start Staff in supporting the families we serve. The techniques presented will be used consistently throughout the program. Staff, as individuals, will need to deal with their own personal feelings about behavior management and resolve any difficulties they might have so that the policies are consistently used in the program. Staff training and support services are available to help facilitate this.

In C-HCCAA Head Start the person responsible for a child's care is as follows:

- On the bus going to and from the Head Start site, the bus driver is the person primarily responsible for the child's care.
- When the child has been delivered to the site, the teaching staff is responsible for the child's care. This responsibility extends until the time the child is picked up by the child's parent, guardian or the Head Start bus drivers.
- Any other professionals working with the children are asked to check in with the teaching staff before taking the child from the group and to check them back in when the session is completed.
- In addition, it is the responsibility of *all staff* to ensure that *all children* enrolled or associated with our program are safe and supervised at all times.

A. LEVEL ONE GUIDANCE TECHNIQUES

All staff and parents need to be positive behavioral coaches at all times for all children. Staff consistency is very important. That is, if "ignoring" is the plan for a particular behavior, ALL STAFF must ignore according to the plan.

1. *Positive Modeling:* Staff will model behavior that is consistent with the behavior that is expected from the children at all times. For example, if children are expected to speak in a quiet voice, the teacher will not yell to get the children's attention, but will use a firm quiet voice. This extends to any interactions that a child may witness, including interactions between staff members, volunteers and any other persons present in the center. It may be necessary at times for the adult to set up a role-play or a demonstration of appropriate behavior for a child. The child can attend to what is being modeled, i.e. she may say, "Watch how I ask to use that toy."

2. *Developmental Appropriateness:* Staff will use techniques that are appropriate for all of the children with whom they work. Some appropriate teaching techniques include:

    - Redirect child to another acceptable activity;
    - Give child a choice of two or more acceptable activities;
    - Give descriptive feedback of desirable behaviors without placing any value judgments on the behavior to promote the child's ability to own behavior;

- Give encouragement and reinforcement for desirable behavior;
- Discuss child's feelings and help the child with words to express these feelings;
- Explain expected behavior to children and provide immediate, consistent and related consequences for a child's unacceptable behavior;
- Establish routines and rituals that make the day predictable. Use the same words to introduce new activities and use the modeling to match the words. Begin and end each day in the same way;
- Anticipate and eliminate potential problems by creating a room arrangement that is conducive to a child's self-control;
- Ensure that children and staff have an environment and activities that are safe and accessible so there are no areas that are "off limits";
- Plan the daily schedule so as to allow the children a successful mixture of choice and structure;
- Plan adequate time, space and materials daily for gross motor play and energy release either indoors or outdoors;
- Ignore attention-getting behavior, when appropriate.

In addition, activities planned for children at C-HCCAA Head Start must be developmentally appropriate—and interesting. The session should have a minimum of transitions in the day, have adequate materials, and be child directed whenever possible. One cause of behavior problems in children is frustration when they are not capable of performing tasks that are assigned because they are not developmentally appropriate.

Another crucial factor in avoiding conflict in the classroom is to provide adequate supervision. Adults must be strategically positioned in the classroom. There is to be no more than one teacher-directed activity underway in the classroom at a time. This allows one staff to supervise the activity while the second staff person acts as a "floater." The floater is responsible for spotting potential conflicts and helping children resolve the issue before conflict occurs.

3. *Use of Attention to Teach:* Pre-school children are naturally wiggly and can be non-conforming at times. When appropriate, pay attention to the positive activities that are present in the room and not to the child's negative behavior. This is effective when a child refuses to join the group or comply with a request but is not disruptive or unsafe. Simply state that the child is always welcome to join in and then give attention to those who are participating. When it is known that a child's behavior tends to escalate in this situation, this technique will not be effective and another strategy will be chosen.

4. *Verbal Intervention (Teaching Techniques):* A number of verbal techniques can be used to guide children's behavior including:

- Setting clear expectations at the beginning of the year with rule reminders as needed
- Arranging compromises (Example: A child is not listening to a story. The teacher states, "As soon as we read the story, we can go to the playroom.")
- Positive rewards for behavior such as: "The quietest child will be the leader today."
- Discussion of the consequences of behavior with other children as in, "Tell Johnny how it made you feel when he took your toy."

5. *Physical Intervention (Teaching Techniques):* Some physical techniques can be used to guide children who do not catch the verbal cues including:

   • Provide physical proximity to teacher by moving next to child, holding child's hand companionably, allowing child to sit on lap, or placing hand lightly on child's shoulder;
   • Positive replacement of behavior by asking child to play with teacher, to accomplish a task or hold a position of responsibility for the teacher;
   • Modeling of appropriate behavior: Show children what they are to do physically such as in covering mouth to indicate quiet and then praising other children who are being quiet;
   • Removal of dangerous or misused objects or toys until child can agree on and/ or demonstrate appropriate use of that object;
   • Physical calming techniques such as rubbing child's back or forehead, slow rocking, using a soothing voice, firm pressure top to bottom on either side of spinal column;
   • Asking child to choose another area in which to play and watching to be sure that they go to that area;
   • Setting up natural consequences for behavior such as having child pick up objects thrown or dropped or going to the back of the line if unable to wait appropriately.

6. *Physical Management Techniques:*

   • Offering child a choice of appropriate behavior or consequence (Example—Child is spooning cereal on the table instead of eating. "You can eat the cereal or I will have to put the bowl away.")
   • Keeping child from engaging in a favored activity because of a contingency such as, "Children who participate in small group activity may go to the playground." Child does not engage in activity, therefore does not go to the playground.
   • Setting up a method for restitution if another child is involved such as helping other child with a job in the classroom or giving up a toy to that child.

7. *Separation:* Protecting the safety of children and staff is very important. If methods of guiding children's behavior have been unsuccessful and the child's *behavior threatens the safety and well being of others,* separation from the group may be necessary. *Separation must meet the following guidelines:*

   a. The child must be in a part of the classroom where a staff person in the child's assigned room continuously monitors him in an assigned room or in another classroom in the center.
   b. The child's return to the group must be contingent upon the child's stopping or bringing under control the behavior in question.
   c. The child must be returned to the group as soon as the behavior stops or lessens to a degree that the child poses no threat to self or others.
   d. Document any separation. Document the child's name, staff person's name, time, date, what less intrusive methods were tried and how the child's behavior threatened child's own well-being or that of the other children or staff, and how the parent was notified.

e. If a child is separated three (3) or more times in one day, the child's parents will be notified and notation of this will be documented.

f. If a child is separated five (5) or more times in one week, or eight (8) or more times in two (2) weeks, a parent conference must be held and a behavior plan written and followed.

8. *Physical Restraint:* Staff must have received and reviewed procedures through training and practice. ***A signed verification of training hours in restraint techniques on preschool children is required BEFORE any physical restraint is practiced on any Head Start enrollee.*** Sometimes it may become necessary to restrain a child physically to keep him/her from harming him/herself or others. This should be used as a *last resort* and should never be done in the Head Start Center by using artificial restraints. The child should be contained with your body—crossing child's arms in front and holding the child's back against you, putting your head in a position to minimize the chance of being hit by the child's head. *Talk should always be positive.* Help the child gain control by firm, but supportive restraint. Encourage the child to breathe deeply, to count slowly and to talk to you about the problem.

You want the child walking away from this crisis feeling good about himself or herself and about you. Watch for signs that the crisis is passing. For example: relaxed muscles, decreased body rigidity, or a more regulated breathing pattern. As soon as possible, gradually terminate holding the child.

If the use of physical restraint on a child causes a severe reaction such as fear, extreme anger, etc., contact the child's parents and office staff. Do not continue the use of physical restraint in these instances until further advised. Document the reaction in detail and place in the child's file.

Whenever physical restraint is used in the classroom, the child's parents must be notified. The use and results of physical restraint need to be documented and kept in the child's file.

If a child's parent(s) objects to the use of physical restraint on their child when the child's behavior becomes uncontrollable, the parents will need to provide suggestions for acceptable behavior management methods, which will keep the child from harming him/herself or others.

B. LEVEL TWO GUIDANCE TECHNIQUES

There are children who come to Head Start with behaviors that do not respond to any of the above techniques. When these attempts have been unsuccessful more systematic planning and follow through needs to occur to guide children to more socially acceptable behavior. Remember that the longer you wait to intervene, the worse the problem becomes and the ranges of options become smaller. Do not wait to take action.

It is important for staff to understand that there is usually a reason for a child's behavior. Each child has a unique way of looking at the world based on many different factors. Inability to control behavior can be caused by one of more of the following reasons:

1. *Organic causes* that include brain damage, prenatal exposure to drugs or alcohol, chemical imbalances, genetic disorders, etc. A child's inability or lack of opportunity to form attachments early in life may result in an organic inability to bond to others, to show compassion or empathy.

2. *Emotional causes* can include mental illness, physical or sexual abuse or neglect, witnessing violence or excessive stress in the family that is long term.

3. *Situational causes* such as a short-term crisis like temporary homelessness, some minor traumas such as bullying, divorce, death of a loved one or other losses can also be a reason for inappropriate behaviors.

4. The *social causes* in our culture are the violence that happens all the time in homes or in the media. Inappropriate behavior is modeled and encouraged in some homes.

When a child presents with behaviors that do not respond to the guidance techniques outlined earlier, a more methodical and aggressive approach must be developed.

Phase I—Investigation Phase

Step 1.   *Identify and Define the Behavior:* Analyze the situation in which the behavior occurs by doing 3–4 written observations. The observations should include:

- When the behavior occurs;
- What happens immediately before the behavior;
- What happens immediately after the behavior;
- What happens during the behavior;

Spend time getting to know the child—what is a motivator for the child, what is the child's temperament and learning style, what are the child's strengths, and whom does the child respond to most willingly.

Step 2.   *Analyze the Classroom Environment* to determine its role in the child's behavior:

- Ensure that classroom expectations and consequences are clearly stated to and understood by the child.
- Evaluate the physical characteristics in the classroom.
- Consult with Education Team Leader, Mental Health Consultant, Education Manager, or other expert for suggestions to improve the physical environment.
- Consult with Education Team Leader, Mental Health Consultant, Education Manager, or other expert for suggestions to improve the room set up, daily schedule, lesson planning, classroom rules, etc. to more closely meet the child's needs.
- Request a visit to another program or classroom that is a model for working with children who have challenging behaviors or seek additional resources or other research for use in classroom planning.

- Look for interactions with other children or with staff that may be provoking inappropriate behavior. Would another room be a better fit?

Step 3. *Request that an Individual Observation* be done by the Education Team Leader assigned to your center.

Step 4. *Consult with Parents* either by telephone or by meeting. Remember that they are the Captains of the team. If they do not buy into the process it will not be successful. It is important that they be informed every step of the way. One staff person should be designated as the parents' contact and any conversation with the parent should include this person. This could be the Teacher, Site Manager or Family Service Worker. Any contact made with the parent will be documented in the child's file. Initial conversations should include questions about the behaviors at home (What are mealtimes/bedtimes like?), family routines, any recent changes or stresses in the family, and any other factors that could be affecting the child. Inquire about the health of child.

Step 5. *Complete a Request for Mental Health Consultant Form* and submit to the Health Team Leader. Attach the observations of the Health Team Leader to this form and describe at least three of the interventions described above that have been attempted with the child.

Step 6. *Request a Screening* be done to rule out language delays or any other delays that would make the child more prone to frustration. Look at results of child's physical exam to rule out any other organic conditions that could be of concern. Determine, as a team, if a referral to another community resource should be made.

Phase II—Guidance Plan

Step 1. *Develop a Behavior Management Plan* for the child in consultation with the parents, classroom staff, Site Manager, Health Services Manager, Mental Health Consultant, any other professionals involved and any others that would be appropriate to the team.

- Site Manager or another designated staff person if appropriate, will act as a facilitator for the team meeting.
- The facilitator will review with the parents, C-HCCAA Head Start's behavior guidance policy.
- All collected information concerning the challenging behavior(s) will be shared with the parent(s).
- Parent(s) will provide information concerning strategies used at home by parent(s) and/or other caregivers.
- Behavior Management Strategies will be developed by the team. There will be at least two (2) desired behaviors identified in the Head Start Center to be addressed by staff.

- There will also be at least one (1) desired behavior identified to be addressed in the home or community environment by the parent(s).
- Parent(s) may also be asked to be available to transport child or to participate in center's special activities field trips to be responsible for the supervision of the child.
- Set a date(s) for follow up to determine if the plan is working.

Step 2.   If the team determines that an additional *Child Support Person* should be assigned to the classroom, a request for this must be made to the Co-Associate Directors of Self-Administered. Include in the request all of the documentation accumulated to this point.

A Child Support person may be utilized in one of several ways:

- To work individually with the child to coach social interactions, act as a conflict mediator or act as child's special friend.
- To relieve Teacher or Assistant Teacher so that staff person may provide individual attention to the child.
- To serve as an additional person in the classroom that interacts and is involved with all of the children.
- When appropriate, this staff person will ride the bus with the child to ensure the safety of all children when coming to or going from the Head Start Center.

Child Support Staff must have a written plan for their involvement and will be included in all staffing and other discussions pertaining to the child. They are to be supervised daily by the Teacher and Site Manager, but *will* ultimately be responsible to the Health Services Manager. The Health Services Area and teaching staff will evaluate effectiveness of this approach every six (6) weeks.

Step 3.   If the child's behavior continues to endanger the safety and/or well-being of themselves, other children or staff, *A Contract Will Be Entered into with the Parent* requiring the parent and child to receive appropriate counseling in regards to the child's behavior. Staff will provide a list of possible therapy sources and will facilitate the initiation of this service in any way possible.

C. INAPPROPRIATE GUIDANCE TECHNIQUES

C-HCCAA Head Start Staff will use guidance techniques that show respect for children and encourage self-control, self-direction, self-esteem and cooperation. This means that the *following techniques will not be acceptable in our program:*

1. Hitting, striking, biting, pinching, grabbing by the arm, shoulder or hair, pulling child roughly or inflicting a form of corporal punishment,
2. Restricting a child's movement by binding or tying the child,
3. Inflicting mental or emotional punishment, such as humiliating, shaming or threatening a child,

4. Depriving a child of meals, snacks, exercise, rest or necessary toilet use,

5. Separating child from the group except when outlined procedures are followed, or

6. Confining a child in an enclosed area, such as a closet, locked room, box or similar cubicle.

Staff that uses any of these prohibited actions or direct another person to use these actions will be subject to disciplinary action.

D. BUS POLICIES

The time spent on the Head Start bus can be significant in a child's day. It is imperative that the children are safe and supervised during this time. Bus drivers are the first Head Start staff seen in the child's day and the last person seen at the end of the day. In order for all of the children to have a positive experience on the bus, the following policies will be followed:

- Techniques outlined above will be used by bus drivers and bus monitors as they work with children;
- Communicate the rules of the bus to the children as they begin in the program;
- All children must be seated and have seat belts fastened whenever the bus is moving;
- Using a box at the front of the bus for backpacks will eliminate the opportunity to use a backpack for hitting;
- Assigned seats would help to always know where children are and eliminate the need to find a seat for everyone each day;
- Knowing children by name, greeting them as they board and sending them off with encouragement will help them feel welcome;
- Rewards such as stickers, or a comment to the child and the parent about a specific good behavior will be a part of each day;
- Enlist parents' and teachers' help to talk with the child about appropriate behavior;
- When problems occur, the bus should pull over to the side of the road and wait until the conflict is resolved before continuing.

Chapter 10

Determining When
Outside Help Is Needed

Mary B. Boat, Victoria Carr,
Lawrence J. Johnson, and Dawn Denno

Teachers and administrators sometimes need outside help in working with a young child who exhibits challenging behavior. However, outside resources may appear inaccessible or nonexistent for that particular child's situation. This chapter begins by discussing issues related to working with outside agencies. It outlines the best way to collaborate from an administrative point of view. Then, it discusses sources and dimensions of support inside and outside the early childhood program and factors related to the decision making necessary for seeking outside help.

WHAT ISSUES SHOULD EDUCATORS CONSIDER WHEN WORKING WITH OTHER PROGRAMS AND AGENCIES?

A critical administrative role is the management of collaborations across programs and/ or agencies. One program cannot do it all, and the administrator must be able to manage collaboration. Johnson, Tam, Zorn, LaMontagne, and Johnson (2003) examined factors that contributed to or inhibited interagency or cross-program collaborations. Data from this investigation revealed factors related to successful interagency collaboration: commitment, communication, involvement of key decision makers, understanding the culture of collaborating agencies, engaging in serious preplanning, providing adequate support for collaboration, and minimizing turf issues. (For clarity, the term *interagency collaboration* is used throughout the chapter to refer to collaborations across different programs or agencies.)

Commitment

Commitment is a critical factor that provides the foundation for successful interagency collaborations, and it is typically missing when such collaborations fail. If significant numbers of individuals within collaborating agencies do not have a commitment to the collaboration, the process will probably fail. To develop this commitment, it is critical for members of each agency to share in the development of the goals of the collaboration to facilitate a high level of trust and to encourage mutual responsibility for these goals. Examples of detrimental and trust-destroying behaviors include developing or following one's own agenda at the expense of other collaborators, displaying an unwillingness to examine or modify an agency's procedures that are unnecessarily inhibiting or detrimental to a collaborating agency, and failing to provide incentives and/or consequences for cooperative and uncooperative behaviors of agency members.

There are a few important suggestions related to building and maintaining commitment. It is necessary to encourage willingness to compromise on important differences and to develop strategies for this purpose. Participating agencies should clarify which issues cannot be compromised. Furthermore, the goals and the potential positive outcomes of the collaboration must be in mind at all times. Revisiting these goals is particularly critical when members of the collaboration face a difficult issue.

Communication

Open communication is another critical component of successful collaborations. It enables people to resolve the differences that will undoubtedly arise between collaborating agencies. Certain activities can enhance communication. For instance, being up front about issues and potential differences develops a proactive approach to communication. Each party must be aware of potential problems and ways to address these problems early in the collaborative process. The collaborators should create frequent opportunities for communication (e.g., e-mail, mail, regular meetings, telephone calls). In addition, developing personal connections promotes a cohesive working relationship and maximizes informal communication links (e.g., occasionally meeting for a cup of coffee or lunch). Most important, giving agency partners written updates about necessary information minimizes miscommunications. This element is critical in the early stages of interagency collaboration.

Involvement of Key Decision Makers

Upper management must be involved and committed to the collaboration or the collaboration will eventually fail. This requires enlisting someone who has a broad perspective on the agency's position and priorities. It is also important to involve someone with enough authority to make decisions on behalf of the agency. Furthermore, the group should include someone who can provide immediate and direct assistance when problems arise.

Finally, it is important to engage someone who can authorize the utilization of the agency's resources to support the collaboration.

Understanding of Each Agency's Culture

Each agency has its own organizational culture, including language and communication patterns, values or priorities, rules and regulations, ways of doing business, organizational structure, and even definitions of *collaboration*. It is important that individuals within agencies attempt to understand the culture of collaborating agencies. Moreover, when individuals adopt this perspective, they are less likely to characterize the rules, values, communication patterns, and structures of other agencies as wrong. Rather, using a cultural view encourages these individuals to seek solutions that are sensitive to the unique cultures of the collaborating agencies.

Certain steps can enhance an understanding of the culture of collaborating agencies. First, staff should take time to learn and comprehend each agency's mission, priorities, and technical language. Activities to accomplish this goal include the following:

- Develop a staff loan program in which a representative of a collaborating agency is loaned to another agency and housed in that agency's office.
- Have each collaborating agency provide a presentation about the agency in the early stages of the collaboration.
- Take care to ensure that definitions of common terms are understood by collaborating agencies. For example, the term *empowerment* has a positive connotation for those working in early intervention, whereas the term carries a negative connotation for those working in areas related to substance abuse.

In addition, staff should review pertinent agency rules and regulations prior to the collaborative effort. They must ensure that the collaboration process does not inadvertently violate any existing rules and regulations.

Adequate Resources for Collaboration

As discussed in Chapter 2, it is important for administrators to recognize that collaboration is difficult and time consuming. Adequate resources and support must be identified and applied if the collaboration is to be successful. Administrators should provide time and additional resources for those engaging in the collaboration. It is critical to recognize the increased time that is required for collaboration. A pitfall to avoid is asking individuals to engage in a difficult task while they are still accountable for the responsibilities they had prior to the collaborative effort.

Minimizing Turf Issues

Even in optimum collaborative circumstances, turf issues are likely to occur and cannot be ignored. The best way to minimize these issues is to anticipate their appearance and to find a solution, developing a plan for addressing them as they emerge. Providing staff members with a positive view of the collaboration is an important step in forming such a plan. This is accomplished by engaging staff in goal development and the identification of potential positive outcomes of the collaboration. Revisiting these goals and outcomes is critical when turf issues arise. It is also useful to disseminate examples of positive outcomes from previous collaborations. In addition, a system of rewards and consequences may be implemented for individuals participating in the collaboration. Finally, it is necessary to engage in serious preplanning to anticipate and address potential turf issues. This can avoid many problems and provide the foundation for a successful collaboration. One suggestion for accomplishing preplanning is to form a steering committee to identify potential problems, key issues, and similarities and differences among the cultures of participating agencies. Another approach is to clearly articulate the developing goals and anticipated outcomes of the collaboration.

CLASSROOM APPLICATION

Have factors related to successful interagency collaboration been addressed?

Are there high levels of commitment from key members of the agencies who are involved in the collaboration?

Have effective and ongoing methods of communication been established among these key members?

Is there administrative involvement from each collaborative agency? Have the administrative personnel committed sufficient time and resources for the collaboration to succeed?

Are those involved in the collaborative process familiar with the values, structure, and language of the participating agencies?

Has preplanning identified key issues in the process? Do the collaborating agencies share a vision of involvement and desired outcomes?

WHAT ARE SOURCES OF OUTSIDE SUPPORT?

It is a given that the entire process for collaborating with outside agencies requires commitment, communication, leadership, planning, and allocating adequate resources for personnel and funding. Yet, one of the biggest challenges in obtaining outside support for addressing challenging behaviors is identifying which resources are available to early childhood programs. This process often is complicated by the numerous factors that make specific resources available only to specific children. For example, children and families who qualify for services under the Individuals with Disabilities Education Act (IDEA) Amendments of 1997 (PL 105-17) are entitled to particular services, free of charge (or on a sliding fee scale for children birth to 3 years of age), depending on their qualifications (Sections 602 & 631). In addition, children who receive social services or are from certain

Table 10.1.   Services available to children and their families under Individuals with Disabilities Education Act (IDEA) Amendments of 1997 (PL 105-17)

Services available under Part B (Ages 3–21 years)	Services available under Part C (Ages birth–3 years)
Special instruction	Family training, counseling, and home visits
Speech-language pathology, audiology	Special instruction
	Speech-language pathology, audiology
Occupational therapy	Occupational therapy
Physical therapy	Physical therapy
Psychological services	Psychological services
Recreation, therapeutic recreation	Service coordination
Social work services	Medical services for diagnostic and evaluation purposes
Counseling services	Early identification, screening, and assessment services
Orientation and mobility services	Health services necessary for the infant or toddler to benefit from other early intervention services
Medical services for diagnostic and evaluation purposes	
	Social work services
Early identification and assessment of conditions that may cause disability	Vision services
	Assistive technology devices and services
	Transportation and related costs to receive other early intervention services

economic strata may qualify for specifically defined sources of support. In general, outside resources for challenging behaviors are either legally mandated/entitlement services or fee-based services. Some of the resources may be obtained through health insurance. Additional support also may be available through charitable or volunteer organizations.

IDEA lists a range of services available to young children and their families who qualify for those services. For children ages 3–21, any services for which they qualify under IDEA Part B must be provided at no cost to the family. For children ages birth to 3 and their families, services supported by IDEA, Part C must be available to families free of charge or on a sliding fee scale. These services are summarized in Table 10.1.

WHAT SUPPORTS ARE AVAILABLE TO TEACHERS?

A multitude of factors may influence the types of resources available to early childhood teachers. Support options range from informal to formal and local to national. Regardless of the options available, teachers need to take the initiative to mobilize support for themselves and the children in their classrooms.

Informal Supports

Teachers often underutilize informal support systems. Informal supports are relationships that are not professionally dictated or paid. Thus, co-workers may provide informal supports to teachers. For example, teachers may chat during lunch or engage in discussion and problem solving simply as colleagues and friends, not to fulfill requirements of their jobs. One co-worker may be aware of resources with which another is unfamiliar, and each may provide the other with valuable information.

Co-workers are not the only informal supports for addressing challenging behaviors in the classroom. The families of children exhibiting these behaviors are important resources as well. In fact, The Division of Early Childhood (DEC) of the Council for Exceptional Children Position Statement on Interventions for Challenging Behaviors clearly states that families are vital partners in the process of creating and implementing interventions for challenging behaviors (Brault et al., 1999). Relationships with the children's parents and other family members may provide informal support systems for teachers by providing feedback and reinforcing shared expectations. Each relationship may lead to the creation of more formal support structures. For example, parents may provide a teacher with information from and access to service providers outside of the system, such as physicians and mental health professionals. The best outcomes result from family members and professionals working together to identify and address challenging behaviors. If a collaborative family–professional relationship does not yet exist, gathering as much information as possible from family members and primary caregivers is critical as part of the problem-solving process. In addition, teachers and other professionals can gain access to many resources that exist for families. Parent support organizations may have information about current issues and research related to specific behavioral concerns.

Formal Supports

Teachers need access to more formal support systems as well. The range of formal support systems can be conceptualized as a ladder that moves progressively away from the immediate resources available to teachers, classrooms, and programs (see Figure 10.1). The first step on the ladder is to look for support internally. The teacher may ask whether anyone in the program has experience in the area of concern or whether an appropriate intervention can be found by brainstorming about the issue with colleagues. The second step involves gaining access to expertise that is contained within the program but is not necessarily part of the program's day-to-day operations. For example, speech-language pathologists or other therapists who work for or contract with the program might serve as resources for support. The next step involves going outside the program to other individuals, programs, or agencies. This step is necessary when the program does not have the expertise to successfully address challenging behaviors, and it may include gaining access to programs such as local mental health agencies and local health organizations. The last is obtaining outside support from a limited community of experts. In this case, a child may have specific physical or psychological needs that are beyond the knowledge base of general practitioners in that field. Such expertise may be found locally, regionally, nationally, or internationally and is possessed by a limited number of individuals. It is likely to be affiliated with a research organization or with a specialized clinical or educational setting.

Some early childhood programs may already have support teams or problem-solving teams in place (i.e., the first and second steps on the ladder). These teams may serve as forums for discussing behavioral concerns and may include professionals from other fields such as special education, counseling, and speech-language pathology. Such collaborative

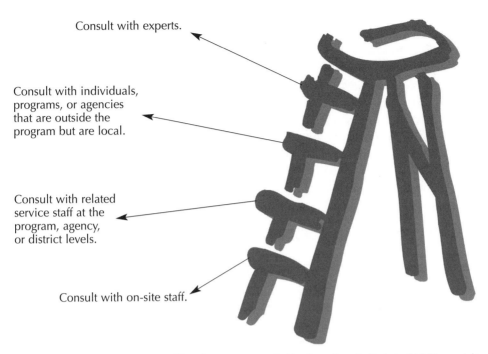

Consult with experts.

Consult with individuals, programs, or agencies that are outside the program but are local.

Consult with related service staff at the program, agency, or district levels.

Consult with on-site staff.

Figure 10.1. The progressive range of formal support systems. (Ladder clip art from *Art Explosion* [Vol. 2], copyright © 1995–2001 Nova Development Corporation.)

efforts are more likely to occur in large programs and in those that receive public funds to support children with special needs. It also is possible for such teams to form in districts and program areas (i.e., local or regional teams). For example, teacher assistance teams (TATs) are school-based teams designed to assist general educators in addressing the needs of children who are at risk for referral to special education (Cosden & Semmel, 1992).

The categories identified in Figure 10.1 are not necessarily mutually exclusive. One example of interaction between the steps is the collaborative problem-solving group initiated by Hobbs and Westling (see Westling, Herzog, Cooper-Duffy, Prohn, & Ray, 2002). They created a regional forum for teachers to utilize one another's expertise in addressing classroom concerns regarding issues related to special education. Interested individuals met weekly to problem-solve collaboratively, with facilitation by a nationally recognized expert in special education who was on the faculty of a local university. Participation was voluntary and could be counted as part of a graduate level course.

Other types of supports may be obtained through local groups formed to support parents and professionals as they work with children who have autism, ADHD, or other mental health diagnoses. In addition, an Internet search often leads to multiple sources of informational support and professional organizations that may list local, regional, and national resources.

Teachers facing challenging behavior in the classroom may feel isolated and perceive that little help or hope is available. However, the potential sources of support for early childhood teachers (e.g., professional organizations) are significant. Knowing when and how to obtain those resources is the difficult part. In at least some cases, legislation exists to guide the referral, evaluation, and intervention processes. Yet, teachers often recognize that each situation is unique and the product of system factors that reflect the dynamics of human interactions as well as differences in resource availability. The difficulties surrounding challenging behaviors are not consistent enough for one individual, or even one discipline, to have all of the expertise needed to effectively address every situation (Rosenfield & Gavois, 1996). Thus, teachers often are forced to rely on subjective information in determining when to request help. Although informed judgment plays a critical role in determining how to proceed in working with young children with challenging behaviors, teachers must have some consistent information on which to base their decisions so they know the best avenues for addressing their concerns and engaging in collaborative problem solving. Creating an environment in which teachers can consistently articulate their concerns and issues is the cornerstone of this process.

CLASSROOM APPLICATION

Have available supports been considered?

What resources are available within the program?

Who within the program can assist with finding outside help?

Who within the program can be a support person?

What resources are available on the Internet?

WHAT ARE SOME COMMON MISPERCEPTIONS ABOUT CHILDREN WITH CHALLENGING BEHAVIORS?

Identifying and gaining access to support often is hindered by teacher concerns and misperceptions regarding the children with challenging behaviors and by the process of getting support. For example, research on the referral for evaluation of preschool-age children suggests that emotional and behavioral problems are underreferred (Fantuzzo et al., 1999; Piotrkowski, Collins, Knitzer, & Robinson, 1994; Yoshikawa & Knitzer, 1997). Although a number of factors usually contribute to this outcome, one element may be that teachers are concerned about the stigma associated with identified behavior problems and often hope that these children will grow out of the behavior (Mallory & Kerns, 1988; Yoshikawa & Knitzer, 1997). Concern about the accuracy and long-term effect of labeling young children is clearly admirable, but research suggests that emotional and behavioral challenges in preschool are likely to persist and, if not addressed, are related to negative outcomes (Rose, Rose, & Feldman, 1989).

Another common misperception among teachers is that addressing challenging behaviors is no longer their concern once a referral has been made. This belief is not surprising given that referral and evaluation often bring other service systems into play and, historically, these systems have not included the early childhood teachers in their activities. Furthermore, if a child is identified as needing additional supports, these supports often are provided by other service systems. Most human services systems parallel one another and have limited infrastructure to support collaboration. Therefore, classroom teachers must be active partners in the collaborative process to address the needs of young children with challenging behaviors in the classroom.

A final misperception is about the capacity of specific interventions to thoroughly address all factors that contribute to challenging behaviors. Consider the example of methylphenidate (Ritalin), the psychoactive medication prescribed for increasing numbers of young children diagnosed as having ADHD. Many professionals and parents expect the drug to completely eliminate hyperactivity and the problems associated with ADHD. However, it is likely that some, if not most, of the difficult behaviors exhibited by a child with ADHD have been learned as a result of the child's inability to regulate his or her activity level. Although children may have biological predispositions or conditions that contribute to challenging behaviors, the behaviors themselves are created and shaped by the children's environments. Children who take medication still need to learn appropriate behaviors.

CLASSROOM APPLICATION

Have misperceptions about children with challenging behavior been addressed?

What perceptions exist about the group of children in this class? What perceptions exist about specific children in the class?

Are these perceptions individually, developmentally, and culturally appropriate?

What perceptions exist about the referral and evaluation process? What perceptions exist about the agencies and interventions involved? Are these perceptions valid?

HOW CAN TEACHERS DECIDE WHEN TO SEEK ADDITIONAL SUPPORT?

Identifying the source(s) of teacher concern regarding child behavior is the critical step in determining the next action to take. Consider the factors that may contribute to a teacher's decision to seek additional support:

1. Are the other children in danger?
2. Is the child's behavior inappropriate in a way that embarrasses the teacher?
3. Does the teacher feel that his or her time is being inequitably distributed?

The best support options stem from situations in which teachers and staff can provide concrete information about the concerning situation(s). Thus, in thinking about a particular child, teachers must be able to systematically analyze the situation. This includes being able to identify and organize information about the teacher, classroom, and child factors that affect child behavior. To facilitate this process, teachers can ask

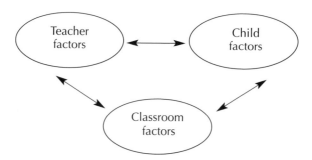

Figure 10.2. Separate yet interrelated factors that affect child behavior.

themselves a series of organizing or framing questions about these components, which are separate yet interrelated (see Figure 10.2).

The following areas for gathering information in no way address all of the influences on child outcomes. Rather, the areas reflect the types of information teachers are most likely to possess and the spheres in which teachers have the most influence. Addressing challenging behaviors in early childhood settings requires the collaborative efforts of professionals and families to define child outcomes from a systems perspective.

Teacher Factors

Daily decision making is based on teacher perceptions of given realities at particular points in time; therefore, thoughts about the importance and functions of child behavior are guided to some degree, by teacher tolerance for differences. According to Strain and Hemmeter, "We each define challenging behaviors based upon our unique set of past experiences, values, instructional practices, and institutional guidelines" (1999, p. 17). Individual teachers have dispositions that affect how they handle stressful situations and beliefs and values that affect how they interpret child behavior. Reactions to challenging behaviors also are altered by teacher perceptions of their capacities to deal with stressors in their lives. Everyone needs support to navigate the challenges of life. Just as it is important to recognize that some children may need more support than others at different points to be successful in school, it also is important to recognize that some teachers may need more support than others at different points to be successful in their classrooms. This reality mirrors the needs of adults in general and should not be used to condemn teachers who need support. Rather, this information should be used to identify and build support systems. Dealing with challenging behaviors is a system problem that requires system solutions. Early childhood programs cannot support children without also supporting their teachers.

How does a teacher develop a better understanding of his or her challenges and needs? Teachers should be able to identify the most pressing concerns and convey the parameters of the situation to others, framed in terms of needs for support. To consistently articulate the challenges in the classroom, teachers can ask themselves several guiding questions:

1. "What specific challenges does this child's behavior present to me as teacher in this classroom?" In asking this question, the teacher should address issues such as extensive

time demands; safety of the child, his or her peers, and the staff; and concern about knowing the best way to approach challenging behavior.

2. "What have I done to address the situation?" Answers should include identifying the kinds of interventions previously attempted and the frequency, duration, and intensity with which those interventions were implemented.

3. "How have I documented my concerns?" This question addresses the ways in which the teacher has gathered information to support his or her assertions. Examples include recording behavioral concerns to identify patterns and specifying, or at least approximating, the qualitative and quantitative characteristics of the concerning behaviors.

Classroom Factors

In addition to identifying teacher factors, it is important to determine dimensions of the classroom context that may exacerbate or mitigate challenging behaviors. As discussed extensively in Chapters 4 and 5, classroom factors may include classroom materials, schedules and routines, classroom staff, and peers (Bailey, Harms, & Clifford, 1983; McEvoy, Fox, & Rosenburg, 1991; Twardoz, 1984). Guiding questions that teachers can ask to assess possible classroom factors include the following:

1. Are specific materials associated with the challenging behaviors?
2. Are specific activities associated with the challenging behaviors?
3. Are challenging behaviors more likely to occur at certain times of the day?
4. In which situations are the behaviors likely (and unlikely) to occur?
5. Are challenging behaviors more likely to occur when the child interacts with specific staff members?
6. Are there enough staff members to cover the classroom when difficult events or crises occur?
7. Are staff members qualified to perform the duties required of them when teacher attention is focused on a problem situation?
8. Are challenging behaviors more likely to occur when the child interacts with certain peers?
9. Do episodes of challenging behavior involve the classroom environment (i.e., are objects, peers, or staff targeted)?

The responses to these questions help teachers articulate the type and extent of support needed regarding classroom factors.

Child Factors

In determining the need for support, early childhood staff often focus exclusively on child or child-related (often family) factors. These factors are critically important but only can be evaluated in the context of their relationship to teacher and classroom factors. To help others understand the challenges posed by child behaviors within the classroom, the teacher must be able to explain the concerning behaviors to others. In trying to systematically describe the child's role in the problem situation, consider the following previously mentioned questions:

1. What are the specific behavioral concerns?

2. What is the frequency, duration, and intensity of those concerns?

3. Are identifiable patterns related to the behavior(s)?

4. What are some possible functions of the behavior for the child (e.g., obtaining an object or staff attention, escaping an activity or person, expressing frustration)?

5. What typically precedes the challenging behaviors?

6. What events follow the challenging behaviors?

7. Do any signals suggest that challenging behaviors are going to occur (e.g., forewarning behaviors)?

In addition to identifying patterns related to a child's challenging behaviors, a teacher can directly observe and document the sequences of events related to those behaviors through an A-B-C analysis (Bijou, Peterson, & Ault, 1968; see also Chapter 6). When conducting an A-B-C analysis, the teacher must first identify and operationally define the target behavior(s). Operational definitions are observable, measurable descriptions of a behavior that enable multiple observers to be certain that they are focusing on the same behavior.

The next step is to consistently observe the child to determine the factors that precede and follow an occurrence of the target behavior. These observations should occur across *at least* five observation periods. As discussed in Chapter 8, another option is using *frequency counts* (or *tallies*), simply recording the information each time that the behavior occurs. This approach allows teachers and staff to remain engaged in classroom activities while visually monitoring the environment to document the antecedents and consequences of the behavior.

The final step is to analyze the findings for patterns. These patterns may help teachers make decisions about possible interventions or may provide teachers with more information to share with outside sources of support. Two vignettes of children with challenging behaviors are presented as illustrations of this process. Consider the following questions when reading each vignette:

1. How might the guiding questions for teacher, classroom, and child factors be answered for Jerome and for Christopher? What would the situation profile look like?

2. How are the cases of Jerome and Christopher similar and different?

3. What types of support are needed to address Jerome's and Christopher's situations?

Vignettes

Jerome, age 4, attends a full-day, full-week early childhood program at a large child development center. The center provides a developmentally appropriate inclusive learning environment for children ages 3–5. The lead classroom teachers have bachelor's degrees in early childhood education and work in teams to create an integrated curriculum. The staff is required to participate in monthly in-service trainings on a variety of topics.

Jerome began attending the center's half-day program when he was 3 years old. His individual development profile (collection of assessment data illustrating his developmental skill levels) from the previous year stated that Jerome was a "sweet boy" who loved blocks, singing, and helping the teachers at snack time. The profile also indicated that Jerome initially had difficulty separating from his mother or father at drop off time (i.e., he sat by the coat room and cried for 5–20 minutes); however, these episodes decreased in length and intensity until they disappeared 3 weeks into the year. When discussing Jerome's strengths and areas for growth, the teachers indicated that Jerome interacted well with his peers, adapted well to the program's demands, and engaged in preferred activities for prolonged periods of time. However, the teachers described Jerome as rather stubborn, particularly when asked to stop a preferred activity. The teachers also indicated that Jerome often was unwilling to try new activities but typically enjoyed these experiences once he engaged in them.

Jerome is currently 2 months into the year in his new full-day class, and his teachers are becoming increasingly frustrated with his outbursts. Almost every day—and often several times per day—Jerome gets upset and throws items (typically whatever is in his hand). He then drops to the floor and cries. Jerome's outbursts do not target the staff or his peers, but he has accidentally hit others with the thrown objects more than once. Sometimes, it takes the teachers 20–30 minutes to help Jerome calm down and become reengaged; occasionally, Jerome cries himself to sleep. The teachers have noted that these episodes are more likely to occur at transition times, particularly in the late morning and during the afternoon. The teachers initially attributed Jerome's behavioral outbursts to his transition to a new class with new children and a longer schedule. In fact, the teachers believe that it is common for some children to exhibit this behavior as they make the transition to a new school year. Yet, the teachers also believe that Jerome's outbursts should have decreased by this point in the year.

Jerome's teachers discuss their concerns about and frustration with the amount of time spent attending to Jerome's outbursts. The lead teacher decides to conduct an A-B-C analysis. First, she operationally defines *tantrum* because the word's general definition is too vague for independent observers to provide consistent findings. The teacher more specifically describes Jerome's behaviors of dropping to the floor and crying or throwing objects inappropriately. However, she realizes that *inappropriately* is also vague and that she must further define this criterion as well. She determines that *throwing inappropriately* means 1) throwing objects during any activity for which throwing is not an acceptable form of participation or 2) throwing objects that are not meant to be thrown.

To gather the A-B-C data, the teacher observes Jerome consistently or at intervals (for 10 minutes, every 20 minutes, or across a 1-hour time period) during the times when the tantrums are most likely to occur. Analyzing the A-B-Cs of Jerome's tantrums may reveal that his actions are often preceded by other children approaching him or trying to use materials that he is using. The process also indicates that Jerome's tantrums always result in attention from staff. Such information informs the teacher of factors that may be precipitating and maintaining the undesirable behaviors. The teacher then synthesizes and analyzes these teacher, classroom, and child factors for themes.

It is important to remember that the guiding questions for teacher, classroom, and child factors are intended to provide a sketch of the situation that facilitates further information gathering. The questions are neither exhaustive nor necessarily sufficient to promote intervention. In all likelihood, outside professionals or agencies with which teachers or early childhood education programs collaborate will have their own processes for gathering needed information. The next vignette exemplifies collaboration with additional professionals.

Christopher is an active 4-year-old who is in Jerome's class and is new to the early childhood center. Christopher has an open file with child protective services and has lived in three different foster homes in the past 2 years. Over the summer, he was placed with his aunt and her four children, ages 1–7 years.

Christopher previously attended several different Head Start programs but never for more than 3 months at a time. His attendance always was disrupted by moves or changes in foster care placement. Christopher started attending his current program after his social services plan was changed to require attendance in a qualified full-day preschool. Staff at the current program have been unable to obtain any additional information from his previous early childhood settings.

During the first week of the program, Christopher appears to be pleased with his new school. He is affectionate with the staff and is inquisitive, frequently asking the teachers questions about the current and upcoming activities. The teachers note that Christopher has a high energy level and difficulty sitting still during large group activities and stories. The teachers also note that Christopher has poor peer interaction skills and requires significant intervention for success with peers. Given his circumstances, however, the teachers believe that Christopher is doing remarkably well.

A few days into the second week, however, the teachers begin voicing concerns about Christopher's behavior. Specifically, Christopher is becoming more aggressive with his peers, using profanity and occasionally hitting and kicking them. As the weeks progress, Christopher's expressions of anger increase in intensity and scope. Two months into the school year, Christopher is exhibiting verbal and physical aggression toward peers and staff daily. The frequency of these outbursts varies from two to ten times per day. Christopher is often removed from the classroom and spends one-to-one time with staff. He becomes very upset when he is removed from the classroom, yet when spending individual time with a staff member, he rarely shows aggression.

The teachers and staff note several important observations about Christopher's behavior. First, they cannot identify consistent patterns in his outbursts, although they tend to be less common during times of active play (e.g., outdoor time). Second, the targets for Christopher's aggression appear to be random. There are no specific children or adults toward whom he consistently is aggressive. Finally, once Christopher calms down, he does not appear to have any remorse about hurting others; in some cases, he does not display any memory of having done so.

The teachers meet with administrators and Christopher's aunt to discuss the situation. At this meeting, Christopher's teachers state that they are concerned about Christopher's behavior and the other children's safety. They report that their assessments have identified no consistently effective intervention strategies and that they have decided to seek outside help.

The teachers determine that a team should be formed to collect more specific data about Christopher's behaviors and to provide intervention within the classroom. The teacher is identified as the principal assessor/ interventionist because the team members strongly believe that given his foster care background, Christopher needs to build a relationship with one person. This approach eliminates having multiple adults ask questions and isolating Christopher from a secure environment. The mental health professional who visits the center weekly and the speech-language pathologist who also provides services to children in the program outline specific tasks for the teacher to implement when assessing language development and self-regulatory skills. These can be carried out within the natural classroom routines. During this scheduled intervention-based assessment time, the team, including Christopher's aunt, observe the interactions, collect data, make comments based on Christopher's responses, and discuss new issues as they might arise. From this data, the team develops a behavioral intervention plan that includes ongoing assessment and evaluation of the plan.

CONCLUSION

Children with challenging behaviors present early childhood programs with unique opportunities for collaborating with internal and external support systems. It is important to recognize and understand the teacher, child, and classroom factors that contribute to each situation and to identify the resources that are available to teachers and programs. When collaborating with outside agencies, seeking to understand the culture of the agency and building a relationship based on commitment and communication best ensures success and support for children and teachers.

Chapter 11

Putting it All Together

Susan Hart Bell

This final chapter summarizes and integrates the ideas presented throughout *Challenging Behavior in Early Childhood Settings: Creating a Place for All Children*. A complete assessment and intervention plan includes attention to factors associated with the child, the family, the early childhood classroom, the program's policies and procedures, and the unique characteristics of other agencies with whom the center collaborates. This chapter revisits important aspects of each element, highlighting the most important questions that the caregiver and/or the collaborative assessment team should address. The chapter also reiterates the elements of an individualized assessment plan to form interventions for challenging behaviors.

WHAT ARE THE INITIAL STEPS FOR ASSESSING A PROBLEMATIC CLASSROOM SITUATION?

The initial steps for assessing challenging behavior include an examination of the child's enrollment records and identification of classroom features that may affect the behavior. Each topic is explored in the following subsections.

Examine the Child's Enrollment Records

The first step in evaluating a problem situation is examining the enrollment records of the child involved. These documents may provide pertinent information about the child and his or her family.

Child Characteristics

As the early childhood teacher begins to assess challenging behavior in the classroom, it is essential to become as familiar as possible with the characteristics of the child involved. The first step is a thorough review of enrollment materials, including the child's medical and social histories. As detailed in Chapter 1, this includes an examination of the child's file for information such as medical diagnoses of congenital problems or sensory impairments; chronic or episodic illnesses and current medications; and professional and/or parental concerns regarding developmental delays, especially in the cognitive or communication domains. The teacher may look for evidence of previous child care or preschool enrollment. Parental concerns about behavior management at home may be noted as well. Center records may indicate a history of contributing factors to the child's behavior, allowing the early childhood teacher to investigate relevant information through contacts with the child's parents and, given appropriate consent, with the child's current and previous medical and child care providers. This can be helpful in planning a behavioral assessment (e.g., observing differences in behavior on days with and without medication) and can serve as an excellent source for intervention ideas (e.g., rearranging the classroom schedule to match the fluctuating energy levels associated with a child's health condition). In general, examining the center records for child characteristics allows the administrator or classroom teacher to identify factors that influence the child's potential success in the classroom. Illness, identified language delays, medication effects, or limited social skills might indicate a need to modify expectations (e.g., provide additional time for classroom transitions), to modify the daily schedule (e.g., provide additional opportunities for unstructured, open-ended activities), or to mobilize additional strategies for engagement (e.g., intentional teacher scaffolding of play entry).

Family Information

Enrollment applications and center documentation of home visits, parent conferences, telephone contacts, and casual communication also may contain valuable family information. This information is important to consider when planning an assessment and intervention because it often reveals the individual at home who is most vested in the child's success. Typically, this is the individual with whom the most successful center contacts have been made. Family involvement efforts are most effective when they target this individual as the key contact person. In some instances, given appropriate consent from the child's parent or guardian, consulting with a maternal grandmother or a concerned uncle, for instance, facilitates family contact.

As discussed extensively in Chapters 1 and 3, several characteristics affect how the teacher chooses to engage the parent in intervention planning. Concerned and involved parents provide valuable insights into their child's preferences and typical behaviors. They are invaluable sources of information regarding the child's communicative style, causes of frustration, and previous social experiences with peers and siblings. In addition, they may suggest effective intervention strategies used within the home and community contexts. They also may support classroom interventions in diverse ways, such as using the intervention language and conflict negotiation strategies at home, introducing curricular activities at home in preparation for classroom participation, observing or assisting in the classroom during strategic time periods, or supporting appropriate classroom behavior through home reinforcement.

Parents who seem inexperienced or less skilled may need considerable guidance in understanding appropriate developmental and behavioral expectations and acceptable strategies. They may require extensive support in understanding the need for interventions and the importance of their role in developing and implementing such plans. Preferred styles of home–school communication can vary across families and may be noted in each child's file. Information regarding cultural practices and the availability of translators may be contained in the center records as well. Families with multiple challenges (e.g., extreme financial stress, parental substance abuse, marital conflict, parental physical or mental illness) may be unavailable for direct involvement in the child's classroom programming and may need referrals to appropriate resources for assistance. In extreme cases, the center may need to consider contacting a social services agency to ensure the child's safety and well-being.

Examine Classroom Elements

The next step in evaluating a child's challenging behavior is to examine how classroom attributes may influence the behavior. These components include teacher characteristics, aspects of the daily schedule or classroom activities, and the consistency of staff responses during crises.

Teacher Characteristics

The center administrator or classroom teacher should scrutinize closely the actions of teachers and other staff members who are directly involved with a child who exhibits challenging behavior. It is critical that these individuals have a broad knowledge base regarding theories of early child development, knowledge about effective practices regarding specific disabilities (when children with such disabilities are included in the classroom), and extensive training in the center's policies and procedures. These individuals also should have experience in developmentally appropriate practices for the age groups with which they work. If gaps in knowledge or ability are identified, opportunities for professional development should be provided for staff members. As discussed in Chapters 3 and 7, these educational efforts can include planning refresher in-service sessions for the entire staff, arranging for tuition and/or release time to attend relevant college courses, establishing mentoring relationships with experienced and effective staff members, or providing specific corrective feedback for individual staff members regarding variation from established practices.

As discussed extensively in Chapters 1, 4, and 6, direct observation by administrative or classroom staff can target numerous child or classroom factors, including the following:

- The amount of time that caregivers spend in close proximity to children, visually scanning the area and preempting problem situations
- The timing, frequency, style, and content of verbal directions that are given to the group as a whole and to individual children

- The amount of time that caregivers devote to prompting or facilitating play interactions and participation in the daily routines
- The responsiveness of the caregivers to child concerns and requests for assistance
- The manner in which child conflicts are typically handled
- The variety of strategies that are used to move children efficiently through the daily routines

In addition, conversations with classroom personnel might reveal staff member beliefs or emotions that interfere with successful resolution of the problem situation. The administrator or classroom teacher might find that staff member attitudes or feelings necessitate a change in assignment before effective intervention can begin (i.e., either the staff member or the child can be moved to another classroom).

Aspects of the Daily Schedule or Classroom Activities

As discussed in great detail in Chapters 4, 5, and 6, center administration and classroom personnel should take care in creating a predictable and age-appropriate daily routine. Children should be given a variety of activities with sufficient time allotted for creative exploration and constructive play. Activities should be selected with individual child abilities and interests in mind, flowing from a developmentally appropriate centerwide curriculum. Limits should encourage self-regulation while ensuring safety at all times. Direct observation by the administrative or classroom staff can identify hot spots for the group as a whole. Small changes in 1) the physical layout of the classroom; 2) the order or length of daily activities; 3) the number, content, and variety of materials available; 4) the manner in which children transition between activities; or 5) the grouping of children (e.g., the placement of children at group time, naptime, or snack time) may significantly improve the problem situation.

Consistency of Staff Responses During Crises

Challenging behaviors can escalate into crisis situations. Chapter 9 discusses the importance of preparing classroom personnel for unpredictable events that can exacerbate a problem situation. The chapter includes a model for administrative procedures that covers policies ranging from positive guidance for minor disruptive behavior to staff management of crises. Administrators must ensure that early childhood programs have comprehensive policies and procedures covering predictable classroom crises. These procedures must be accessible to classroom teachers, and personnel must be trained in their implementation. Crisis drills allow teachers to implement procedures effectively and prepare them to act automatically in high-stress situations. When challenging behaviors precipitate a classroom crisis, the center must have a clearly stated set of procedures for addressing the victim, isolating the perpetrator, getting medical attention as needed, and summoning extra staff when necessary. The center should include a policy on physical restraint, designating proper procedures to ensure that neither staff nor children sustain injury during implementation.

Summary

The initial steps for assessing a problematic classroom situation are to examine center records for helpful information regarding child and family characteristics, assess the willingness of family members to participate in discussions of the challenging situation, and identify classroom variables that might be easily amenable to change. Attention to changes indicated by the record review, suggested by parents or other caregivers, or identified through initial observation of caregiver behaviors and classroom variables may provide early resolution of a challenging classroom situation, but staff must be trained in established procedures for handling crises.

WHAT ADDITIONAL INFORMATION SHOULD BE COLLECTED BEFORE DEVELOPING AN INTERVENTION PLAN?

If the initial steps do not successfully address the problem situation, further assessment and intervention are indicated. Chapters 5 and 6 provide many suggestions for assessment strategies. Initial examination of the child's performance within the daily routines can be documented through anecdotal notes, journal entries, videotaping, or frequency counts of specific behaviors (e.g., counting the number of tantrums per day, tallying the number of reminders that a child needs during transitions). These general observations can be shared with parents in the initial stages of assessment and can help parents and center personnel jointly decide which behaviors require more intensive, planned observations.

Form an Effective Assessment Team

Chapter 2 emphasizes the importance of obtaining administrative support for assessment and intervention. Observation by administrative personnel or involvement of outside consultants (often at additional expense to the program or the parents) may be critical in mobilizing expertise during the assessment phase. Administrators also authorize additional staff coverage for team planning time and, when necessary, for assistance in implementing the intervention plan.

Many of the chapters in this book have emphasized the importance of engaging parents in the assessment and intervention process. Chapter 3 highlights the parent- and teacher-identified barriers to home–school collaboration and gives recommendations for creating a welcoming atmosphere, overcoming logistical barriers for parent involvement, and improving communication between the educational and home environments. Chapter 5 gives specific guidelines for interviewing parents to obtain relevant assessment information and engage family members in the assessment process.

Chapter 7 provides additional guidelines for selecting the stakeholders who will be part of the assessment and intervention team. It is important to identify team members who can provide information that is relevant to problem definition and analysis as well as individuals who can contribute intervention ideas during plan development and implementation. Chapter 10 provides a decision framework for the classroom teacher, allowing him or her to problem-solve the need for outside support and providing suggestions for effective interagency collaboration. Issues such as securing a commitment for full participation and ensuring effective communication between agencies are addressed.

Select Targeted Behaviors

As discussed in Chapters 1 and 7, careful attention should be devoted to identifying child behaviors that are amenable to change, measurable, observable, and identified as problematic by the classroom staff and the parents. Aggressive or noncompliant behaviors that do not differ from those typically observed in preschool settings are best addressed with classwide interventions (e.g., changes in the daily schedule, teacher strategies in response to classwide disruptive behaviors). Individual child behaviors that vary in frequency, duration, intensity, or form (e.g., sexually sophisticated play, self-injurious behaviors) from developmental expectations are those that are usually targeted for individualized intervention planning. Behaviors that endanger the safety or comfort of the child, other children in the classroom, or the classroom personnel are of highest priority for change.

Identify Elements that Trigger and Maintain Behavior

Chapter 6 provides detailed information regarding the identification of elements that likely trigger and maintain the problem situation. A functional assessment implemented early in the intervention planning process can assist the intervention team in identifying the antecedents (e.g., child fatigue, room crowding, staff absence, schedule changes) and consequences (e.g., teacher attention, obtaining a turn with a preferred activity, escape from a nonpreferred activity) instigating and maintaining the problem behaviors. The classroom teacher or administrative personnel can observe the situation to identify the antecedent elements, specify the child's behaviors, and identify typical teacher and peer responses to the behaviors of concern. The team can then brainstorm alternative strategies (discussed at length in Chapter 6) that the classroom teacher can use to interrupt, extinguish, decrease, or redirect the child's behavior.

After defining and prioritizing the behaviors of concern, it is important for the team to record pertinent characteristics of these behaviors (i.e., frequency, duration, intensity, latency, variability) to provide a baseline. (Strategies for baseline data collection are discussed in Chapter 7.) A careful comparison of subsequent observations with baseline data allows the intervention team to measure the effectiveness of any plan that is implemented.

HOW IS THE PLAN IMPLEMENTED AND EVALUATED?

Chapter 7 addresses the issue of putting a behavioral plan into place within the classroom. The intervention team first reviews the information collected during baseline to ensure that the behaviors are well defined and appropriately prioritized. The team then reviews the functional assessment to identify significant antecedents and consequences maintaining (or preventing/interrupting) the behavior. Strategies may include rearranging the physical environment or daily schedule, altering the group composition, and introducing teacher strategies that reduce incidences of the disruptive behavior while teaching alternative behaviors.

The most effective plans are detailed action scripts that include the classroom staff's usual language and actions and follow center policies regarding the implementation of strategies such as physical restraint. This allows for little departure from current classroom practices and increases the probability of consistent implementation across classroom settings and personnel. Plans should include "if–then" scenarios to allow the least intrusive intervention based on child behavior. For example, the teacher will remind the child to use "friendly words" in a conflict situation; if the child exhibits physically aggressive behavior, then he or she will be removed from the activity center and taken to the cool-down area.

Assess the Plan's Effectiveness

The data collection begun during baseline should be continued as the plan is implemented. This allows the team members to see any changes caused by factors such as classroom scheduling or teacher strategies. However, child behavior may change for reasons unrelated to the planned classroom modifications. Chapter 8 discusses methods for recording the plan's intervention integrity. To link child changes to the strategies included in the intervention plan, the team must measure how often the plan is actually used with the child and how faithfully the steps are followed. Plans may be agreed on during team meetings but implemented occasionally, incompletely, or not at all. This outcome may be related to the staff members' level of comfort with the language and actions specified in the plan. Initial implementation followed by replanning can allow the classroom staff to try it out before suggesting changes that make the plan fit more naturally into the classroom routines.

Decide When to Discontinue the Plan

As the problem situation responds to a specific intervention, the team must plan for fading specific elements of the plan. The team might experiment with deleting steps to determine whether a streamlined plan will be equally effective. The team might introduce elements of self-monitoring—revising the plan so the child takes over the planning, evaluating his or her behavior in specific situations. The goal is to return the child to the levels of teacher proximity and scaffolding provided to other children within the classroom.

Faithfully implemented plans that result in little change may need modification. The team can reconvene to step up the intrusiveness and artificiality of the intervention strategies. Chapter 6 discusses the range of teacher strategies that can be included in an intervention plan. Team members can request additional personnel as the interventions become more time consuming and individualized.

As increasingly costly and time-consuming plans fail to address the behavior, the team might consider the appropriateness of the child's placement in the current early childhood program. At this point, the intervention team should consider the need for further professional evaluation and should provide the parents with appropriate referrals to community resources. This action may result in the child's continuing within the early childhood program with substantial support from outside agencies. Conversely, it may be determined that the child would be better served within another community program. This is a tough decision that should be made in consultation with the parents and only after substantial efforts have been devoted to sustain the child within the current setting.

CLOSING THOUGHTS

A parent enrolls her child in an early childhood program seeking a chance for him to experience the outside world, to adjust to school limits and expectations, and to learn to negotiate social interactions with other children and adults. A teacher greets this child with the confidence that she has prepared an effective learning environment within which the child will thrive. The teacher has planned a developmentally appropriate sequence of novel activities within a safe and attractive classroom setting and anticipates that the child is able and willing to be engaged. The child enters the room—perhaps fearfully, perhaps enthusiastically, but wanting above all to enjoy the time that he spends there. Violations of these expectations form the basis for a problem situation. The child may be unable or unwilling to become engaged in the classroom activities or to follow the classroom limits, and school ceases to be an enjoyable and safe place for him. The teacher finds that classroom management strategies that she has used so successfully with other children are inadequate and ineffective, and she loses confidence in her ability to manage the interactions within the classroom. The parent then realizes that her efforts to introduce her child to other children and adults and to provide him with the skills for negotiating the outside world has resulted in the child's first experience with failure. This book has introduced strategies for early childhood programs to use to address such violations of expectations and to create a place for all children—restoring the parent's hope, the teacher's confidence, and the child's joy.

References

Abelson, M.A., & Woodman, R.W. (1983). Review of research on team effectiveness: Implications for teams in schools. *School Psychology Review, 12,* 125–136.

Ackerman, B.P., Kogos, J., Youngstrom, K.S., Schoff, K., & Izard, C. (1999). Family instability and the problem behaviors of children from economically disadvantaged families. *Developmental Psychology, 35,* 258–268.

Albin, R.W., Lucyshyn, J.M., Horner, R.H., & Flannery, K.B. (1996). Contextual fit for behavioral support plans: A model for "goodness of fit." In L.K. Koegel, R.L. Koegel, & G. Dunlap (Eds.), *Positive behavioral support: Including people with difficult behavior in the community* (pp. 81–98). Baltimore: Paul H. Brookes Publishing Co.

American Psychiatric Association. (2000). *Diagnostic and statistical manual of mental disorders* (4th ed., Text Rev.). Washington, DC: Author.

Anastopoulos, A.D., Klinger, E.E., & Temple, E.P. (2001). Treating children and adolescents with attention-deficit/hyperactivity disorder. In J.N. Hughes, A.M. LaGreca, & J.C. Conoley (Eds.), *Handbook of psychological services for children and adolescents* (pp. 245–266). New York: Oxford University Press.

Arndorfer, R.E., & Miltenberger, R.G. (1993). Functional assessment and treatment of challenging behavior: A review with implications for early childhood. *Topics in Early Childhood Special Education, 13,* 82–105.

Arnold, D.H., Griffith, J.R., Ortiz, C., & Stowe, R.M. (1998). Day care interactions and teacher perceptions as a function of teacher and child ethnic group. *Journal of Research in Childhood Education, 12,* 143–154.

Arnold, D.H., McWilliams, L., & Arnold, E.H. (1998). Teacher discipline and child misbehavior in day care: Untangling causality with correlational data. *Developmental Psychology, 34,* 276–287.

Baer, R.A., Williams, J.A., Osnes, P.G., & Stokes, T.F. (1985). Generalized verbal control and correspondence training. *Behavior Modification, 9,* 477–489.

Bagley, D.M., & Klass, P. (1997). Comparison of the quality of preschoolers' play in housekeeping and thematic sociodramatic play centers. *Journal of Research in Childhood Education, 12,* 71–77.

Bagnato, S., Neisworth, J., & Munson, S. (1989). *Linking developmental assessment and early intervention.* Gaithersburg, MD: Aspen Publishers.

Bailey, D.B., Jr. (1994). Working with families of children with special needs. In M. Wolery & J.S. Wilbers (Eds.), *Including children with special needs in early childhood programs* (pp. 23–44). Washington, DC: National Association for the Education of Young Children.

Bailey, D.B., Jr., Harms, T., & Clifford, R.M. (1983). Matching changes in preschool environments to desired changes in child behavior. *Journal of the Division of Early Childhood, 7,* 61–68.

Bailey, D.B., Jr., Skinner, D., Rodriguez, P., Gut, D., & Correa, V. (1999). Awareness, use, and satisfaction with services for Latino parents of young children with disabilities. *Exceptional Children, 65*(3), 367–381.

Bandura, A. (1977). *Social learning theory.* Upper Saddle River, NJ: Prentice Hall.

Barkley, R.A. (1996). Attention deficit/hyperactivity disorder. In E.J. Mash & L.G. Terdal (Eds.), *Child psychopathology* (pp. 63–112). New York: The Guilford Press.

Barnett, D. (1999, December). *Scripting inclusionary practices for disruptive and dangerous behaviors.* Paper presented at the annual meeting of the Division for Early Childhood, Council for Exceptional Children, Washington, DC.

Barnett, D.W., Bauer, A.M., Ehrhardt, K.E., Lentz, F.E., & Stollar, S.A. (1996). Keystone targets for change: Planning for widespread positive consequences. *School Psychology Quarterly, 11,* 95–117.

Barnett, D.W., Bell, S.H., & Carey, K.T. (1999). *Designing preschool interventions: A practitioner's guide.* New York: The Guilford Press.

Barnett, D.W., Bell, S.H., Gilkey, C.M., Lentz, F.E., Graden, J.L., Stone, C.M., Smith, J.J., & Macmann, G.M. (1999). The promise of meaningful eligibility determination: Functional intervention-based multi-factored preschool evaluation. *The Journal of Special Education, 33,* 112–124.

Barnett, D.W., Carey, K.T., & Hall, J.D. (1993). Naturalistic intervention design for young children: Foundations, rationales, and strategies. *Topics in Early Childhood Special Education, 13,* 430–444.

Barnett, D.W., Ehrhardt, K.E., Stollar, S.A., & Bauer, A.M. (1994). PASSKey: A model for naturalistic assessment and intervention design. *Topics in Early Childhood Special Education, 14,* 350–373.

Barnett, D.W., Lentz, F.E., Bauer, A.M., Macmann, G., Stollar, S. & Ehrhardt, K.E. (1997). Ecological foundations of early intervention: Planned activities and strategic sampling. *The Journal of Special Education, 30,* 471–490.

Batshaw, M.L. (Ed.). (2002). *Children with disabilities* (5th ed.). Baltimore: Paul H. Brookes Publishing Co.

Bauer, A., & Shea, T. (1999). *Learners with emotional and behavioral disorders.* Upper Saddle River, NJ: Prentice Hall.

Baumrind, D. (1967). Child care practices anteceding three patterns of preschool behavior. *Genetic Psychology Monographs, 75,* 43–88.

Baumrind, D. (1996). The discipline controversy revisited. *Family Relations, 45,* 405–415.

Beirne-Smith, M., Ittenbach, R.F., & Patton, J.R. (1998). *Mental retardation* (5th ed.). Columbus, OH: Merrill.

Bell, S. (1997). *Parent preferences for involvement in assessment and intervention design.* Unpublished doctoral dissertation, University of Cincinnati, OH.

Bell, S.H., & Barnett, D.W. (1999). Peer micronorms in the assessment of young children: Methodological review and examples. *Topics in Early Childhood Special Education, 19,* 112–122.

Berg, I.K. (1994). *Family based services: A solution-focused approach.* New York: W.W. Norton & Company.

Berk, L.E. (1997). *Child development* (4th ed.). Boston: Allyn & Bacon.

Berk, L.E., & Winsler, A. (1995). *Scaffolding children's learning: Vygotsky and early childhood education.* Washington, DC: National Association for the Education of Young Children.

Bhavnagri, N.P., & Gonzalez-Mena, J. (1997). The cultural context of infant caregiving. *Childhood Education, 74,* 2–8.

Bierman, K.L. (1996). Family-school links: An overview. In A. Booth & J.F. Dunn (Eds.), *Family–school links: How do they affect educational outcomes?* (pp. 275–287). Mahwah, NJ: Lawrence Erlbaum Associates.

Bijou, S.W., Peterson, R.F., & Ault, M.H. (1968). A method to integrate descriptive and experimental field studies at the level of data and empirical concepts. *Journal of Applied Behavior Analysis, 1,* 175–191.

Boekaerts, M., & Roder, I. (1999). Stress, coping and adjustment in children with a chronic disease: A review of the literature. *Disability and Rehabilitation, 21*(7), 311–337.

Borgia, P.T. (1992). Communicating with camcorders. *Young Children, 47*(2), 29.

Boulware, G., Schwartz, I., & McBride, B. (1999). Addressing challenging behaviors at home. In S. Sandall & M. Ostrosky (Eds.), *Young exceptional children: Practical ideas for addressing challenging behaviors* (Monograph Series 1, pp. 29–40). Denver, CO: Division for Early Childhood of the Council for Exceptional Children.

Boyajian, A.E., DuPaul, G.J., Handler, M.W., Eckert, T.L., & McGoey, K.E. (2001). The use of classroom-based brief functional analyses with preschoolers at-risk for attention deficit hyperactivity disorder. *School Psychology Review, 30,* 278–293.

Boyer, W.A.R. (1997). Enhancing playfulness with sensory stimulation. *Journal of Research in Childhood Education, 12,* 78–87.

Brault, L., Carta, J., Hemmeter, M.L., McEvoy, M., Neilson, S., Rous, B., Smith, B., Strain, P., & Timm, M. (1999). Division for Early Childhood (DEC) concept paper on the identification of and intervention with challenging behavior. In S. Sandall & M. Ostrosky (Eds.), *Young exceptional children: Practical ideas for addressing challenging behaviors* (Monograph Series 1, pp. 63–70). Denver, CO: Division for Early Childhood of the Council for Exceptional Children.

Bredekamp, S., & Copple, C. (Eds.). (1997). *Developmentally appropriate practice in early childhood programs* (Rev. ed.). Washington, DC: National Association for the Education of Young Children.

Brenner, V., & Fox, R.A. (1998). Parental discipline and behavior problems in young children. *The Journal of Genetic Psychology, 159*(2), 251–256.

Bricker, D., Pretti-Frontczak, K., & McComas, N. (1998). *An activity-based approach to early intervention* (2nd ed.). Baltimore: Paul H. Brookes Publishing Co.

Bronfenbrenner, U. (1975). Is early intervention effective? In B. Friedlander, G. Sterritt, & G. Kirk (Eds.), *Exceptional infant: Vol. 3. Assessment and intervention* (pp. 449–475). Philadelphia: Brunner/Routledge.

Bronfenbrenner, U. (1979). *The ecology of human development: Experiments by nature and design.* Cambridge, MA: Harvard University Press.

Bronson, M.B. (2000). *Self-regulation in early childhood: Nature and nurture.* New York: The Guilford Press.

Brook, J.S., Zheng, L., Whiteman, M., & Brook, D.W. (2001). Aggression in toddlers: Association with parenting and marital relations. *The Journal of Genetic Psychology, 162*, 228–241.

Brotherson, M.J., & Goldstein, B.L. (1992). Time as a resource and constraint for parents of young children with disabilities: Implications for early intervention services. *Topics in Early Childhood Special Education, 12*, 508–527.

Brown, J., & Murray, D. (2001). Strategies for enhancing play skills for children with Autism Spectrum Disorder. *Education and Training in Mental Retardation and Developmental Disabilities, 36*(3), 312–317.

Brown, M., Bauer, A., & Kretschmer, R. (1995). Dual agenda: Social participation and academic instruction in a developmental kindergarten, *Qualitative Studies in Education, 8*, 265–280.

Brown, R.T., & Anderson, D.L. (1999). Cognition in chronically ill children: A collaborative endeavor of pediatrics and psychology. In R.T. Brown (Ed.), *Cognitive aspects of chronic illness in children* (pp. 1–11). New York: The Guilford Press.

Brown, R.T., & DuPaul, G.J. (1999). Introduction to the miniseries: Promoting school success in children with chronic medical conditions. *School Psychology Review, 28*, 175–181.

Brown, R.T., & Macias, M. (2001). Chronically ill children and adolescents. In J.N. Hughes, A.M. La Greca, & J.C. Conoley (Eds.), *Handbook of psychological services for children and adolescents* (pp. 353–372). New York: Oxford University Press.

Brown, R.T., Tanaka, O.F., & Donegan, J.E. (1998). Pain management. In L. Phelps (Ed.), *Health-related disorders in children and adolescents* (pp. 501–513). Washington, DC: American Psychological Association.

Brown, W., Odom, S., & Holcombe, A. (1996). Observational assessment of young children's social behavior with peers. *Early Childhood Research Quarterly, 11*(1), 19–40.

Brown, W.H., Odom, S.L., Li, S., & Zercher, C. (1999). Ecobehavioral assessment in early childhood programs: A portrait of preschool inclusion. *The Journal of Special Education, 33*, 138–153.

Bruder, M.B. (1994). Working with members of other disciplines: Collaboration for success. In M. Wolery & J.S. Wilbers (Eds.), *Including children with special needs in early childhood programs* (pp. 45–70). Washington, DC: National Association for the Education of Young Children.

Bruner, J.S. (1966). *Toward a theory of instruction.* Cambridge, MA: Belknap Press.

Bryant, D., Vizzard, L.H., Willoughby, M., & Kupersmidt, J. (1999). A review of interventions for preschoolers with aggressive and disruptive behavior. *Early Education and Development, 10*, 47–68.

Buhs, E.S., & Ladd, G.W. (2001). Peer rejection as an antecedent of young children's social adjustment: An examination of mediating processes. *Developmental Psychology, 37*, 550–560.

Bulach, C., Pickett, W., & Boothe, D. (1998). *Mistakes educational leaders make* (Report No. ED0-EA-98-6). Washington, DC: Office of Educational Research and Improvement. (ERIC Document Reproduction Service No. ED422604)

Cairns, R.B., & Cairns, B.D. (1991). Social cognition and social networks: A developmental perspective. In D.J. Pepler & K.H. Rubin (Eds.), *The development and treatment of childhood aggression* (pp. 249–278). Mahwah, NJ: Lawrence Erlbaum Associates.

Campbell, S.B. (1990). *Behavior problems in preschool children: Clinical and developmental issues.* New York: The Guilford Press.

Campbell, S.B., Shaw, D.S., & Gilliom, M. (2000). Early externalizing behavior problems: Toddlers and preschoolers at risk for later maladjustment. *Development & Psychopathology, 12*, 467–488.

Carey, W.B. (1998). Temperament and behavior problems in the classroom. *School Psychology Review, 27*, 522–533.

Carson, J.L., & Parke, R.D. (1996). Reciprocal negative affect in parent–child interactions and children's peer competency. *Child Development, 67*, 2217–2226.

Carr, E.G., Taylor, J.C., & Robinson, S. (1991). The effects of severe behavior problems in children on the teaching behavior of adults. *Journal of Applied Behavior Analysis, 24,* 523–535.

Cellitti, A. (1998). Teaching peace concepts to children. *Dimensions of Early Childhood, 26*(2), 20–22.

Chavkin, N.F., & Williams, D.L. (1993). Minority parents and the elementary school attitudes and practices. In N.F. Chavkin (Ed.), *Families and schools in a pluralistic society* (pp. 73–84). Albany: State University of New York Press.

Chess, S., & Thomas, A. (1991). Temperament and the concept of goodness of fit. In J. Strelau & A. Angleitner (Eds.), *Explorations in temperament: International perspectives on theory and measurement. Perspectives on individual differences* (pp. 15–28). New York: Kluwer Academic/Plenum Publishers.

Christenson, S.L., Rounds, T., & Franklin, M.J. (1992). Home–school collaboration: Effects, issues, and opportunities. In S.L. Christenson & J.C. Conoley (Eds.), *Home–school collaboration: Enhancing children's academic and social competence* (pp. 19–47). Bethesda, MD: National Association of School Psychologists.

Church, E.B. (1996). Group rules and routines. *Scholastic Early Childhood Today, 11,* 68–69.

Cincinnati-Hamilton County Community Action Agency Head Start. (2000). *Positive guidance policy.* Cincinnati, OH: Author.

Coll, C.G., & Magnuson, K. (2000). Cultural differences as sources of developmental vulnerabilities and resources. In J.P. Shonkoff & S.J. Meisels (Eds.), *Handbook of early childhood intervention* (2nd ed., pp. 94–114). New York: Cambridge University Press.

Collins, W.A., Maccoby, E.E., Steinberg, L., Hetherington, E.M., & Bornstein, M.H. (2000). Contemporary research on parenting: The case for nature and nurture. *American Psychologist, 55,* 218–232.

Cosden, M.A., & Semmel, M.I. (1992). Teacher assistance teams: A conceptual and empirical review. *Special Services in the Schools, 6*(3/4), 5–25.

Coutinho, M.J., Oswald, D.P., Best, A.M., & Forness, S.R. (2002). Gender and sociodemographic factors and the disproportionate identification of culturally and linguistically diverse students with emotional disturbance. *Behavioral Disorders, 27,* 109–125.

Covey, S.R. (1990). *The seven habits of highly effective people: Restoring the character ethic.* New York: Simon & Schuster.

Covey, S.R. (1991). *Principle-centered leadership.* New York: Summit Books.

Crick, N.R., Casas, J.F., & Ku, H. (1999). Relational and physical forms of peer victimization in preschool. *Developmental Psychology, 35,* 376–385.

Crosser, S. (1992). Managing the early childhood classroom. *Young Children, 47*(2), 23–29.

Czaja, C.F. (1999). The effect of teacher style on interactive engagement: Comment. *Early Childhood Research Quarterly, 14,* 71–74.

Daigre, I.R., Johnson, L.J., Bauer, A.M., & Anania Smith, D. (1998). Developing an inclusive, prosocial curriculum. In L.J. Johnson, M.J. LaMontagne, P.M. Elgas, & A.M. Bauer, *Early childhood education: Blending theory, blending practice* (pp. 173–186). Baltimore: Paul H. Brookes Publishing Co.

Dauber, S.L., & Epstein, J.L. (1993). Parents' attitudes and practices of involvement in inner-city elementary and middle schools. In N.F. Chavkin (Ed.), *Families and schools in a pluralistic society* (pp. 53–72). Albany: State University of New York Press.

Davies, D. (1997). Crossing boundaries: How to create successful partnerships with families and communities. *Early Childhood Education Journal, 25*(1), 73–77.

Davies, S.L., Glaser, D., & Kossoff, R. (2000). Children's sexual play and behavior in pre-school settings: Staff's perceptions, reports, and responses. *Child Abuse & Neglect, 24,* 1329–1343.

Davis, C.A., Reichle, J.E., & Southard, K.L. (2000). High-probability requests and a preferred item as a distractor: Increasing successful transitions in children with behavior problems. *Education & Treatment of Children, 23,* 423–441.

Davis, S.H. (1997). The principal's paradox: Remaining secure in a precarious position. *NASSP Bulletin 81*(592), 73–80.

De Shazer, S. (1985). *Keys to solution in brief therapy.* New York: W.W. Norton & Co.

DeJong, P., & Miller, S.D. (1995). How to interview for client strengths. *Social Work, 40*(6), 729–736.

DeKlyen, M., Biernbaum, M.A., Speltz, M.L., & Greenberg, M.T. (1998). Fathers and preschool behavior problems. *Developmental Psychology, 34,* 264–275.

Division for Early Childhood of the Council for Exceptional Children. (1999). Position statement on interventions for challenging behavior. In S. Sandall & M. Ostrosky (Eds.), Practical ideas for addressing challenging behaviors. *Young Exceptional Children Monograph*(Series No. 1), 3–4.

Doggett, R.A., Edwards, R.P., Moore, J.W., Tingstrom, D.H., & Wilczynski, S.M. (2001). An approach to functional assessment in general education classroom settings. *School Psychology Review, 30,* 313–328.

Dole-Kwan, J., Chen, D., & Hughes, M. (2001). A national survey of service providers who work with young children with visual impairments. *Journal of Visual Impairment and Blindness, 95,* 325–337.

Donohue, K.M., Weinstein, R.S., Cowan, P.A., & Cowan, C.P. (2000). Patterns of teachers' whole-class perceptions and predictive relationships between teachers' and parents' perceptions of individual child competence. *Early Childhood Research Quarterly, 15,* 279–305.

Dooley, P., Wilczenski, F.L., & Torem, C. (2001). Using an activity schedule to smooth school transitions. *Journal of Positive Behavior Interventions, 3,* 57–61.

Dunlap, G., & Kern, L. (1996). Modifying instructional activities to promote desirable behavior: A conceptual and practical framework. *School Psychology Quarterly, 11,* 297–312.

Dunn, J., & Hughes, C. (2001). "I got some swords and you're dead!": Violent fantasy, antisocial behavior, friendship, and moral sensibility in young children. *Child Development, 72,* 491–505.

Dunst, C.J., Bruder, M.B., Trivette, C.M., Hamby, D., Raab, M., & McLean, M. (2001). Characteristics and consequences of everyday natural learning opportunities. *Topics in Early Childhood Special Education, 21,* 68–92.

Dunst, C.J., Trivette, C.M., & Deal, A.G. (1988). *Enabling and empowering families: Principles and guidelines for practice.* Newton-Upper Falls, MA: Brookline Books.

Dunst, C.J., Trivette, C.M., Starnes, A., Hamby, D.W., & Gordon, N.J. (1993). *Building and evaluating family support initiatives: A national study of programs for persons with developmental disabilities.* Baltimore: Paul H. Brookes Publishing Co.

Durand, V.M. (1990). *Severe behavior problems: A functional communication training approach.* New York: The Guilford Press.

Dyer, K., & Larsson, E.V. (1997). Developing functional communication skills: Alternatives to severe behavior problems. In N.N. Singh (Ed.), *Prevention and treatment of severe behavior problems: Models and methods in developmental disabilities* (pp. 121–148). Belmont, CA: Brooks/Cole.

Edwards, C., Gandini, L., & Forman, G. (1998). *The hundred languages of children: The Reggio Emilia Approach—Advanced reflections* (2nd ed.). Westport, CT: Ablex.

Edwards, O.W. (2000). Grandparents raising grandchildren. In M.J. Fine & S.W. Lee (Eds.), *Handbook of diversity in parent education: The changing faces of parenting and parent education* (pp. 199–211). San Diego: Academic Press.

Edwards, R. (1995). Psychologists foster the new definition of family. *APA Monitor on Psychology, 26,* 38.

Ehrhardt, K.E., Barnett, D.W., Lentz, F.E., Stollar, S.E., & Reifen, L. (1996). Innovative methodology in ecological consultation: Use of scripts to promote treatment acceptability and integrity. *School Psychology Quarterly, 11,* 149–168.

Elgas, P., Prendeville, J., Moomaw, S., & Kretschmer, R. (2002). Early childhood classroom setup. *Child Care Information Exchange, 143,* 17–20.

Elkind, D. (1981). *The hurried child.* Boston: Addison-Wesley.

Epps, S., & Jackson, B. (2000). *Empowered families, successful children: Early intervention programs that work.* Washington, DC: American Psychological Association.

Fagan, J., Newash, N., & Schloesser, A. (2000). Female caregivers' perceptions of fathers' and significant adult males' involvement with their Head Start children. *Families in Society, 81,* 186–196.

Fantuzzo, J., Stoltzfus, J., Lutz, M.N., Hamlet, H., Balraj, V., Turner, C., et al. (1999). An evaluation of the special needs referral process for low-income preschool children with emotional and behavior problems. *Early Childhood Research Quarterly, 14,* 465–482.

Farver, J.M. (1996). Aggressive behavior in preschoolers' social networks: Do birds of a feather flock together? *Early Childhood Research Quarterly, 11,* 333–350.

Fawcett, S.B. (1991). Social validity: A note on methodology. *Journal of Applied Behavior Analysis, 24,* 235–239.

Feldman, M.A., & Griffiths, D. (1997). Comprehensive assessment of severe behavior problems. In N.N. Singh (Ed.), *Prevention and treatment of severe behavior problems: Models and methods in developmental disabilities* (pp. 24–48). Belmont, CA: Brooks/Cole.

Feldman, M.A., Hancock, C.L., Rielly, N., Minnes, P., & Cairns, C. (2000). Behavior problems in young children with or at risk for developmental delay. *Journal of Child and Family Studies, 9,* 247–261.

Ferro, J., Foster-Johnson, L., & Dunlap, G. (1996). Relation between curricular activities and problem behaviors of students with mental retardation. *American Journal on Mental Retardation, 101,* 184–194.

Field, T. (1999). Music enhances sleep in preschool children. *Early Childhood Development and Care, 150,* 65–68.

Filla, A., Wolery, M., & Anthony, L. (1999). Promoting children's conversations during play with adult prompts. *Journal of Early Intervention, 22,* 93–108.

Fine, M.J., & Wardle, K.F. (2000). A psychoeducational program for parents of dysfunctional backgrounds. In M.J. Fine & S.W. Lee (Eds.), *Handbook of diversity in parent education: The changing faces of parenting and parent education* (pp. 133–153). San Diego: Academic Press

Finney, J.W. (1991). On further development of the concept of social validity. *Journal of Applied Behavior Analysis, 24,* 245–249.

Forehand, R., & McMahon, R.J. (1981). *Helping the noncompliant child: A clinician's guide to parent training.* New York: The Guilford Press.

Fox, L., Little, N., & Dunlap, G. (2001). Starting early: Developing school-wide behavioral support in a community preschool. *Journal of Positive Behavior Interventions, 3,* 251–254.

Franco, N., & Levitt, M.J. (1997). The social ecology of early childhood: Preschool social support networks and social acceptance. *Social Development, 6,* 292–306.

Frosch, C.A., & Mangelsdorf, S.C. (2001). Marital behavior, parenting behavior, and multiple reports of preschoolers' behavior problems: Mediation or moderation? *Developmental Psychology, 37,* 502–519.

Galensky, T.L., Miltenberger, T.G., Stricker, J.M., Garlinghouse, M.A., & Koegel, R.L. (2001). Functional assessment and treatment of mealtime behavior problems. *Journal of Positive Behavior Interventions, 3,* 211–225.

Gartrell, D. (1995). Misbehavior or mistaken behavior? *Young Children, 50*(5), 27–34.

Gartrell, D. (1997). Beyond discipline to guidance. *Young Children, 52*(6), 34–42.

Girolametto, L., Weitzman, E., Lieshout, R., & Duff, D. (2000). Directiveness in teachers' language input to toddlers and preschoolers in day care. *Journal of Speech, Language & Hearing Research, 43,* 1101–1114.

Goldstein, A.P. (2001). Low-level aggression. In J.N. Hughes, A.M. LaGreca, & J.C. Conoley (Eds.), *Handbook of psychological services for children and adolescents* (pp. 161–181). New York: Oxford University Press.

Gonzalez-Mena, J., & Bhavnagri, N.P. (2001). Cultural differences in sleeping practices. Helping early childhood educators understand. *Child Care Information Exchange, 138,* 91–93.

Gould, P., & Sullivan, J. (1999). *The inclusive early childhood classroom: Easy ways to adapt learning centers for all children.* Beltsville, MD: Gryphon House.

Gray, C.A., & Garand, J.D. (1993). Social stories: Improving responses of students with autism with accurate social information. *Focus on Autistic Behavior, 8,* 1–10.

Greene, L., Kamps, D., Wyble, J., & Ellis, C. (1999). Home-based consultation for parents of young children with behavior problems. *Child and Family Behavior Therapy, 21*(2), 19–45.

Gresham, F.M. (1989). Assessment of treatment integrity in school consultation and prereferral intervention. *School Psychology Review, 18,* 37–50.

Gresham, F.M., MacMillan, D.L., Beebe-Frankenberger, M.E., & Bocian, K.M. (2000). Treatment integrity in learning disabilities intervention research: Do we really know how treatments are implemented? *Learning Disabilities Research & Practice, 15,* 198–205.

Gresham, F.M., Watson, T.S., & Skinner, C.H. (2001). Functional behavioral assessment: Principles, procedures, and future directions. *School Psychology Review, 30,* 156–172.

Grossman, S., Osterman, K., & Schmelkin, L.P. (1999, April). *Parent involvement: The relationship between beliefs and practices.* Paper presented at the Annual Meeting of the American Educational Research Association. (ERIC Document Reproduction Service No. ED433326)

Hanson, M.J., & Carta, J.J. (1996). Addressing the challenges of families with multiple risks. *Exceptional Children, 62,* 201–212.

Harden, B.J., Winslow, M.B., Kendziora, K.T., Shahinfar, A., Rubin, K.H., Fox, N.A., Crowley, M.J., & Zahn-Waxler, C. (2000). Externalizing problems in Head Start children: An ecological exploration. *Early Education & Development, 11,* 357–385.

Harding, J.W., Wacker, D.P., Berg, W.K., Cooper, L.J., Asmus, J., Mlela, K., & Muller, J. (1999). An analysis of choice making in the assessment of young children with severe behavior problems. *Journal of Applied Behavior Analysis, 32,* 63–82.

Harry, B. (1992). Restructuring the participation of African-American parents in special education. *Exceptional Children, 59*(2), 123–131.

Hartle, L.C. (1996). Effects of additional materials on preschool children's outdoor play behaviors. *Journal of Research in Childhood Education, 11,* 68–81.

Hawkins, J.D., Catalano, R.F., & Miller, Y. (1992). Risk and protective factors for alcohol and other drug problems in adolescence and early adulthood: Implications for substance abuse prevention. *Psychological Bulletin, 112,* 64–105.

Herrenkohl, R.C., & Russo, M.J. (2001). Abusive early child rearing and early childhood aggression. *Child Maltreatment, 6,* 3–16.

Hewitt, D. (1995). *So this is normal too?* St. Paul, MN: Redleaf Press.

Hinojosa, J., Bedell, G., Buchholz, E.S., Charles, J., Shigaki, I.S., & Brochieri, S.M. (2001). Team collaboration: A case study of early intervention. *Qualitative Health Research, 11,* 206–220.

Holbrook, M.C (1996). *Children with visual impairments: A parents' guide.* Bethesda, MD: Woodbine House.

Honig, A.S. (2001). Building relationships through music. *Early Childhood Today, 15*(4), 24–25.

Hord, S.M. (1997). *Professional learning communities: Communities of continuous inquiry and improvement.* Southwest Educational Development Laboratory. (ERIC Document Reproduction Service No. ED410659)

Horton, C.B. (1996). Children who molest other children: The school psychologist's response to the sexually aggressive child. *School Psychology Review, 25,* 540–557.

Hourcade, J.J., Parette, H.P., & Huer, M.B. (1997). Family and cultural alert! Considerations in assistive technology assessment. *Teaching Exceptional Children, 30*(1), 40–44.

Howe, N., Moller, L., Chambers, B., & Petrakos, H. (1993). The ecology of dramatic play centers and children's social and cognitive play. *Early Childhood Research Quarterly, 8,* 235–251.

Howlin, P., Baron-Cohen, S., & Hadwin, J. (1999). *Teaching children with autism to mind-read: A practical guide.* New York: John Wiley & Sons.

Hoyson, M., Jamieson, B.V., Strain, P.S., & Smith, B.J. (1998). Duck, duck: Colors and words of early childhood inclusion. *Teaching Exceptional Children, 30*(4), 66–71.

Individuals with Disabilities Education Act (IDEA) Amendments of 1997, PL 105-17, 20 U.S.C. §§1400 *et seq.*

Ivory, J.J., & McCollum, J.A. (1999). Effects of social and isolate toys on social play in an inclusive setting. *The Journal of Special Education, 32,* 238–243.

Jackson, A.P., Brooks-Gunn, J., Huang, C., & Glassman, M. (2000). Single mothers in low-wage jobs: Financial strain, parenting, and preschoolers' outcomes. *Child Development, 71,* 1409–1423.

Jackson, L., & Panyan, M.V. (2002). *Positive behavioral support in the classroom: Principles and practices.* Baltimore: Paul H. Brookes Publishing Co.

Johnson, L.J. & Hawkins, A. (2001). School–family collaboration. In M.C. Pugach & L.J. Johnson (Eds.), *Collaborative practitioners, collaborative schools* (pp. 201–226). Denver, CO: Love Publishing Co.

Johnson, L.J., Zorn, D., Tam, B.K.Y., LaMontagne, M., & Johnson, S.A. (2003). Stakeholders' views of factors that impact successful interagency collaboration. *Exceptional Children, 69*(2), 195–209.

Kahle, A., & Jones, G.N. (1999). Adaptation to parental chronic illness. In A.J. Goreczny & M. Hersen (Eds.), *Handbook of pediatric and adolescent health psychology* (pp. 387–399). Boston: Allyn & Bacon.

Kaiser, A.P., & Hester, P.P. (1997). Prevention of conduct disorder through early intervention: A social-communicative perspective. *Behavioral Disorders, 22,* 117–130.

Kaiser, B., & Rasminsky, J.S. (1999). *Meeting the challenge: Effective strategies for challenging behaviors in early childhood environments.* Washington, DC: National Association for the Education of Young Children.

Karpowitz, D.H. (2000). American families in the 1990's and beyond. In M.J. Fine & S.W. Lee (Eds.), *Handbook of diversity in parent education: The changing faces of parenting and parent education* (pp. 1–14). San Diego: Academic Press.

Katz, L.G. (1975). *Some generic principles of teaching: Second collection of papers for teachers.* Urbana: University of Illinois, College of Education. (ERIC Document Reproduction Service No. 119807)

Katz, L.G., & McClellan, D.E. (1997). *Fostering children's social competence: The teacher's role.* Washington, DC: National Association for the Education of Young Children.

Kazdin, A.E. (2001). *Behavior modification in applied settings* (6th ed.). Belmont, CA: Wadsworth.

Kellegrew, D.H. (1998). Creating opportunities for occupation: An intervention to promote the self-care independence of young children with special needs. *American Journal of Occupational Therapy, 52*(6), 457–465.

Kelman, A. (1990). Choices for children. *Young Children, 45*(3), 42–45.

Kochanska, G., Coy, K.C., & Murray, K.T. (2001). The development of self-regulation in the first four years of life. *Child Development, 72,* 1091–1111.

Koegel, L.K., Koegel, R.L., Kellegrew, D.H., & Mullen, K. (1996). Parent education for prevention and reduction of severe problem behaviors. In L.K. Koegel, R.L. Koegel, & G. Dunlap (Eds.), *Positive behavioral support: Including people with difficult behavior in the community* (pp. 3–30). Baltimore: Paul H. Brookes Publishing Co.

Kohler, F.W., Anthony, L.J., Steighner, S.A., & Hoyson, M. (2001). Teaching social interaction skills in the integrated preschool: An examination of naturalistic tactics. *Topics in Early Childhood Special Education, 21,* 93–105.

Kohler, F.W., & Strain, P.S. (1997). Procedures for assessing and increasing social interaction. In N.N. Singh (Ed.), *Prevention and treatment of severe behavior problems: Models and methods in developmental disabilities* (pp. 49–59). Belmont, CA: Brooks/Cole.

Kohler, F.W., & Strain, P.S. (1999). Maximizing peer-mediated resources in integrated preschool classrooms. *Topics in Early Childhood Special Education, 19,* 92–102.

Kontos, S. (1984). Congruence of parent and early childhood staff perceptions of parenting. *Parenting Studies, 1,* 5–10.

Kontos, S., & Dunn, L. (1989). Attitudes of caregivers, maternal experiences with day care, and children's development. *Journal of Applied Developmental Psychology, 10,* 37–51.

Kontos, S., Moore, D., & Giorgetti, K. (1998). The ecology of inclusion. *Topics in Early Childhood Special Education, 18,* 38–48.

Kontos, S., Raikes, H., & Woods, A. (1983). Early childhood staff attitudes toward their parent clientele. *Child Care Quarterly, 12,* 45–58.

Kontos, S., & Wells, W. (1986). Attitudes of caregivers and the day care experiences of families. *Early Childhood Research Quarterly, 1,* 47–67.

Kontos, S., & Wilcox-Herzog, A. (1997). Influences on children's competence in early childhood classrooms. *Early Childhood Research Quarterly, 12*(3), 247–262.

Koralek, D.G., Colker, L.J., & Dodge, D.T. (1995). *The what, why and how of high-quality early childhood education: A guide for on-site supervision.* Washington, DC: National Association for the Education of Young Children. (ERIC Document Reproduction Service No. ED417029)

Kuebli, J. (1994). Young children's understanding of everyday emotions. *Young Children, 49*(3), 36–47.

Kupersmidt, J.B., Bryant, D., & Willoughby, M.T. (2000). Prevalence of aggressive behaviors among preschoolers in Head Start and community child care programs. *Behavioral Disorders, 26,* 42–52.

Kutash, K., & Duchnowski, A.J. (1997). Create comprehensive and collaborative systems. *Journal of Emotional and Behavioral Disorders, 5,* 66–75.

La Paro, K., & Pianta, R. (2000). Predicting children's competence in the early school years: A meta-analytic review. *Review of Educational Research, 70,* 443–484.

Lara, S.L., McCabe, L.A., & Brooks-Gunn, J. (2000). From horizontal to vertical management styles: A qualitative look at Head Start staff strategies for addressing behavior problems. *Early Education and Development, 11,* 283–306.

Lawry, J., Danko, C.D., & Strain, P.S. (2000). Examining the role of the classroom environment in the prevention of problem behaviors. *Young Exceptional Children, 3,* 3–19.

Lee, S.W., & Guck, T.P. (2000). Parenting chronically ill children. In M.J. Fine & S.W. Lee (Eds.), *Handbook of diversity in parent education: The changing faces of parenting and parent education* (pp. 277–297). San Diego: Academic Press.

Lewis, M.C. (1993). *Beyond barriers: Involving Hispanic families in the education process.* Washington, DC: National Committee for Citizens in Education. (ERIC Document Reproduction Service No. ED385660)

Lieber, J., Capell, K., Sandall, S.R., Wolfberg, P., Horn, E., & Beckman, P. (1998). Inclusive preschool programs: Teachers' beliefs and practices. *Early Childhood Research Quarterly, 13*(1), 87–105.

Lightfoot, S.L. (1978). *Worlds apart: Relationships between families and schools.* New York: Basic Books.

Linan-Thompson, S., & Jean, R.E. (1997). Completing the parent participation puzzle: Accepting diversity. *Teaching Exceptional Children, 30*(2), 46–50.

Luciano, M.C., Herruzo, J., & Barnes-Holmes, D. (2001). Generalization of say-do correspondence. *The Psychological Record, 51,* 111–130.

Luria, A.R. (1961). *The role of speech in the regulation of normal and abnormal behavior.* New York: Pergamon Press.

Lynch, E.W., & Hanson, M.J. (1998). *Developing cross-cultural competence: A guide for working with children and their families* (2nd ed.). Baltimore: Paul H. Brookes Publishing Co.

Lynch, E.W., & Stein, R. (1987). Parent participation by ethnicity: A comparison of Hispanic, Black and Anglo families. *Exceptional Children, 54*(2), 105–111.

Maccoby, E.E., & Martin, J.A. (1983). Socialization in the context of the family: Parent–child interaction. In P.H. Mussen (Series Ed.) & E.M. Hetherington (Vol. Ed.), *Handbook of child psychology: Vol. 4. Socialization, personality, and social development* (4th ed., pp. 1–101). Hoboken, NJ: John Wiley & Sons.

MacDonald, S. (1997). *The portfolio and its use: A road map for assessment.* Beltsville, MD: Gryphon House.

Mace, F.C., Hock, M.L., Lalli, J.S., West, B.J., Belfiore, P., Pinter, E., & Brown, D.K. (1988). Behavioral momentum in the treatment of noncompliance. *Journal of Applied Behavior Analysis, 21,* 123–141.

Mahoney, A., Jouriles, E.N., & Scavone, J. (1997). Marital adjustment, marital discord over childrearing, and child behavior problems: Moderating effects of child age. *Journal of Clinical Child Psychology, 26,* 415–423.

Malaguzzi, L. (1993). For an education based on relationships. *Young Children, 49*(1), 9–12.

Mallory, B.L., & Kerns, G.M. (1988). Consequences of categorical labeling of preschool children. *Topics in Early Childhood Education, 8,* 39–50.

Malmskog, S., & McDonnell, A.P. (1999). Teacher-mediated facilitation of engagement by children with developmental delays in inclusive preschools. *Topics in Early Childhood Special Education, 19,* 203–216.

Margolis, H., & Shapiro, A. (1988). Systematically resolving parental conflict with the goal-output-process-input-procedure. *High School Journal, 71,* 88–96.

Marion, M. (1995). *Guidance of young children.* Upper Saddle River, NJ: Prentice Hall.

Matson, J.L., & Duncan, D. (1997). Aggression. In N.N. Singh (Ed.), *Prevention and treatment of severe behavior problems: Models and methods in developmental disabilities* (pp. 217–236). Belmont, CA: Brooks/Cole.

McCabe, J.R., Jenkins, J.R., Mills, P.E., Dale, P.S., & Cole, K.N. (1999). Effects of group composition, materials, and developmental level on play in preschool children with disabilities. *Journal of Early Intervention 22,* 164–178.

McCartney, K., Scarr, S., Rocheleau, A., Phillips, D., Abbott-Shim, M., Eisenberg, M., Keefe, N., Rosenthal, S., & Ruh, J. (1997). Teacher–child interaction and child-care auspices as predictors of social outcomes in infants, toddlers, and preschoolers. *Merrill-Palmer Quarterly, 43,* 426–450.

McCormick, L., Noonan, M.J., & Heck, R. (1998). Variables affecting engagement in inclusive preschool classrooms. *Journal of Early Intervention, 21,* 160–176.

McDonnell, A.P., & Brownell, K.L. (1997). Teaching experience and specialist support: A survey of preschool teachers employed in programs accredited by NAEYC. *Topics in Early Childhood Special Education, 17,* 263–285.

McEvoy, M.A., Fox, J.J., & Rosenburg, M.S. (1991). Organizing preschool environments: Effects on the behavior of preschool children with handicaps. *Topics in Early Childhood Special Education, 11*(2), 18–28.

McGaha, C.G., & Farran, D.C. (2001). Interactions in an inclusive classroom: The effects of visual status and setting. *Journal of Visual Impairment and Blindness, 95,* 80–94.

McGinnis, E., & Goldstein, A.P. (1990). *Skillstreaming in early childhood: Teaching prosocial skills to the preschool and kindergarten child.* Champaign, IL: Research Press.

McWilliam, R.A. (1991). Targeting teaching at children's use of time: Perspectives on preschoolers' engagement. *Teaching Exceptional Children, 23*(4), 42–43.

McWilliam, R.A., & Bailey, D.B., Jr. (1995). Effects of classroom social structure and disability on engagement. *Topics in Early Childhood Special Education, 15,* 123–147.

McWilliam, R.A., Trivette, C.M., & Dunst, C.J. (1985). Behavior engagement as a measure of the efficacy of early intervention. *Analysis and Intervention in Developmental Disabilities, 5,* 33–45.

Mesibov, G.B., Browder, D.M., & Kirkland, C. (2002). Using individualized schedules as a component of positive behavioral support for students with developmental disabilities. *Journal of Positive Behavior Interventions, 4,* 73–79.

Miceli, P.J., Rowland, J.F., & Whitman, T.L. (1999). In T.L. Whitman, T.V. Merluzzi, & R.D. White (Eds.), *Chronic illnesses in childhood: Life-span perspectives on health and illness* (pp. 165–186). Mahwah, NJ: Lawrence Erlbaum Associates.

Miller, K. (1996). *The crisis manual for early childhood teachers: How to handle the really difficult problems.* Beltsville, MD: Gryphon House.

Miltenberger, R.G. (2001). *Behavior modification: Principles and procedures* (2nd ed.). Belmont, CA: Wadsworth.

Moles, O.C. (1993). Collaboration between schools and disadvantaged parents: Obstacles and openings. In N.F. Chavkin (Ed.), *Families and schools in a pluralistic society* (pp. 21–51). Albany: State University of New York Press.

Moomaw, S., & Hieronymus, B. (2001). *More than letters.* St. Paul, MN: Redleaf Press.

Mukherjee, S., & Lightfoot, J. (2000). The inclusion of pupils with a chronic health condition in mainstream school: What does it mean for teachers? *Educational Research, 42,* 59–72.

Murray, C.G. (2000). Learning about children's social and emotional needs at snack time: Nourishing the body, mind and spirit of each child. *Young Children, 55*(2), 43–52.

National Association for the Education of Young Children. (2001, November). *NAEYC standards for early childhood professional preparation: Baccalaureate or initial licensure level.* Retrieved January 18, 2003, from www.ncate.org/standard/new%20program%20standards/naeyc%202001.pdf

National Institute of Child Health and Human Development. (1998). Early child care and self-control, compliance and problem behavior at twenty-four and thirty-six months. *Child Development, 69,* 1145–1170.

Neilsen, S., Olive, M., Donovan, A., & McEvoy, M. (1999). Challenging behaviors in your classroom? Don't react—teach instead. In S. Sandall & M. Ostrosky (Eds.), *Young exceptional children: Practical ideas for addressing challenging behaviors* (Monograph Series 1, pp. 5–15). Denver, CO: Division for Early Childhood of the Council for Exceptional Children.

Newcomb, A.F., Bukowski, W.M., & Pattee, L. (1993). Children's peer relations: A meta-analytic review of popular, rejected, neglected, controversial, and average sociometric status. *Psychological Bulletin, 113,* 99–128.

Nicolau, S., & Ramos, C.L. (1990). *Together is better: Building strong relationships between schools and Hispanic parents.* Washington, DC: Hispanic Policy Development Project. (ERIC Document Reproduction Service No. ED325543)

Odom, S., & Diamond, K. (1998). Inclusion of young children with special needs in early childhood education: The research base. *Early Childhood Research Quarterly, 13*(1), 3–25.

Odom, S.L., McConnell, S.R, McEvoy, M.A., Peterson, C., Ostrosky, M., Chandler, L.K., Spicuzza, R.J., Skellenger, A., Creighton, M., & Favazza, P.C. (1999). Relative effects of interventions supporting the social competence of young children with disabilities. *Topics in Early Childhood Special Education, 19,* 75–91.

O'Leary, S.G., Slep, A.M.S., & Reid, M.J. (1999). A longitudinal study of mothers' overreactive discipline and toddler's externalizing behavior. *Journal of Abnormal Child Psychology, 27,* 331–341.

Olmi, K.J., Sevier, R.C., & Nastasi, D.F. (1997). Time-in/time-out as a response to noncompliance and inappropriate behavior with children with developmental disabilities: Two case studies. *Psychology in the Schools, 34,* 31–39.

O'Neill, R.E., Horner, R.H., Albin, R.W., Sprague, J.R., Storey, K., & Newton, J.S. (1997). *Functional assessment and program development for problem behavior: A practical handbook* (2nd ed.). Belmont, CA: Brooks/Cole.

Orlebeke, J.F., Knol, D.L., Boomsma, D.I., & Verhulst, F.C. (1998). Frequency of parental report of problem behavior in children decreases with increasing maternal age at delivery. *Psychological Reports, 82,* 395–404.

Paine, S.C., Radicchi, J., Rosellini, L.C., Deutchman, L., & Darch, C.B. (1983). *Structuring your classroom for academic success.* Champaign, IL: Research Press.

Patterson, G.R., DeBaryshe, B.D., & Ramsey, E. (1989). A developmental perspective on antisocial behavior. *American Psychologist, 44,* 329–335.

Peters, C. (1995). *Preschool activity centers: Effects on opportunities to engage in social interactions.* Unpublished doctoral dissertation, University of Cincinnati, OH.

Petrakos, H., & Howe, N. (1996). The influence of the physical design of the dramatic play center on children's play. *Early Childhood Research Quarterly, 11,* 63–77.

Phelps, L. (1998). *Health-related disorders in children and adolescents.* Washington, DC: American Psychological Association.

Phelps, L., Brown, R.T., & Power, T.J. (2002). *Pediatric psychoparmacology: Combining medical and psychosocial interventions.* Washington, DC: American Psychological Association.

Piazza, C.C., Hanley, G.P., Bowman, L.G., Ruyter, J.M., Lindauer, S.E., & Saiontz, D.M. (1997). Functional analysis and treatment of elopement. *Journal of Applied Behavior Analysis, 30,* 653–672.

Piotrkowski, C.S., Collins, R.C., Knitzer, J., & Robinson, R. (1994). Strengthening mental health services in Head Start. *American Psychologist, 49,* 133–139.

Porterfield, J.K., Herbert-Jackson, E., & Risley, T.R. (1976). Contingent observation: An effective and acceptable procedure for reducing disruptive behavior of young children in a group setting. *Journal of Applied Behavior Analysis, 9,* 55–64.

Powell, D.R. (1990). *Families and early childhood programs.* Washington, DC: National Association for the Education of Young Children.

Premack, D. (1959). Toward empirical behavior laws: I. Positive reinforcement. *Psychological Review, 66,* 219–233.

Pugach, M., & Johnson, L.J. (1995). *Collaborative practitioners, collaborative schools.* Denver, CO: Love Publishing Co.

Raspa, M., McWilliam, R.A., & Ridley, S.M. (2001). Child care quality and children's engagement. *Early Education and Development, 12,* 209–224.

Read, K.H. (1992). The nursery school: A human relations laboratory. *Young Children, 47*(3), 4–5.

Reguero de Atiles, J.T., Stegelin, D.A., & Long, J.K. (1997). Biting behaviors among preschoolers: A review of the literature and survey of practitioners. *Early Childhood Education Journal, 25,* 101–105.

Reichle, J., & Wacker, D.P. (Eds.). (1993). *Communication and language intervention series: Vol. 3. Communicative alternatives to challenging behavior: Integrating functional assessment and intervention strategies.* Baltimore: Paul H. Brookes Publishing Co.

Reimers, T.M., Wacker, D.P., & Koeppl, G. (1987). Acceptability of behavioral interventions: A review of the literature. *School Psychology Review, 16,* 212–227.

Repetti, R.L., McGrath, E.P., & Ishikawa, S.S. (1999). Daily stress and coping in childhood and adolescence. In A.J. Goreczny & M. Hersen (Eds.), *Handbook of pediatric and adolescent health psychology* (pp. 343–360). Boston: Allyn & Bacon.

Roberts, M.L., Marshall, J., Nelson, J.R., & Albers, C.A. (2001). Curriculum-based assessment procedures embedded within functional behavioral assessments: Identifying escape motivated behaviors in a general education classroom. *School Psychology Review, 30,* 264–277.

Roberts, S.B., Brown, P.M., & Rickards, F.W. (1996). Social pretend play entry behaviors of preschoolers with and without impaired hearing. *Journal of Early Intervention, 20*(1), 52–64.

Rose, S.L., Rose, S.A., & Feldman, J.F. (1989). Stability of behavior problems in very young children. *Development and Psychopathology, 1,* 5–19.

Rosenfield, S.A., & Gavois, T.A. (1996). *Instructional consultation teams: Collaborating for change.* New York: The Guilford Press.

Rosenkoetter, S.E., & Fowler, S.A. (1986). Teaching mainstreamed children to manage daily transitions. *Teaching Exceptional Children, 19,* 20–23.

Rushton, S., & Larkin, E. (2001). Shaping the learning environment: Connecting developmentally appropriate practices to brain research. *Early Childhood Education Journal, 29,* 25–33.

Sainato, D.M. (1990). Classroom transitions: Organizing environments to promote independent performance in preschool children with disabilities. *Education & Treatment of Children, 13,* 288–297.

Sainato, D.M., & Lyon, S.R. (1989). Promoting successful mainstreaming transitions for handicapped preschool children. *Journal of Early Intervention, 13,* 305–314.

Sainato, D.M., & Strain, P.S. (1992). Increasing integration success for preschoolers with disabilities. *Teaching Exceptional Children, 25,* 36.

Saleeby, D. (1992). *The strengths perspective in social work practice.* New York: Longman Publishing.

Sandall, S.R. (1997a). Early intervention contexts, content, and methods. In A.H. Widerstrom, B.A. Mowder, & S.R. Sandall (Eds.), *Infant development and risk: An introduction* (2nd ed., pp. 261–286). Baltimore: Paul H. Brookes Publishing Co.

Sandall, S.R. (1997b). The family service team. In A.H. Widerstrom, B.A. Mowder, & S.R. Sandall (Eds.), *Infant development and risk: An introduction* (2nd ed., pp. 155–172). Baltimore: Paul H. Brookes Publishing Co.

Scheinfeld, D.R. (1993). *New beginnings: A guide to designing parenting programs for refugee and immigrant parents.* New York: International Catholic Child Bureau. (ERIC Document Reproduction Service No. ED367507)

Schmit, J., Alper, S., Raschke, D., & Ryndak, D. (2000). Effects of using a photographic cueing package during routine school transitions with a child who has autism. *Mental Retardation, 38,* 131–137.

Schreibman, L., Koegel, R.L., Mills, J.I., & Burke, J.C. (1984). Training parent–child interactions. In E. Schopler & G.B. Mesibov (Eds.), *The effects of autism on the family* (pp. 187–205). New York: Kluwer Academic/Plenum Publishers.

Schuman, W.B., & La Greca, A.M. (1999). Social correlates of chronic illness. In R.T. Brown (Ed.), *Cognitive aspects of chronic illness in children* (pp. 289–311). New York: The Guilford Press.

Schwartz, I.S. (1999). Controversy or lack of consensus? Another way to examine treatment alternatives. *Topics in Early Childhood Special Education, 19,* 189–193.

Schwartz, I.S., & Baer, D.M. (1991). Social validity assessments: Is current practice state of the art? *Journal of Applied Behavior Analysis, 24,* 189–204.

Schwartz, I.S., & Olswang, L.B. (1996). Evaluating child behavior change in natural settings: Exploring alternative strategies for data collection. *Topics in Early Childhood Special Education, 16,* 82–101.

Schwartz, W. (1995). *A guide to communication with Asian American families: For parents/about parents.* New York: Office of Educational Research and Improvement. (ERIC Document Reproduction Service No. ED396014)

Seefeldt, C. (1990). Assessing young children. In C. Seefeldt (Ed.), *Continuing issues in early childhood education* (pp. 311–330). Columbus, OH: Merrill.

Seligman, M. (2000). *Conducting effective conferences with parents of children with disabilities: A guide for teachers.* New York: The Guilford Press.

Sergiovanni, T.J. (1996). *Leadership for the schoolhouse: How is it different? Why is it important?* San Francisco: Jossey-Bass.

Sethi, A., Mischel, W., Aber, J.L., Shoda, Y., & Rodriguez, M.L. (2000). The role of strategic attention deployment in development of self-regulation: Predicting preschoolers' delay of gratification from mother-toddler interactions. *Developmental Psychology, 36,* 767–777.

Shahinfar, A., Fox, N.A., & Leavitt, L.A. (2000). Preschool children's exposure to violence: Relation of behavior problems to parent and child reports. *American Journal of Orthopsychiatry, 70,* 115–125.

Shaw, D.S., Winslow, E.B., Owens, E.B., & Hood, N. (1998). Young children's adjustment to chronic family adversity: A longitudinal study of low-income families. *Journal of the American Academy of Child and Adolescent Psychiatry, 37,* 545–553.

Shim, S., Herwig, J.E., & Shelley, M. (2001). Preschoolers' play behaviors with peers in classroom and playground settings. *Journal of Research in Childhood Education, 15,* 149–163.

Shriberg, L.D., Flipsen, P., Thielke, H.M., Kwiatkowski, J., Kertoy, M.K., Katcher, M.L., Nellis, R.A., & Block, M.G. (2000). Risk for speech disorder associated with early recurrent otitis media with effusion: Two retrospective studies. *Journal of Speech, Language, and Hearing Research, 43,* 79–99.

Shure, M.B. (2001). *I can problem solve: An interpersonal cognitive problem-solving program* (kindergarten and primary grades). Champaign, IL: Research Press.

Siemoens, S. (2001). *Class-wide interventions for challenging behaviors: An extension of PASSKey procedures.* Unpublished doctoral dissertation, University of Cincinnati, OH.

Singh, N.N. (1997). Enhancing quality of life through teaching and habilitation. In N.N. Singh (Ed.), *Prevention and treatment of severe behavior problems: Models and methods in developmental disabilities* (pp. 1–22). Belmont, CA: Brooks/Cole.

Sirridge, S.T. (2000). Parent education for fathers. In M.J. Fine & S.W. Lee (Eds.), *The changing faces of parenting and parent education* (pp. 179–197). San Diego: Academic Press.

Slaby R., Roedell, D., Arezzo, D., & Hendrix, K. (1995). *Early violence prevention: Tools for teachers of young children.* Washington, DC: National Association for the Education of Young Children.

Spaggiari, S. (1998). The community-teacher partnership in the governance of the schools: An interview with Lella Gandini. In C. Edwards, L. Gandini, & G. Forman (Eds.), *The hundred languages of children: The Reggio Emilia Approach—Advanced reflections* (2nd ed., pp. 99–112).Westport, CT: Ablex Publishing.

Spieker, S.J., Larson, N.C., Lewis, S.M., Keller, T.E., & Gilchrist, L. (1999). Developmental trajectories of disruptive behavior problems in preschool children of adolescent mothers. *Child Development, 70,* 443–458.

Spodek, B., & Saracho, O.N. (1990). Preparing early childhood teachers for the twenty-first century: A look to the future. In B. Spodek & O.N. Sacharo (Eds.), *Yearbook in Early Childhood Education: Vol. 2* (pp. 45–66). New York: Teachers College Press.

Stainback, W., Stainback, S., & Froyen, L. (1987). Structuring the classroom to prevent disruptive behaviors. *Teaching Exceptional Children, 19,* 12–16.

Sterling-Turner, H., & Watson, T.S. (1999). Consultant's guide for the use of time-out in the preschool and elementary classroom. *Psychology in the Schools, 36,* 135–148.

Sterling-Turner, H.E., Robinson, S.L., & Wilczynski, S.M. (2001). Functional assessment of distracting and disruptive behaviors in the school setting. *School Psychology Review, 30,* 211–226.

Stone, J. (1993). Caregiver and teacher language: Responsive or restrictive? *Young Children, 48*(4), 12–18.

Stormont, M. (1998). Family factors associated with externalizing disorders in preschoolers. *Journal of Early Intervention, 21,* 232–251.

Stormont, M., Zentall, S., Beyda, S., Javorsky, T., & Belfiore, P. (2000). Playground contexts for aggression for preschoolers with hyperactivity. *Journal of Behavioral Education, 10,* 37–48.

Stormshak, E.A., Bellanti, C.J., & Bierman, K.L. (1996). The quality of sibling relationships and the development of social competence and behavioral control in aggressive children. *Developmental Psychology, 32,* 79–89.

Strain, P.S., & Hemmeter, M.L. (1999). Keys to being successful when confronted with challenging behaviors. In S. Sandall & M. Ostrosky (Eds.), *Young exceptional children: Practical ideas for addressing challenging behaviors* (Monograph Series 1, pp. 17–27). Denver, CO: Division for Early Childhood of the Council for Exceptional Children.

Strayer, F.F. (1980). Child ethology and the study of preschool social relations. In H.C. Foot & A.J. Chapman (Eds.), *Friendship and social relations in children* (pp. 235–265). Piscataway, NJ: Transaction Publishers.

Stremel, K., Matthews, P., Wilson, R., Molden, R., Yates, C., Busbea, B., & Holson, J. (1992, December). *Facilitating infant/toddler skills in family-child routines.* Paper presented at the Council for Exceptional Children Division of Early Childhood International Conference on Children with Special Needs, Washington, DC.

Swaggart, B.L., & Gagnon, E. (1995). Using social stories to teach social and behavioral skills to children with autism. *Focus on Autistic Behavior, 10,* 1–10.

Swap, S.M. (1993). *Developing home–school partnerships: From concepts to practice.* New York: Teachers College Press.

Taylor, D. (1993). Family literacy: Resisting deficit models. *TESOL Quarterly, 27*(3), 550–553.

Taylor, J.C., Ekdahl, M.M., Romanczyk, R.G., & Miller, M.L. (1994). Escape behavior in task situations: Task versus social antecedents. *Journal of Autism and Developmental Disorders, 24,* 331–344.

Thies, K.M. (1999). Identifying the educational implications of chronic illness in school children. *Journal of School Health, 69,* 392–397.

Thomasgard, M., & Metz, W.P. (1997). Parental overprotection and its relation to perceived child vulnerability. *American Journal of Orthopsychiatry, 67,* 330–335.

Thomasgard, M., Shonkoff, J.P., Metz, W.P., & Edelbrock, C. (1995). Parent–child relationship disorders: Part II. The vulnerable child syndrome and its relation to parental overprotection. *Journal of Developmental and Behavioral Pediatrics, 16,* 251–256.

Thompson, S. (1992). Building on a foundation of respect for families and children: A roundtable discussion. *Equity and Choice, 8*(3), 37–40.

Trivette, P.S. (1998). Otitis media (ear infections). In L. Phelps (Ed.), *Health-related disorders in children and adolescents* (pp. 494–500). Washington, DC: American Psychological Association.

Tuckman, B.W. (1965). Developmental sequence in small groups. *Psychological Bulletin, 63,* 384–399.

Tuckman, B.W., & Jensen, M.A. (1977). Stages of small-group development revisited. *Group & Organization Studies, 2,* 419–427.

Turnbull, A.P., & Turnbull, H.R. (2001). *Families, teachers, and exceptionality: Collaborating for empowerment* (4th ed.). Columbus, OH: Merrill.

Turnbull, A.P., Turnbull, H.R., Shank, M., & Leal, D. (1995). *Exceptional lives: Special education in today's schools.* Columbus, NJ: Merrill.

Twardoz, S. (1984). Environmental organization: The physical, social, and programmatic context of behavior. In M. Hersen, R.M. Eisler, & P.M. Miller (Eds.), *Progress in behavior modification: Vol. 18* (pp. 123–161). San Diego: Academic Press.

Umbreit, J. (1996). Functional analysis of disruptive behavior in an inclusive classroom. *Journal of Early Intervention, 20*(1), 18–29.

Umbreit, J., & Blair, K.S. (1997). Using structural analysis to facilitate treatment of aggression and noncompliance in a young child at-risk for behavioral disorders. *Behavioral Disorders, 22,* 75–86.

U.S. Census Bureau. (1995). *Statistical abstract of the United States.* Washington, DC: Author.

VanDerHeyden, A.M., Witt, J.C., & Gatti, S. (2001). Descriptive assessment method to reduce overall disruptive behavior in a preschool classroom. *School Psychology Review, 30,* 548–567.

Vaughn, E. (1990). Everything under the sun: Outside learning. *Dimensions, 18*(4), 20–22.

Vig, S. (1996). Young children's exposure to community violence. *Journal of Early Intervention, 20,* 319–328.

Vygotsky, L. (1962). *Thought and language.* Cambridge, MA: The MIT Press.

Webster-Stratton, C. (1990a). Long-term follow-up of families with young conduct problem children: From preschool to grade school. *Journal of Clinical Child Psychology, 19,* 144–149.

Webster-Stratton, C. (1990b). Stress: A potential disruptor of parent perceptions and family interactions. *Journal of Consulting and Clinical Psychology, 62,* 583–593.

Webster-Stratton, C. (1998). Preventing conduct problems in Head Start children: Strengthening parenting competencies, *Journal of Consulting and Clinical Psychology, 66,* 715–730.

Webster-Stratton, C. (2000). Oppositional-defiant and conduct-disordered children. In M. Hersen & R.T. Ammerman (Eds.), *Advanced abnormal child psychology* (2nd ed., pp. 387–412). Mahwah, NJ: Lawrence Erlbaum Associates.

Webster-Stratton, C., Reid, M.J., & Hammond, M. (2001). Preventing conduct problems, promoting social competence: A parent and teacher training partnership in Head Start. *Journal of Clinical Child Psychology, 30,* 283–302.

Welch, M. (1994). Ecological assessment: A collaborative approach to planning instructional interventions. *Intervention in School and Clinic, 29,* 160–164.

Westling, D.L., Herzog, M.J., Cooper-Duffy, K., Prohn, K., & Ray, M. (2002). *The teacher support program: A proposed need for the special education profession and an initial validation.* Unpublished manuscript, Western Carolina University, NC.

Whaley, K.T., & Bennett, T.C. (1991). Promoting engagement in early childhood special education. *Teaching Exceptional Children, 23*(4), 51–54.

White-Clark, R., & Decker, L.E. (1996). *The "hard-to-reach" parent: Old challenges, new insights.* Boston: Middle-Atlantic Center for Community Education.

Whitman, T.L., Borkowski, J.G., Keogh, D.A., & Weed, K. (2001). *Interwoven lives: Adolescent mothers and their children.* Mahwah, NJ: Lawrence Erlbaum Associates.

Wilcox-Herzog, A., & Kontos, S. (1997). Influences on children's competence in early childhood classrooms. *Early Childhood Research Quarterly, 12*(3), 247–262.

Wilde, L.D., Koegel, L.K., & Koegel, R.L. (1992). *Increasing success in school through priming: A training manual.* Santa Barbara: University of California.

Willoughby, M., Kupersmidt, J., & Bryant, D. (2001). Overt and covert dimensions of antisocial behavior in early childhood. *Journal of Abnormal Child Psychology, 29,* 177–187.

Wittmer, D., & Honig, A. (1994). Encouraging positive social development in young children, *Young Children, 49*(5), 4–12.

Wolery, M. (1994). Assessing children with special needs. In M. Wolery & J.S. Wilbers (Eds.), *Including children with special needs in early childhood programs* (pp. 71–96). Washington, DC: National Association for the Education of Young Children.

Wolery, M., Anthony, L., Caldwell, N.K., Snyder, E.D., & Morgante, J.D. (2002). Embedding and distributing constant time delay in circle time and transitions. *Topics in Early Childhood Special Education, 22,* 14–25.

Wolery, M., Anthony, L., & Heckathorn, L. (1998). Transition-based teaching: Effects on transitions, teachers' behavior, and children's learning, *Journal of Early Intervention, 21,* 117–131.

Wolery, M., & Fleming, L.A. (1992). Preventing and responding to problem situations. In D.B. Bailey, Jr., & M. Wolery (Eds.), *Teaching infants and preschoolers with disabilities* (2nd ed., pp. 363–406). New York: Macmillan/McGraw-Hill.

Wolery, M., & McWilliam, R.A. (1998). Classroom-based practices for preschoolers with disabilities. *Intervention in School and Clinic, 34,* 95–104.

Wolery, M., & Wilbers, J.S. (1994). Introduction to the inclusion of young children with special needs in early childhood programs. In M. Wolery & J.S. Wilbers (Eds.), *Including children with special needs in early childhood programs* (pp. 1–22). Washington, DC: National Association for the Education of Young Children.

Wolery, M., & Winterling, V. (1997). Curricular approaches to controlling severe behavior problems. In N.N. Singh (Ed.), *Prevention and treatment of severe behavior problems: Models and methods in developmental disabilities* (pp. 87–120). Belmont, CA: Brooks/Cole.

Wolf, M.M. (1978). Social validity: The case for subjective measurement or How applied behavior analysis is finding its heart. *Journal of Applied Behavior Analysis, 11,* 203–214.

Wright, C.A., George, T.P., Burke, R., Gelfand, D.M., & Teti, D.M. (2000). Early maternal depression and children's adjustment to school. *Child Study Journal, 30,* 153–168.

York, S. (1997). When a child won't nap. *Scholastic Early Childhood Today, 11,* 16.

Yoshikawa, H., & Knitzer, J. (1997). *Lessons from the field: Head Start mental health strategies to meet the changing needs.* New York: National Center for Children in Poverty.

Zeece, P.D., & Corr, M. (1988). *Group time techniques: Implications for learning.* Nebraska: Elementary and Childhood Education. (ERIC Document Reproduction Service No. ED301330)

Zinn, M.B., & Eitzen, D.S. (1993). *Diversity in families* (3rd ed.). New York: HarperCollins Publishers.

Index

Page references followed by *t* or *f* indicate tables or figures, respectively.

A-B-C analysis, *see* Antecedent-behavior-consequence analysis
Active learning, facilitating, 58–59
Active listening, 38, 44
ADHD, *see* Attention-deficit/hyperactivity disorder
Administrative leadership, *see* Leadership, administrative
African American families, challenges to participation of, 35–36, 46
Aggressive behaviors, 7–8, 12, 55, 67; *see also* Challenging behaviors
Alternate behaviors, as part of an intervention plan, 132–133
Anecdotal records, 51, 91
Antecedent-behavior-consequence (A-B-C) analysis, 99–101, 180
Arrangements, classroom, *see* Classroom environments, supportive
Asian families, challenges to participation of, 36
Assessment process
  for challenging behavior
    antecedent-behavior-consequence (A-B-C) analysis, 99–101, 180
    and baseline observations, 130–131, 144–145
    curriculum based, 105
    functional analysis, 101–103, 150
    functional assessment, 8, 101, 129–130, 190
    initial steps for, 185–187, 187–189
    teacher's role in, 97–98
    vignettes about, 98–99, 100, 103, 130
  for intervention plan effectiveness
    acceptability/social validity, 142–144
    classroom applications regarding, 142, 144, 146
    educational benefits, 137–138
    elements of, 144–146, 190–191
    measuring intervention integrity, 140–141, 141*f*
    need for further evaluation, 135, 146–147, 191–192
    procedures for fading, 146–147
    scripted interventions, 138–140
    selected behaviors, 138
    vignettes about, 138, 139–140, 141, 143–144, 145
Assistive technology, 46
Attention span, as group time consideration, 74

Attention-deficit/hyperactivity disorder (ADHD), 5, 175, 177
Atypical developmental delays, 3–4
Autism, 175

Baseline data, 68, 130–131, 144–145
Behavior management crises, *see* Crisis intervention
Behavior of concern
  classroom applications regarding, 18
  defining elements of, 17–18, 124, 129, 130
  warning signs, 18, 121–122
  see also Challenging behaviors
Behavior plans, *see* Individualized behavior plan
Behavioral intervention
  alternate behaviors, presenting, 132–133
  classroom modifications
    activity engagement levels, 104–105
    child groupings, 106–107
    classroom applications regarding, 107
    daily schedules, 106
    physical arrangement, 103–104
    play materials, 105–106
    vignettes about, 105–106, 107
  defining, 122
  effectiveness of types
    overcorrection, 117–118
    punishment, 115
    reinforcers, 114, 134
    reprimands, 115
    response–cost, 115–116
    restraint policies, 118, 135, 155–156
    rewards, 113–114
    say-do correspondence, 114–115
    time-out, 116–117, 135
    vignettes about, 113–114, 116, 117, 118
  engaging families in, 45–48
  positive guidance approaches, 98–99
  teacher's role in, 97–98
    classroom limits, 108–109
    monitoring strategies, 109–110
    naturalistic teaching strategies, 109
    peer interaction, 110–111
    peer modeling, 112
    play partnering, 111–112
    scaffolded play entry, 111
    social skills training, 112–113
    vignettes about, 109, 110, 112
  vignettes about, 47–48, 98–99
  see also Crisis intervention; Individualized behavior plan

Beliefs and expectations, for children, 63
Biases, personal, 63–64

Caregiving, sensitivity, 15
Centerwide support, developing
    classroom applications regarding, 25, 32
    components for, 25–32
    principle-centered leadership, 21–25
    vignettes about, 26, 30
Challenging behaviors
    characteristics
        child factors, 1–9, 122, 179–180, 186
        classroom applications regarding, 4, 8–9,
            13, 16–17, 18
        classroom factors, 13–17, 123, 179,
            187–189
        defining elements, 17–18
        home factors, 9–13
        teacher factors, 178–179, 182, 187–188
        vignettes about, 2–3, 4, 6, 7, 10–11, 12,
            14–15, 16, 122–123
    data collection methods for clarifying
        anecdotal records, 51, 91
        frequency counts, 91–92, 131f, 180
        journaling, 94–95
        need for, 68, 90–91
        parent interviews, 92–94
        videotaping, 95–96
        vignette about, 94
    misperceptions about, 176–177
    preventive strategies for school
        choice time, 80–83
        classroom applications regarding, 72–73,
            76, 79–80, 83, 85–86, 87, 89–90
        gross motor time, 83–86
        group time, 73–76
        lunch/snack time, 88–90
        naptime, 76–80
        outside play, 86–87
        transition problems, 69–73
        vignettes about, 72, 75–76, 79, 82–83, 85,
            87, 89
    types
        antisocial behavior, 8
        biting, 8
        conduct disorder, 67
        hostile aggression, 8
        oppositional defiant disorder, 67
        running, 8, 124
        verbal behaviors, inappropriate, 8
        violent pretend play, 6–7
    see also Behavioral intervention;
        Individualized behavior plan
Charts, classroom, 70
Child care quality, 13–14
Child characteristics of challenging behaviors
    atypical development, 3–4
    classroom applications regarding, 4, 8–9
    guiding questions about, 179–180, 182

identified health conditions/disabilities, 2–3,
    122
inappropriate play themes, 6–7
reviewing enrollment records, 186
safety-related responses, 7–8
separation anxiety, 7
social interaction difficulties, 4–6
unidentified disabilities/impairments, 3
vignettes about, 2–3, 4, 6, 7
Child-rearing practices, 9–10, 29
Choice time challenges, 80–83, 109–110
Classroom environments, supportive
    classroom applications regarding, 53, 55, 56,
        57–58, 60, 62
    interdependent elements of, 49–50
        child groupings, 55–56
        curricular activities, 58–60
        daily routines, 16, 50–53, 188
        physical arrangements, 15–16, 56–58, 81,
            103–104
        rules and limits, 16, 60–62
        teacher–child relationships, 62–64, 77–78
        transition routines, 53–55
    vignettes about, 52, 55, 59–60
Classroom factors of challenging behaviors
    classroom applications regarding, 16–17
    and daily routines, 16, 188
    guiding questions about, 179, 182
    physical arrangement, 15–16
    staff sensitivity, 15
    staff training, 14
    teacher characteristics, 178–179, 187–188
    teacher–child ratio, 13–14
    vignettes about, 14–15, 16
    see also Classroom environments, supportive
Classroom management, 60
Classwide intervention, 123–124, 190
Collaborative problem solving, see Problem
    solving, collaborative
Communication issues, 38–39, 41–43, 46, 63,
    78
Community, sense of, 82–83
Community violence, 12–13
Conduct disorder, 67
Conference planning, phases of, 43–45
Confidentiality, 92
Conflict resolution, 154
    see also Crisis intervention
Consequences, establishing, 134
    see also Behavioral intervention
Contextual fit, 46–47, 47t
Cooperative play, 105
Coping skills, 149–150
Crisis intervention
    alternative plan for, 155
    classroom applications regarding, 151–152,
        156–157
    comprehensive goal of, 135, 149–150
    conflict resolution, 154

engaging parents as partners in, 156
initial plan procedures, 153–154
management plan for, 152–153
promoting self-regulation, 150–151
restraining policies, 118, 135, 155–156
staff availability for, 155
teacher strategies to address, 152, 188
vignette about, 153
Cross-program collaborations, *see* Outside
agency resources
Cultural issues, and challenging behaviors,
35–37, 38, 46
Curricular activities
best practice guidelines for, 58–60
engagement level of, 51–52, 74–75, 104–105
play materials and, 59–60
Curriculum enrichment model, 34

Daily routines
best practice guidelines for, 50–53, 188
disruption of, 123
family support in, 45
predictability of, 16, 52, 106
preventing transition problems in, 69–73
Data collection methods
anecdotal records, 51, 91
frequency counts, 91–92, 131*f*, 180
and graphing, 144–145, 145*f*
journaling, 94–95
need for, 68, 90–91
parent interviews, 92–94
videotaping, 95–96
vignettes about, 94, 95
Developmental disabilities, 3, 4
Differential positive reinforcement, 113–114
Disciplinary methods, ineffective, 9–10
Distraction, factors contributing to, 75
Documentation, *see* Information-gathering
process
Domestic violence, 12–13
Dramatic play, 58–59
Duration, as characteristic of challenging
behavior, 17, 130

Economic resources, as contributing to
children's challenging behaviors,
10–11, 35
Enablement model, 27
Enrollment records, examining, 185
child information, 186
family information, 186–187
Environmental modifications, *see* Classroom
environments, supportive

Facilitator's role, 127
Fading procedures, 146–147
Family system, components of, 34–37
Family-centered program, 29–31
see also Parent involvement

Feedback, defined, 114–115
Financial concerns, 10–11, 35
Formal support systems, 174–176, 175*f*
Frequency, as characteristic of challenging
behavior, 17, 130
Frequency counts, 91–92, 131*f*, 180
Functional analysis, 101–103, 150
Functional assessment, 8, 101, 129–130, 190
Funding, for additional staff, 27–28

Grant funding, 27–28
Gross motor time challenges, 83–86
Grouping of children
best practice guidelines for, 55–56
interventions for, 73–74, 84–85, 88, 106–107
Group time challenges, 73–76, 104
Guidance approaches, 98–99, 149–150

Health concerns, as contributing to children's
challenging behaviors, 2–3, 122
Home factors, as contributing to children's
challenging behaviors
child-rearing practices, 9–10, 29
classroom applications regarding, 13
financial concerns, 10–11
multiple family concerns, 12
neighborhood/community violence, 12–13
parental chronic illness, 11
parental substance abuse, 11
siblings, 12
vignettes about, 10–11, 12, 122–123
Home–school relationships, *see* Parent
involvement

IDEA, *see* Individuals with Disabilities
Education Act Amendments of 1997
(PL 105-17)
IEP, *see* Individualized education program
Inclusion, benefits of, 97–98
Individualized behavior plan
assessment of
acceptability/social validity, 142–144
classroom applications regarding, 142,
144, 146
educational benefits of, 137–138
effectiveness of elements, 144–146,
190–191
measuring intervention integrity,
140–141, 141*f*
need for further evaluation, 135, 146–147,
191–192
procedures for fading, 146–147
scripted interventions, 138–140
selected behaviors, 138
vignettes about, 138, 139–140, 141,
143–144, 145
components of
alternate behaviors, 132–133
antecedents and practices, 133–134

Individualized behavior plan—*continued*
  classroom applications regarding,
    134–135
  consequences, 134
  consistency and specific changes, 133
  prioritized behaviors, 131–132, 190
  prosocial replacement behaviors, 132–133
  selected intervention strategies, 132, 190
  vignettes about, 132–133, 134
  crisis response system, 135, 149–150, 188
  deciding indicators for
    classroom applications regarding,
      124–125
    classroom factors, 123
    deviation from peer norms, 123–124
    parent factors, 122–123
    severity of the behavior, 124
    vignettes about, 122–123, 124
  development process for
    classroom applications regarding, 128
    collaborative problem solving, 125–126
    facilitator's role in, 127
    partnership with parents, 126
    planning time, 127
    professional development and training,
      127–128
    stages of, 126–127
    and team members, 125, 135–136,
      189–190
  implementation of, 121–122
  techniques for gathering information
    baseline observations, 68, 130–131
    classroom applications regarding, 131
    contributing conditions, 129–130
    defining the target behavior, 129
    functional assessment, 130, 190
    problem-solving sequence, 128
    vignettes about, 129, 130
Individualized education program (IEP), 45,
  46
Individuals with Disabilities Education Act
  (IDEA) Amendments of 1997 (PL
  105-17), 172–173, 173*t*
Informal support systems, 173–174
Information-gathering process
  methods of observation, 91–96
  need for, 68, 90–91
  parent communication, 90–91
  vignette about, 94
Instructional techniques, *see* Behavioral
  intervention
Interagency collaboration, 169–170
  see also Outside agency resources
Intervention plans, *see* Behavioral intervention;
  Individualized behavior plan
Interviewing parents, *see* Parent interviews

Journaling, for home–school communication,
  94–95

Language delays, 3, 150
Latino/Hispanic families, challenges to
  participation of, 36–37, 46
Leadership, administrative
  classroom applications regarding, 25, 32
  consistency of, 188
  principle centered, 21–25
  for providing centerwide support, 25–32
  vignettes about, 26, 30
Lunch time challenges, 88–90

Materials, classroom, 59–60, 104, 105–106
Medical conditions, as contributing to
  children's challenging behaviors, 2–3,
  122
Medication side effects, as contributing to
  children's challenging behaviors, 2
Mental health issues
  parental, as contributing to children's
    challenging behaviors, 11–12
  supports for children with, 175
Misbehavior, consequences for, 61–62
Modeling, as a behavioral support, 88, 112
Monitoring strategies, for preventing
  behavioral escalation, 109–110

Naptime challenges, 76–80
Naturalistic teaching strategies, 109
Neighborhood safety, as contributing to
  children's challenging behaviors,
  12–13

Observation methods, for documenting
  challenging behaviors
  anecdotal records, 51, 91
  baseline data, 68, 130–131, 144–145
  checklists, 51, 99–100
  frequency counts, 91–92, 131*f*, 180
  home–school journaling, 94–95
  parent interviews, 92–94
  within the sociocultural context, 27
  videotaping, 95–96
  vignette about, 94
Oppositional defiant disorder, 67
Outside agency resources
  areas for gathering information, 177–178,
    178*f*
    child factors, 179–180
    classroom factors, 179
    teacher factors, 178–179
  classroom applications regarding, 172, 176
  collaboration considerations of, 169–172
  common misperceptions about, 176–177
  identifying sources, 172–173
  teacher support options, 173–176
  vignettes about, 180–183
Outside play challenges, 86–87
Overcorrection, 117–118

Parent apathy, 40
Parent conference planning, phases of, 43–45
Parent hostility, 40–41
Parent interviews, 92–94
Parent involvement
    administrator's role in, 28–29
    in changing behavior, 33–34
        assessing contextual fit, 46–47, 47t
        benefits of, 45–46, 156, 186
        classroom applications regarding, 37,
            39–40, 43
        parent-identified barriers to, 28, 37–39
        teacher-identified barriers to, 28, 40–43
        vignettes about, 42–43, 47–48
    family-centered approach to, 29–31
Parent-identified barriers to family
        participation, 28, 37–39
Parent–professional partnerships, 126, 174
Parent–school interaction, models of, 33–34
Parental substance abuse, as contributing to
        children's challenging behaviors,
        11–12
Participation, family, see Parent involvement
Partnership model, 34
Partnerships, parent–professional, 126, 174
Peer interaction, 110–111
Peer modeling, as a behavioral support, 88,
        112
Physical limitations, as contributing to
        children's challenging behaviors, 2
Physical prompts, as behavioral supports, 133
Picture schedules, as behavioral supports, 52,
        70
PL 105-17, see Individuals with Disabilities
        Education Act Amendments of 1997
Play entry, 5–6, 111
    play partnering, to support, 111–112
Play materials, see Materials, classroom
Play themes, 5, 6–7, 110–111
    see also Social interaction
Playground staffing, for adequate supervision,
        86–87
Positive reinforcement, 113–114, 134
Premack principle, 114
Pretend play, 6–7
Preventive strategies, see Challenging behaviors
Principle-centered leadership, 21–25
Problem solving, collaborative
    administrative phases of, 25–32
    and intervention team, 125–126, 140
    typical sequence of, 128
    vignettes about, 26
Professional development opportunities,
        31–32, 127–128, 136
Prompts, teacher, as behavioral supports, 61,
        112, 133
Prosocial replacement behaviors, 132–133, 151
Protective model, 33
Punishment procedures, 115, 117, 134

Referrals by teachers, to outside sources,
        176–177
Reinforcers, positive, 113–114, 134
Reprimands, 115
Response–cost, 115–116
Responsive language, 81
Restraint policies, 118, 135, 155–156
Restrictive language, 81
Rewards, for acceptable behavior, 113–114
Routines, see Daily routines
Rules and limits, classroom, 16, 60–62, 80–81,
        108–109
Running, as a challenging behavior, 8, 124

Safety concerns, related to behaviors, 7–8, 115
Say-do correspondence, 114–115
Scaffolding techniques, 110
Schedules, classroom, see Daily routines
Scheduling issues, parent–teacher, 41
School–home communication, 38
School-to-home transmission model, 33
Scripted interventions, 133, 139, 143
Seating arrangements, 73–74, 88
    see also Grouping of children
Self-regulatory skills, 5, 58, 61, 80, 150–151
Sensory impairments, as contributing to
        children's challenging behaviors, 2, 3
Separation anxiety, 7
Setting events, 18
Severity, as characteristic of challenging
        behavior, 17–18, 124
Siblings, as contributing to children's
        challenging behaviors, 12
Single-parent families, 34, 92
Snack time challenges, 88–90
Social development, 58–59, 64, 111
Social interaction, 4–6, 110, 111, 112, 151
Social learning theory, 151
Social preferences, 55–56
Social reinforcers, 113
Social services, 172–173
Social skills training, 112–113
    see also Social interaction
Social stories, as transition tools, 70
Sociocultural contexts, 27
    see also Cultural issues, and challenging
        behaviors
Space, classroom, role in fostering behavior,
        56–58, 81–82, 88–89
Staff training, 14–15, 127–128
    see also Professional development
        opportunities
Staffing patterns, role in behavioral support
        and intervention, 13–14, 26, 27–28,
        152, 155
Storyboards, as transition tools, 70
Substance abuse, parental, as contributing to
        children's challenging behaviors,
        11–12

Tangible reinforcers, 113
Tangible rewards, 113
Tantrums, 8, 124
Target behavior, *see* Behavior of concern
Teacher assistance teams (TATs), 175
Teacher–child ratios, 13–14, 152, 155
Teacher–child relationships, 62–64, 77–78
Teacher-identified barriers to family
    participation, 28, 40–43
Team members, role as
  commitment of, 135–136
  role in collaborative problem solving,
    125–127
  role in developing intervention, 125,
    189–190
Temperament, as contributing to children's
    challenging behaviors, 2, 4–6
Time-out policies, 116–117, 135
Transition routines

best practice guidelines for, 53–55
classroom applications regarding, 72–73
during lunch or snack time, 88
preventing problems during, 69–73, 106
vignette about, 72

Unplanned conferences, with parents, 44–45
Unsafe behavior, 7–8, 115

Verbal behaviors, inappropriate, 8
Verbal prompts, as behavioral supports, 61,
    133
Videotaping, 95–96
Visual boundaries, 81–82
Visual impairments, as contributing to
    children's challenging behaviors, 3
Visual prompts, as behavioral supports, 133

Waiting lists, as behavioral supports, 80–81